(Hetero)sexual Politics

Edited by

Mary Maynard and June Purvis

Taylor & Francis
Publishers since 1798

UK   Taylor & Francis Ltd, 4 John St., London WC1N 2ET
USA   Taylor & Francis Inc., 1900 Frost Road, Suite 101, Bristol, PA 19007

First published 1995

**A Catalogue Record for this book is available from the British
Library**

ISBN 0 7484 0295 0
ISBN 0 7484 0296 9 (pbk)

**Library of Congress Cataloging-in-Publication Data are
available on request**

Typeset in Times by Solidus (Bristol) Limited

*Printed in Great Britain by Burgess Science Press, Basingstoke on
paper which has a specified pH value on final paper manufacture of
not less than 7.5 and is therefore 'acid free'.*

(Hetero)sexual Politics

Feminist Perspectives on The Past and Present Advisory Editorial Board

Contents

Contents

Introduction

A Context for (Hetero)sexual Politics

Mary Maynard and June Purvis

The chapters collected together in this volume were initially given as papers at the annual conference we organized, on behalf of the Women's Studies Network (UK) Association, at the University of Portsmouth in July 1994. Although the main conference topic was 'Women's Studies in an International Context', it soon became clear that there was also a major sub-theme emerging from the various contributions on offer, one focusing on issues to do with sexuality and sexual politics. Now, of course, much has been written on these matters over the last twenty or so years. Feminists, in particular, have been responsible for politicizing the debate, demonstrating how something which is commonly regarded as a private and personal matter is, in fact, a public and a political issue. When the term 'politics' is related to that of the 'sexual' the implication is that relationships of power and the processes through which these are transmitted need to be part of any analysis. Not only are sexual experiences influenced and constrained by dynamics of power which are intrinsic to an immediate relationship itself, they are also affected by factors which lie outside of it. As Humm has noted, Kate Millett's choice of the term 'sexual politics' for the title of her pioneering book indicated that sexuality is not just some natural experience of women and men, but is 'socially constructed with political consequences' as well as being 'politically constructed with social consequences' (Humm, 1992, p. 260). Thus, sexuality has been regarded as an important area for discussion by feminists because it can be seen as one particular site of women's subordination.

Most accounts of the early theorizing and historical development of second-wave feminism appear to imply that a concern for sexuality is primarily a radical feminist preoccupation. It is certainly the case that for

1

many radical feminists sexuality is at the heart of male domination of women and is seen as a primary means of their social control. Attention has been drawn to the ways in which sexual practices are articulated by violence and pornography, the consequences of this in terms of rape, sexual harassment and sexual abuse generally and their significance for the reproduction of patriarchal society (Hanmer and Maynard, 1987). By contrast, it has been suggested that where socialist feminists have written about sexuality they have tended to present sexual relations as being determined by other forms of unequal power relations between men and women, rather than adopting the radical feminist view that sexuality is not simply a reflection of men's power but is also constitutive of it (Richardson, 1993). However, in the 1990s this is now a rather simplistic way of conceptualizing feminists' concerns with sexuality, due to significant changes in focus and emphasis which have occurred over recent years. In any case, those feminists influenced by Freud or other psychoanalytic theorists have always maintained a stoic interest in sexual matters and have kept to this even during times when such concerns were out of current academic and political fashion, as, for example, with the early work of Juliet Mitchell (1974).

The introduction to a book is not the place in which to rehearse in great detail the subtleties and nuances of recent transformations that have taken place in analysing a phenomenon as complex as sexuality. Instead, what follows is a brief account of some of the most important changes that have occurred, particularly in terms of how they have affected feminist thinking.

One important way in which feminists' approach to understanding sexuality has changed is in the recognition, by some, that it is not sufficient to theorize it only as a mechanism of social control used by men against women. Not only can this be seen as thoroughly heterosexist in its assumption of a heterosexual norm and exclusion of other kinds of sexualities, it also plays down the emotional, expressive and possibly pleasurable side of sexual expression. Hence, feminists have been at the forefront of those wishing to re-establish an emphasis on desire and the nature of the erotic (Snitow *et al.*, 1984; Vance, 1984), although such a position is not uncontentious and has been questioned by those who regard the possibility of sexual pleasure for women within patriarchal structures as problematic (Jeffreys, 1990). Focusing on desire, however, does not have to mean that the previous emphasis on how women are constrained and subordinated through the institution of heterosexuality was misplaced or that it has been superseded. The institution of heterosexuality, which is socially constructed rather than inevitable, still creates the expectations, conditions and preconceptions under which women are 'compelled' to 'choose' to

2

become heterosexual (Rich, 1984). Moreover, feminists continue to conduct important research in the area of sexual violence, thereby demonstrating the links between the normative demands of heterosexuality and the abuse of women (Kelly, 1988).

Linked to a concern with the possibilities for pleasure is the increasing feminist interest in matters relating to the body. Although there has been a considerable amount of feminist work which has paid attention to how women's bodies are controlled, through practices such as those involved in the new reproductive technologies and medical interventions, such discussions have rarely taken embodiment *per se* as their starting point (Scott and Morgan, 1993). One reason for this seems to lie in the emphasis towards social constructivist accounts of sexuality and gender relations in feminist writing, together with the tendency, a few notable exceptions apart, to relegate bodily matters to the sphere of biology (Sayers, 1982). But such an approach has unfortunate consequences. Not only does it mean that the body remains undertheorized in feminist thinking, it also helps to reinforce an uncritical polarization between biology and culture. Within such a formulation sexuality is seen *either* as natural *or* as socially constructed. Because feminists have tended to avoid invoking nature in their explanations, due to the supposed dangers of essentialism involved, they have usually opted for a cultural approach. However, as Craib points out, there is no *a priori* reason why sexuality should not be both natural *and* constructed (Craib, 1989). While bodily features and functions might be there as givens, the meanings and significance attributed to these, together with the various ways in which sexuality is expressed, are in some sense 'constructions' because they are historically and culturally located. Further, Craib argues that to acknowledge the existence of something as 'natural' is not necessarily the same as being 'essentialist'. This is because it does not inevitably have to involve reducing our understanding of either the body or sexuality to the result, or cause, of some essential factor. Such arguments are important for feminists as they point the way towards the possibility of 'transcending or blurring the conventional opposition between nature and culture' and between the biological and the social (Scott and Morgan, 1993, p. 6).

A third influence on the way in which the issue of sexuality has been approached lies in the increasing interest expressed by feminists in post-structuralist theory in general and the work of Lacan and Foucault in particular. Here, of course, an emphasis on language and on discourse is especially important. For example, feminists have found Foucault's way of using the concept 'discourse', to refer to specific 'grids' of meaning which underpin, generate and establish all relations, a useful technique for exploring the processes through which sexuality is constituted (Shilling,

1993). Arguing against the repressive hypothesis, which depicts the history of Western European societies since the seventeenth century as a period in which individuals and their bodies were increasingly regulated and constrained, Foucault claims, instead, that there was a proliferation of discourses about sex and sexuality which served to shape sexual values and beliefs (Foucault, 1979). Women's sexuality, he suggests, has not been controlled by denying or ignoring it, as some have suggested. Rather, it is through the changing ways in which the various discourses of the law, the Church, medicine and psychiatry, for instance, created a 'whole grid of observations regarding sex' that sexuality, particularly in relation to women, became an object of administration, management and government (Foucault, 1979, p. 23). It is, therefore, according to Foucault, through discourses on sexuality that sexuality itself is produced. Clearly, such arguments also have significance for those on the body and desire described above.

Other ways in which discussions on sexuality have been influenced relate to questions concerning difference, both in terms of different sexualities between women and how these might, in turn, be understood in relation to dimensions of diversity such as race, class, age and disability. The development of lesbian theory, for example, by providing a political analysis of sexual relationships between women, has helped to de-stigmatize lesbianism, as well as broadening both its meaning and the kinds of relationships defined as being involved (Richardson, 1993). Work on bisexuality has begun to make questions of bisexual identity and behaviour more visible, as well as challenging the conventional boundaries of heterosexual and homosexual relations. Because bisexuality cannot be fully contained within the heterosexual matrix, it is argued that it harbours the possibility of breaking down binary conceptions of sex as the foundation of gender and hence of sexuality (Hemmings, 1993). Other developments involve, for instance, problematizing heterosexuality. The latter, which is usually treated as a taken-for-granted and untheorized given, has been foregrounded as requiring analytic attention because of the ways in which it inscribes women's subordination and male power (Wilkinson and Kitzinger, 1994). In addition, writers as varied as hooks and Ramazanoglu have attempted to assess the implications that women's diverse experiences and political priorities might have for each other in relation to sexuality (hooks, 1991; Ramazanoglu, 1989).

It is against this background that we have put together the contributions to this volume. In doing this, we have paid particular attention to work which has either a material or a practical focus. For, while appreciative of the contributions made to feminist knowledge about sexual politics by those adopting perspectives from discourse and cultural analysis, both of which feature heavily in many of the developments outlined above, we are concerned that there is an increasing and unquestioning acceptance of sexuality as an entirely cultural matter, with little attention being paid either to the historical specificities of culture or to how it is influenced by non-cultural phenomena. Feminism, in our view, urgently needs to pay attention to how we can take the material aspects of sexual politics into account while, at the same time, neither reducing these to biological determinants nor reifying them into ephemeral aspects of discourse. By 'material' we mean events, relations, social and economic formations and bodily experiences which have conditions of existence and real effects outside the sphere of the discursive. Further, we also contend that consideration needs to be given to the practical, methodological and organizational aspects of sexual politics. These points are reflected in the organization of the book.

The first section, 'Analysing (Hetero)sexuality', is concerned with exploring some of the detailed complexities of the material aspects of sexual relations between men and women. The first two chapters address important theoretical issues to which this gives rise. Stevi Jackson, writing of the need critically to assess heterosexuality, without condemning heterosexual women, suggests that adopting a materialist feminist framework, of the kind advocated by the French feminists Christine Delphy and Monique Wittig, enables us to see that both heterosexuality and lesbianism depend for their existence on a social hierarchy of gender. In contrast, Caroline Ramazanoglu, in questioning whether the enormous success of men's power over women is entirely cultural, indicates that feminists have to find ways of theorizing the fact that social lives are lived in material bodies. Taking issue with certain aspects of poststructuralism, Ramazanoglu argues that bodily experiences, in the form of feelings, pains and pleasures, are important aspects of what it means to be a woman. She cautions against ruling out the possibility that some common features of women's experiences as embodied females may provide an important source of feminist knowledge.

The other two chapters in this section focus on more empirical concerns. Julia O'Connell Davidson, in her analysis of the attitudes, motivations and activities of male British sex tourists in Thailand, draws attention to how the consequences of these are racialized and economic, as well as gendered. She argues that the sex tourists themselves are not the only group to benefit from this kind of prostitution, with the economic benefits for national and international capital being equally, if not more, striking. This focus on prostitution is explored further in Jo Phoenix's chapter, where she problematizes existing definitions of what it involves by comparing the different material relationships and activities that occur in two well-known forms of prostitution: street work and parlour work.

The second section of the book, 'Media Discourses of Sexuality', contains analyses regarding women's magazines, television and newspapers. However, although each of the three chapters are concerned with representations of femininity and sexuality, they are as interested in the social and material implications of these as they are in cultural analysis *per se*. Esther Sonnet and Imelda Whelehan, in their piece on women's magazines, explore the implications for feminism and for feminist politics of the current interest in 'post-feminism'. Arguing that the 'heterosexual register' of the latter is 'unmistakable' in the sources they investigated, Sonnet and Whelehan also critique the meanings and images of the term 'lesbianism' as it is frequently portrayed. Similarly, Debbie Epstein and Deborah Lynn Steinberg demonstrate how, far from critiquing or challenging heterosexuality as has been claimed, *The Oprah Winfrey Show* reinscribes and reproduces it in some subtle, and not so subtle, ways. A similar point is made in Christine Forde's analysis of how women soldiers were represented in British newspapers during the Gulf War. Heterosexuality was normalized, she suggests, through a process in which 'representations of women soldiers remain bounded within traditional discourses of sexuality; women soldiers were presented predominantly in terms of victim, mother or, most frequently, sexual object' (p. 119).

The third section of the book focuses on what we have called 'Practising Sexual Politics'. The 'practice' referred to here relates to three kinds of political interventions. The contributions by Ruth Hamson and by Cath Stowers are illustrative of the first in their reflexive awareness of sexual politics in the framing of methodological issues in research. Hamson's work draws on a feminist application of oral history to study the neglected area of women's friendship. The two women who feature in her chapter were friends for nearly half a century and shared a house for twenty-five years. Yet Hamson questions whether their relationship should be referred to as 'lesbian' and discusses the essentialism that is sometimes associated with rigid categorization and labelling. Stowers' concern, on the other hand, is with how to read the fiction of Jeanette Winterson. Arguing that Winterson's lesbianism is frequently displaced in many interpretations of her novels, Stowers, in contrast, offers an analysis centred in a discourse of specifically lesbian desire. She argues that the imagery of exploration and travel, consistently present in Winterson's writing, serves to situate her texts within a complex, but identifiable, context of sexual politics.

The second kind of practice identified in this section refers to the sexual politics of 'practising' Lesbian Studies and Women's Studies. Patsy Staddon draws on her own experiences of setting up Lesbian Studies courses to draw attention to some of the dangers and potentialities which this involves.

Arguing that institutionalizing Women's Studies within the academic domain of higher education has not been politically unproblematic, she sets out some possibilities for 'good practice' which might prevent Lesbian Studies experiencing the same pitfalls. Similarly, Louise Morley, in her discussion of the position of feminism and Women's Studies within the academy, draws attention to the sometimes hidden, but nonetheless significant, micropolitical issues which can arise. She raises questions about the substantive effects of the presence of both liberatory and oppositional discourses within higher educational institutions and explores some of the possible strategies open to feminists who wish to influence change and create new forms of knowledge.

The third form of 'practice' addressed in this section is informed by Jill Radford and Liz Kelly's account of devising a new legal defence to the charge of murder, that of 'self preservation'. Kelly and Radford have been well known for their work on sexual violence for many years, both as activists and researchers. Here, they describe a particular development in feminist jurisprudence which is attempting to bring about change in the law. The proposal has been developed out of the experiences and circumstances of women who have been subjected to continuing violence from male partners whom they are subsequently accused of killing. The purpose of the concept of self preservation is to enable such an act to be seen not only as rational, but also in the context of 'the prevalence and long-term consequences of domestic violence in women's lives and the concerted failure of social institutions and agencies to intervene to protect women and sanction men' (p. 189). It would, therefore, add to the available legal options and increase the number of situations when a shift from a charge of murder to one of manslaughter might be possible.

Together, the three sections of this book contribute to a material understanding of sexuality and sexual politics on various levels. While there is by no means a consensus among the authors as to what this means or should involve, all of them address the issue, whether implicitly or explicitly, at some point in their work. We have called the book as a whole *(Hetero)sexual Politics*. In this we signal the debt owed by feminists to Kate Millett, who drew attention to the symbiotic relationship between 'sexuality' and 'politics' in her early text. Yet, as the chapters in this volume demonstrate, the arguments and debates have moved on apace since this was first published in 1969. In particular, heterosexuality can no longer be taken for granted and needs, along with other forms of sexuality, to be explicitly addressed. This, then, is the particular message we hope to convey in the title of the book.

References

CRAIB, IAN (1989) *Psychoanalysis and Social Theory*, London, Harvester Wheatsheaf.

FOUCAULT, MICHEL (1979) *The History of Sexuality (Vol. 1)*, London, Allen Lane.

HANMER, JALNA and MAYNARD, MARY (Eds) (1987) *Women, Violence and Social Control*, London, Macmillan.

HEMMINGS, CLARE (1993) 'Resituating the Bisexual Body', in BRISTOW, JOSEPH and WILSON, ANGELIA R. (Eds) *Activating Theory: Lesbian, Gay, Bisexual Politics*, London, Lawrence and Wishart.

HOOKS, BELL (1991) *Yearning*, London, Turnaround.

HUMM, MAGGIE (Ed.) (1992) *Feminisms: A Reader*, Hemel Hempstead, Harvester Wheatsheaf.

JEFFREYS, SHEILA (1990) *Anticlimax: A Feminist Perspective on the Sexual Revolution*, London, The Women's Press.

KELLY, LIZ (1988) *Surviving Sexual Violence*, Oxford, Polity.

MILLETT, KATE (1972) *Sexual Politics*, London, Abacus (first Abacus edition).

MITCHELL, JULIET (1974) *Psychoanalysis and Feminism*, Harmondsworth, Penguin.

RAMAZANOGLU, CAROLINE (1989) *Feminism and the Contradictions of Oppression*, London, Routledge.

RICH, ADRIENNE (1984) 'Compulsory Heterosexuality and Lesbian Existence', in SNITOW, ANN, STANSELL, CHRISTINE and THOMPSON, SHARON (Eds) *Desire: The Politics of Sexuality*, London, Virago.

RICHARDSON, DIANE (1993) 'Sexuality and Male Dominance', in RICHARDSON, DIANE and ROBINSON, VICTORIA (Eds) *Introducing Women's Studies*, London, Macmillan.

SAYERS, JANET (1982) *Biological Politics*, London, Tavistock.

SCOTT, SUE and MORGAN, DAVID (Eds) (1993) *Body Matters*, London, Falmer Press.

SHILLING, CHRIS (1993) *The Body and Social Theory*, London, Sage.

SNITOW, ANN, STANSELL, CHRISTINE and THOMPSON, SHARON (Eds) (1984) *Desire: The Politics of Sexuality*, London, Virago.

VANCE, CAROLE (Ed.) (1984) *Pleasure and Danger: Exploring Female Sexuality*, London, Routledge and Kegan Paul.

WILKINSON, SUE and KITZINGER, CELIA (1994) 'Dire Straights? Contemporary Rehabilitations of Heterosexuality', in GRIFFIN, GABRIELE, HESTER, MARIANNE, RAI, SHIRIN and ROSENEIL, SASHA (Eds) (1994) *Stirring It: Challenges for Feminism*, London, Taylor and Francis.

Section I
Analysing (Hetero)sexuality

Chapter 1

Gender and Heterosexuality: A Materialist Feminist Analysis

Stevi Jackson

This chapter is a response to the recent resurgence of debate on feminism and heterosexuality. Although positions within this debate are not as polarized as they were in the early 1980s, there is still a large gulf between radical lesbian feminist critics of heterosexuality (Kitzinger and Wilkinson, 1993) and heterosexual feminists seeking to defend their sexual practices (Hollway, 1993; Segal, 1994). I find myself caught in the middle, dissatisfied with both sides – a white, heterosexual radical feminist, wanting to problematize heterosexuality without damning myself as a failed feminist. I have therefore been looking for means of theorizing heterosexuality critically, exploring the ways in which it is implicated in the subordination of women, but without conflating heterosexuality as an institution with heterosexual practice, experience and identity. I have found a useful starting point in the analyses of gender produced by French materialist feminists, especially Christine Delphy (1984, 1993). In developing this perspective, I shall argue that gender – as a socially constructed product of patriarchal hierarchies – is fundamental to an analysis of sexuality.

The concept of gender has not been uncontested within feminism: the usual distinction between 'sex' as biological difference and culturally constructed 'gender' has proved particularly problematic. There have always been some feminists who disliked this distinction. Psychoanalytic theorists, for example, maintain that sex, gender and sexuality are inextricably linked and cannot be disentangled from each other (Mitchell, 1982). This is the case both for those who see femininity and masculinity as culturally constructed and for those who assume that some essential difference exists prior to cultural influences. Feminists interested in asserting women's 'difference' –

whether from a psychoanalytic perspective or not – often object to the sex gender distinction because they see it as denying the specificity of women's bodily experience (Brodribb, 1992; Gatens, 1983; Irigaray, 1985, 1993).

On the other hand, there are those who reject the sex gender distinction on the grounds that its challenge to essentialism does not go far enough: it still assumes a natural sex onto which gender is grafted. This can all too easily lead to the assumption that heterosexual relations between anatomical males and anatomical females belong in the realm of nature. Hence it is argued that we should question the very existence of gender categories themselves and ask why and how the social world is divided into the two groups we call 'women' and 'men'. This position is often associated with recent writings by poststructuralists and postmodernists, such as Butler (1990), and Riley (1988), but it began to be developed by French radical feminists in the 1970s. These materialist radical feminists differ from poststructuralists and postmodernists in one very crucial respect. The latter see the meaning of social categories as fluid and shifting, constantly being contested and renegotiated. Materialists, while accepting that these categories can and must be challenged, see them as rooted in social practices and structural inequalities which are built into the fabric of society. 'Men' and 'women' are not simply discursive constructs, but are materially existing social groups founded upon unequal, exploitative relationships. It is this perspective that I wish to explore further.

Materialist Feminist Perspectives

Materialist feminism is a form of radical feminism which has been an established current in France since the 1970s. Its exponents include Christine Delphy and Monique Wittig; others, such as Nicole-Claude Mathieu and Colette Guillaumin, are less well known outside France. In the period from 1977 to 1980 this theoretical tendency found a major expression in the journal *Questions Féministes* (*QF*). This journal was dedicated to the analysis of patriarchy as a social system in which men and women constitute classes with opposing interests. This was the starting point for their analysis of men and women as social categories: a radically anti-essentialist perspective on gender.[1]

The form of theory these thinkers have generated confounds popular stereotypes of both radical feminism and 'French feminism'. The former is frequently misrepresented as championing 'women's values' as some essential feminine characteristic – a position to which materialist feminism is fundamentally opposed. The latter, 'French feminism', has come to denote something quite different from feminism in France. It is largely an Anglo-American invention which canonizes some French theorists while completely ignoring others, a misrepresentation perpetuated by some influential anthologies, such as Fraser and Bartky (1992), Jardine and Smith (1987) and Marks and Courtivron (1981). Within France, those engaged in psychoanalytic theorizing about femininity, exploring women's relationships to their body and 'feminine' language, have not generally defined themselves as feminists. Yet this is what is called 'French feminism' outside France, the 'holy trinity' being Hélène Cixous, Julia Kristeva and Luce Irigaray (Landry and MacLean, 1993, p. 54).[2] 'French feminism' can also mean work which draws on the writings of certain male theorists, such as Lacan, Foucault and Derrida. The boundaries of 'French feminism' are thus strangely constructed: some men fall within its definition, as do women who do not call themselves feminists, but those who have always called themselves feminists are excluded. This, as Delphy has pointed out, is a form of imperialism whereby women from outside France define what 'French feminism' really is, while feminists within France are denied the right to be heard (Delphy, forthcoming).

French radical feminism, in particular, suffers from this silencing. Sometimes French radical feminism is reinvented: Chris Weedon even goes so far as to identify the 'trinity', and Irigaray in particular, with radical feminism (Weedon, 1987, p. 9) – apparently because she assumes that anyone asserting women's essential 'difference' must be a radical feminist! Those in France who name themselves radical feminists have always vigorously opposed this point of view. For example, much of the editorial of the first issue of *QF* is devoted to a polemic against this doctrine of 'neo-femininity'. If, as materialist feminists argue, relations between women and men are class relations, then gender divisions have nothing to do with nature but are the product of social and economic structures. Patriarchal domination is not based upon pre-existing sex differences, rather gender exists as a social division because of patriarchal domination. Hence hierarchy precedes division (Delphy, 1993; Delphy and Leonard, 1992). As Delphy and Leonard put it, 'For us "men" and "women" are not two naturally given groups who at some time fell into a hierarchical relationship. Rather the reason the two groups are distinguished socially is because one dominates the other' (Delphy and Leonard, 1992, p. 258). This argument is in keeping with the marxist method of analysis adopted by materialist feminists. For Marxists classes only exist in relation to one another: there can be no bourgeoisie without the proletariat and vice versa. Similarly 'men' and 'women' exist as socially significant categories because of the exploitative relationship which both binds them together and sets them apart from each other. Conceptually there could be no 'women' without the opposing category 'men', and vice versa. As Wittig puts it, 'there are no slaves without masters' (1992, p. 15).

Because they analysed women's oppression in terms of class, French radical feminists emphasized the social aspect of sex categories. From the 1970s they began to speak of social men and social women as distinct from biological males and females (see, for example, Delphy, 1984; Guillaumin, 1987; Mathieu, 1977; Wittig, 1982). The implications of treating 'men' and 'women' as social categories were elaborated in the editorial to the first issue of *Questions Féministes*, in which the collective spelled out their position on sex differences in some detail. They argue that opposition to naturalistic explanations of sexual difference is a basic tenet of radical feminism. Women's oppression derives from a patriarchal social system and 'in order to describe and unmask this oppression, arguments that have recourse to "nature" must be shattered' (*Questions Féministes* collective [1977] 1981, p. 214). Ideas of feminine 'difference' embraced by adherents of 'neo-femininity' derive from patriarchal reasoning which claims that women are different in order to justify and conceal our exploitation. In order to counter this ideology, they argue, radical feminism must refuse any notion of 'woman' that is unrelated to social context.

> The corollary of this refusal is our effort to deconstruct the notion of 'sex differences' which gives a shape and a base to the concept of 'woman' and is an integral part of naturalist ideology. The social mode of being of men and of women is in no way linked to their nature as males and females nor with the shape of their sex organs. (1981, pp. 214–15)

The consequences of this are indeed radical. The political goal envisaged is not the raising of women's status, nor equality between women and men, but the abolition of sex differences themselves. In a non-patriarchal society there would be no social distinctions between men and women, nor between heterosexuality and homosexuality:

> On the level of sexual practices, the distinction between homo- and heterosexuality will be meaningless since individuals will meet as singular individuals with their own specific history and not on the basis of their sexual identity. (1981, p. 215)

To be biologically male or female would no longer define our social or sexual identities. This does not mean women becoming like men 'for at the same time as we destroy the idea of the generic "Woman", we also destroy the idea of "Man"' (1981, p. 215). It cannot be otherwise since the terms woman/ women and man/men are defined in relation to each other: they have no meaning outside this relation. The difference denoted by these terms derives from hierarchy, so that the destruction of sexual hierarchy requires the destruction of difference.

While the collective agreed on these basic premisses, they did not agree on the political consequences of their analysis, particularly for sexuality. In 1980 *QF* ceased publication after an acrimonious dispute over radical lesbianism and heterosexual feminism. This conflict was by no means confined to the *QF* collective – it divided radical feminists as a whole. Nor was this a peculiarly French issue; it was being debated in many Western countries. In Britain, for example, a similarly heated controversy was sparked off by a paper on political lesbianism written by the Leeds Revolutionary Feminists (see Onlywomen Press, 1981).

In France, public debate on this issue was initiated by the publication of two articles in *Questions Féministes* in February 1980. The first of these was Monique Wittig's 'The Straight Mind' in which she challenged the heterosexual thinking she saw as underlying patriarchal culture. The category 'woman', she argued, had no meaning outside 'heterosexual systems of thought'. She concluded that, because they live outside heterosexuality, 'lesbians are not women' (1992, p. 32). The other article, 'Heterosexuality and Feminism' by Emmanuèle de Lesseps, argued against the politics of radical lesbianism. de Lesseps acknowledged the contradictions heterosexual feminists face, but rejected the idea that all feminists should become lesbians or that feminism should exclude heterosexual women. This she saw as turning the feminist movement, which began from womens' common experience, against women.

Each side defended its position in terms of the central tenet of radical feminism: that 'men' and 'women' are classes. As the radical lesbians saw it, they were pushing 'the logic of radical feminist analysis to its conclusion' and identified with 'a lesbian political analysis which considers the *class of men* to be the main enemy' (in Duchen, 1987, p. 85). If men are the class enemy, they argued, feminists should withdraw from any personal relationships with them, should refuse to service them sexually or otherwise and should devote all their energies to the liberation of women. Heterosexuality was 'antagonistic to feminist commitment' (Duchen, 1987, p. 85) and those who did not see this were at best reformist and at worst class 'collaborators' (ibid., p. 87). Those who opposed the radical lesbian position, Delphy and de Lesseps, subsequently launched *Nouvelles Questions Féministes*. In its first editorial they countered the arguments of the radical lesbians, which they saw as incompatible with the premisses of radical feminism: the recognition that women constitute an oppressed class, that we are all oppressed by men as a class and that feminism is the struggle against this *common* oppression of women (in Duchen, 1987, p. 81). While accepting the need for a critique of heterosexuality, they insisted that this should be disassociated from a 'condemnation of heterosexual women' (1987, p. 82).

Since then, theorists on both sides of the debate have held to the position that the categories 'women' and 'men' are the product of class relations, but with differing consequences for the analysis of both lesbianism and heterosexuality (see Delphy, 1984, 1993; Wittig, 1992). It is Delphy's analysis that I am following here, particularly her continued insistence that it is gender division itself, and not just the content of gender categories, that should be the object of scrutiny (Delphy, 1993).

Materialist and Postmodern Perspectives

Although it remains controversial, such radical anti-essentialism has now become more academically fashionable – particularly among poststructuralists and postmodernists. These theorists frequently take their inspiration from the Anglo-American version of 'French feminism' – although Wittig's work has had some influence on theorists such as Diana Fuss (1989) and Judith Butler (1990) who are concerned with the interconnections between gender and sexuality. Reading Wittig in isolation from other materialist feminists, however, leads to interpretations of her work which undermine its materialist foundations. Exploring these perspectives will help to elucidate the differences between postmodern and materialist deconstructions of gender as well as the debates within materialist feminism itself.

Wittig endorses the materialist feminist view that there are no natural sex categories pre-existing hierarchy. 'It is oppression that creates sex and not the contrary' ([1982] 1992, p. 2). Like Delphy she sees men and women as social classes and sexual divisions as a product of this class relationship, but places particular emphasis on heterosexuality as the locus of women's oppression. The category of sex is the political category that founds society as heterosexual' ([1982] 1992, p. 5). Where she differs radically from Delphy is in her assertion that lesbians, fugitives from the heterosexual contract, escape from the category 'women', are not women (1980, 1981). Both Fuss (1989) and Butler (1990) are critical of the essentialism implied by treating lesbianism as lying outside the cultural construction and regulation of gender and sexuality. This is an argument with which Delphy would concur, given that she sees heterosexuality and homosexuality as culturally constructed in the same way as gender – in line with the position originally outlined in *QF*.

Butler's (1990) radical deconstruction of gender owes a great deal to materialist feminism, but is not itself materialist. She does not read Wittig in the context of the thinkers whom Wittig herself (1992, p. xiv) names as her chief political influences, such as Mathieu, Delphy and Guillaumin, but in conjunction with Foucault, Lacan, Derrida, Kristeva and Irigaray. As a result, she filters out much which is fundamental to materialism. In the first place Butler over-sexualizes Wittig's conceptualization of heterosexuality. According to Butler, Wittig sees the binary sexual divide as 'serving the reproductive aims of a system of compulsory heterosexuality (Butler, 1990, p. 19), and as restricting 'the production of identities along the axis of heterosexual desire' (1990, p. 26). Now it is true that Wittig places great emphasis on women's sexual servicing of men, but she also makes it clear that the heterosexual contract involves a good deal more than coitus and reproduction: 'The category of sex is the product of a heterosexual society in which men appropriate for themselves the reproduction and production of women and also their physical persons by means of . . . the marriage contract' (Wittig, [1982] 1992, p. 6). This contract 'assigns the woman certain obligations, including unpaid work' (1992, p. 7). Wittig goes on to argue that it determines control of a woman's children and where she should live, makes her dependent on her husband, subject to his authority, and denies her the full protection of the law if he assaults her. Elsewhere she explains that what lesbians escape from is a relation 'which implies personal and physical obligation as well as economic obligation' ([1981] 1992, p. 20). All this bears comparison with Delphy's (1984) analysis of the class relation between men and women and with Guillaumin's work on sexual difference and on the private and collective appropriation of women's labour (Guillaumin, 1980, 1987).

Butler, however, ignores these material social relations which underpin the category of sex. She does appear to understand that 'materialism takes social institutions and practices . . . as the basis of critical analysis' (1990, p. 125), but she fails to recognize that, for materialists, this implies a system of structural inequalities. Because Wittig's references to such structural inequalities are absent from Butler's summary of her work, we are left with the impression of sexual difference as oppressive, yet not clearly hierarchical. 'Wittig understands "sex" to be discursively produced and circulated by a system of significations oppressive to women, gays and lesbians' (Butler, 1990, p. 113). Wittig's work is thus shaped to fit Butler's own contention that gender is a 'regulatory fiction' to which both women and men are subject, but which is sustained – and can be subverted – through performance.

The association of this deconstruction of gender and sexuality with postmodernism and queer theory explains some feminists' resistance to it –

particularly because queer theory ultimately displaces patriarchal gender hierarchy in favour of heterosexuality as the primary regulatory system. It is vitally important for feminism that we see heterosexuality as a gendered hierarchy and not just as a normative construction of cross-sex desire. For materialist feminists heterosexuality is not simply a matter of the sex-gender-desire matrix which Butler outlines; it certainly includes this, but heterosexuality is founded not only on a linkage between gender and sexuality, but on the appropriation of women's bodies and labour.

Heterosexuality: Institution and Identity

Feminist discussions of heterosexuality frequently distinguish between heterosexuality as institution and as practice or experience (Richardson, 1993; Robinson, 1993). Such distinctions are necessary if we are to deal with the complexities of heterosexuality and not treat it as a monolithic entity. They also help us to avoid conflating the critique of heterosexuality with personal criticism of heterosexual feminists – a problem apparent in earlier debates in Britain, France and elsewhere. I would suggest that, in the light of recent debates, we need to add a further dimension: the social and political identities associated with heterosexuality.[3] Such distinctions are, of course, analytical ones which, as heterosexuality is lived, intersect and interrelate. I would also argue that we should not over-privilege sexuality in relation to other aspects of social life: as institution, identity, practice and experience heterosexuality is not merely sexual. Moreover, while heterosexuality's central institution is marriage, the assumption of normative heterosexuality operates throughout society and even its specifically sexual practice is by no means confined to the private sphere (see, for example, Hearn *et al.*, 1989).

As it is institutionalized within society and culture, heterosexuality is founded upon gender hierarchy: men's appropriation of women's bodies and labour underpins the marriage contract (Delphy and Leonard, 1992). The benefits men gain through their dominant position in the gender order are by no means reducible to the sexual and reproductive use of women's bodies. Men may say that 'women are only good for one thing', but as Delphy (1992) points out, this is no reason why we should accept this at face value. In marriage, for example, the home comforts produced by a wife's domestic labour are probably far more important to a man's well-being and his ability to maintain his position as a man than the sexual servicing he receives. Nonetheless, a man does acquire sexual rights in a woman by virtue of marriage and a woman who is not visibly under the protection of a man can be regarded as fair sexual game by others (Guillaumin, 1980). Fear of sexual violence and harassment is also one means by which women are policed and police themselves through a range of disciplinary practices – from restricting their own access to public space, to where they choose to sit on a bus or train, how they sit and who they avoid eye contact with (Bartky, 1990). Here the macro level of power intersects with its micro practices. The institutionalization of heterosexuality also works ideologically, through the discourses and forms of representation which define sex in phallocentric terms, which position men as sexual subjects and women as sexual objects.

The question of sexual identity, in particular lesbianism as a political identity, has been much debated by feminists. Heterosexuality, however, is still infrequently thought of in these terms and the vast majority of heterosexual women probably do not define themselves as such. Nonetheless, many of the identities available to women derive from their location within heterosexual relations – as wife, girlfriend, daughter or mother. Attachment to these identities affects the ways in which women experience the institution and practices of heterosexuality. For example, women's ambivalent feelings about housework, their unwillingness to be critical of the appropriation of their labour, even when they are aware of the inequity of their situation, springs from their feelings about those they work for and from their desire to be good wives and mothers (Oakley, 1974; Westwood, 1984). In sexual terms, too, women's identities are likely to be shaped by heterosexual imperatives – the need to attract and please a man. The desire to be sexually attractive appears to be profoundly important to women's sense of self worth and closely bound up with the gendered disciplinary practices through which docile, feminine bodies are produced (Bartky, 1990). Hence heterosexuality, while uninterrogated, is pivotal to conventional feminine identities.

To name oneself as heterosexual is to make visible an identity which is generally taken for granted as a normal fact of life. This can be a means of problematizing heterosexuality and challenging its privileged status, but for women being heterosexual is by no means a situation of unproblematic privilege. Heterosexual feminists may benefit from appearing 'normal' and unthreatening, but heterosexuality as an institution entails a hierarchical relation between (social) men and (social) women. It is women's subordination within institutionalized heterosexuality which is the starting point for feminist analysis. It is resistance to this subordination which is the foundation of feminist politics. It is hardly surprising, then, that heterosexual feminists prefer to be defined in terms of their feminism – their resistance – rather than their heterosexuality, their relation to men (Swindells, 1993). Resisting the label heterosexual, though, has its problems. It can imply a refusal to question and challenge both the institution and one's own practice; it can serve to invalidate lesbianism as a form of resistance to patriarchy and

19

to deny the specific forms of oppression that lesbians face. For these reasons Kitzinger and Wilkinson are sceptical about those who 'call for the dissolution of the dichotomous categories "lesbian" and "heterosexual"' (1993, p. 7).

Questioning this binary opposition, however, need not be a way of avoiding the politics of lesbianism or getting heterosexual feminists off the hook, but can represent an honest attempt to problematize heterosexuality (see Young, 1993; Gergen, 1993). Nor is it only heterosexual feminists who are engaged in this deconstructive enterprise, but also lesbian queer theorists such as Diana Fuss (1991) and Judith Butler (1990, 1991). When such arguments are framed from a postmodernist stance, this does make it difficult to account for the systematic structural basis of any form of oppression (see Jackson, 1992). Nonetheless, treating the categories 'lesbian' and 'heterosexual' as problematic is by no means antithetical to radical feminism: indeed, I would argue that it is essential. This is not merely a matter of competing identities, but is fundamental to an appreciation of the social construction of gender and sexual categories.

The categories heterosexual, homosexual and lesbian are rooted in gender – they presuppose gender divisions and could not exist without our being able to define ourselves and others by gender. If we take Delphy's (1984, 1993) argument that 'men' and 'women' are not biologically given entities but social groups defined by the hierarchical and exploitative relationship between them, then the division between hetero and homosexualities is, by extension, also a product of this class relation. Within this perspective it is possible to see gender and sexual categories as both social constructs and material realities. 'Women' are a social rather than natural category defined by their relation to men. Lesbianism by virtue of its location in relation to patriarchal heterosexuality also has a real social existence. This does not mean, as Wittig (1992) would have it, that lesbians are not women – we are all defined by our gender and there is no escaping the patriarchal hierarchy within which we are positioned as women.

Heterosexual Eroticism: Practice and Experience

Recent analyses of heterosexuality, whether attacking it (Kitzinger and Wilkinson, 1993; Kitzinger, 1994) or defending it (Hollway, 1993; Segal, 1994), have tended to focus on sexual experience and practice, particularly on desire and pleasure. These debates have been centrally concerned with power – its structural underpinnings and its micro-practices, the implications of its erotic dimensions and the degree to which women can subvert or challenge it within heterosexual relations. It should be noted that for materialist feminists the experience and practice of heterosexuality is not just about what does or does not happen between the sheets, but about who cleans the bathroom or who performs emotional labour on whom. Because of the prominence of heterosexual eroticism in recent debates, however, I will consider the potential of materialist feminism for furthering our understanding of desire, pleasure and displeasure in heterosexual sex. I will begin from the premiss that gender is fundamental, that as desiring subjects we are gendered, as are the objects of our desire. This is as true of lesbian sexuality as it is of heterosexuality.

To desire the 'other sex' or indeed to desire 'the same sex' presupposes the prior existence of 'men' and 'women' as socially – and erotically – meaningful categories. What is specific to heterosexual desire is that it is premissed on gender *difference*, on the sexual 'otherness' of the desired object. From a materialist feminist perspective this difference is not an anatomical one but a social one; it is the hierarchy of gender which 'transforms an anatomical difference (which is itself devoid of social implications) into a relevant distinction for social practice' (Delphy, 1984, p. 144). Since it is gender hierarchy which renders these anatomical differences socially and erotically significant, it is hardly surprising that heterosexual eroticism is infused with power. However, this eroticization of power is not reducible to the mere juxtaposition of certain body parts. There is nothing intrinsic to male and female anatomy which positions women as passive or privileges certain sexual practices above others. There is no absolute reason why the conjunction of a penis and a vagina has to be thought of as penetration, or as a process in which only one of those organs is active. The coercive equation of sex = coitus = something men do to women is not an inevitable consequence of an anatomical female relating sexually to an anatomical male, but the product of the social relations under which those bodies meet. Those social relations can be challenged. Even the most trenchant critics of heterosexuality and penetrative sex such as Jeffreys (1990) and Dworkin (1987) recognize that it is not male and female anatomy nor even, in Dworkin's case, the act of intercourse itself which constitute the problem, but rather the way in which heterosexuality is institutionalized and practised under patriarchy.

For some feminists anatomical difference, or indeed any form of difference between lovers, is seen as a potential source of power imbalance. Hence they strive to 'eroticise sameness and equality' (Jeffreys, 1990, p. 315). But is 'sameness' necessary for equality? From a materialist feminist perspective it is not difference which produces hierarchy, but hierarchy which gives rise to socially significant differences. All of us are 'different' from each other: no two human beings are 'the same' and a lover is always someone 'other'. The point is that there are some differences which are of little social relevance – such as the colour of our hair – and others which are constructed as socially significant by virtue of hierarchy – such as the configuration of our genitals or our skin pigmentation. Given that gender difference remains a material fact of social life, does this mean that power is an inescapable feature of heterosexual eroticism?

To argue that the power hierarchy of gender is structural does not mean that it is exercised uniformly and evenly at the level of interpersonal sexual relations, nor that our practice and experience is wholly determined by patriarchal structures and ideologies. There is some room for manoeuvre within these constraints. To deny this is to deny heterosexual women any agency, to see us as doomed to submit to men's desires whether as unwilling victims or misguided dupes. Heterosexual feminists, here as elsewhere in their lives, have struggled against men's dominance. We have asserted our right to define our own pleasure, questioned phallocentric models of sexuality, tried to deprioritize penetration or reconceptualize it in ways which did not position us as passive objects (Campbell, 1980; Jackson, 1982; Robinson, 1993). Recently some of us have admitted – cautiously or defiantly – that even penetrative sex with men can be enjoyable and that its pleasure is not merely eroticized submission (Hollway, 1993; Robinson, 1993; Rowland, 1993; Segal, 1994).

Critics of heterosexuality are unimpressed by such claims. Kitzinger and Wilkinson, for example, are scathing about heterosexual feminists' attempts to develop egalitarian sexual practices and to change the meaning of penetration. Such strategies, they say, 'obscure the problem of the *institutionalization* of penile penetration under heteropatriarchy' (1993, p. 21). They see the institution as totally determining practice so that each and every instance of penetration is an enactment of men's power. While it is the case that penetration within patriarchy is loaded with symbolic meanings which encode male power and while it is often in fact coercive, it cannot be assumed that it invariably carries this singular meaning. To argue that it does is to treat the physical act as meaningful in itself, as magically embodying male power without any intervening processes. It is here assumed that the micro-processes of power can simply be read off from the structural level. It certainly cannot be assumed that if women like heterosexual sex we must all be wallowing in a masochistic eroticization of our subordination – the consistent message of the radical lesbian position (Jeffreys, 1990; Kitzinger and Wilkinson, 1993; Kitzinger, 1994).

We need to retain a critical perspective on heterosexual pleasure, but one which is more subtle and less condemnatory. However, we should not underestimate the pervasiveness of male power either. Even if, as Lynne Segal suggests, 'sex places "manhood" in jeopardy', threatening the 'masculine ideal of autonomous selfhood' (1994, p. 255), the hierarchical ordering of gender and sexuality is not as easy to subvert as she implies. Power operates at a variety of levels. Although we can contest it at the level of individual practice (and enhance our sexual pleasure in the process), this may have little effect elsewhere. There are, moreover, very real material constraints on seeking heterosexual pleasure and for many women it remains elusive (Ramazanoglu, 1994). Women often still discipline themselves to fit a model of sexuality which prioritizes male desires and defines women's fulfilment in terms of 'love' and the giving of pleasure (Holland *et al.*, 1994). This attribute of femininity is hardly confined to sexuality: the ethic of service to men is fundamental to other aspects of gender relations, to men's appropriation of women's labour as well as their bodies.

It is difficult to imagine a truly egalitarian form of heterosexuality while gender division persists; and if that division were eradicated heterosexuality would no longer exist in any meaningful sense – and nor would lesbianism. Materialist feminism enables us to see that both heterosexuality and lesbianism depend for their existence on the hierarchy of gender. Sexuality is one site of struggle against that hierarchy, but it is by no means the only one. Nor is sexuality the sole basis of women's subordination. To give too much weight to sexual desire, practice and identity may deflect our attention from the myriad other ways in which the patriarchal ordering of the world into 'men' and 'women' is perpetuated. Heterosexuality helps to sustain that order, but it should be remembered that heterosexuality itself is not merely a sexual institution.

Notes

1   It should be noted that Delphy alone among these theorists used the term 'gender'. As well as being a term which originated in Anglophone theory, French radical feminists felt that, because it was defined in relation to biological sex, it too readily implied a natural distinction which pre-existed the social division of gender (see, for example Wittig, 1992, p. xvi). Delphy on the other hand prefers to use the concept of gender because 'sex' cannot easily be divested of its naturalistic connotations (1993).

2   Of these three, only Irigaray has ever identified as a feminist.

3   Elsewhere, I have also distinguished between practice and experience (Jackson, 1994). I have not explored this here for reasons of space.

References

BARTKY, SANDRA LEE (1990) *Femininity and Domination*, London and New York, Routledge.

BRODRIBB, SOMER (1992) *Nothing Mat(t)ers: A Feminist Critique of Postmodernism*, Melbourne, Spinifex.

BUTLER, JUDITH (1990) *Gender Trouble: Feminism and the Subversion of Identity*, New York, Routledge.

BUTLER, JUDITH (1991) 'Imitation and Gender Insubordination', in FUSS, D. (Ed.) *Inside/Out*, London and New York, Routledge.

CAMPBELL, BEATRIX (1980) 'Feminist Sexual Politics', *Feminist Review*, 5.

DELPHY, CHRISTINE (1984) *Close to Home: A Materialist Analysis of Women's Oppression*, London, Hutchinson.

DELPHY, CHRISTINE (1992) 'Mothers' Union?', *Trouble and Strife*, 24, pp. 12–19.

DELPHY, CHRISTINE (1993) 'Rethinking Sex and Gender', *Women's Studies International Forum*, 16 (1), pp. 1–9.

DELPHY, CHRISTINE (forthcoming) 'The invention of French Feminism: an essential move', in *Yale French Studies*.

DELPHY, CHRISTINE and LEONARD, DIANA (1992) *Familiar Exploitation: A New Analysis of Marriage in Contemporary Western Societies*, Oxford, Polity.

DUCHEN, CLAIRE (Ed.) (1987) *French Connections: Voices from the Women's Movement in France*, London, Hutchinson.

DWORKIN, ANDREA (1987) *Intercourse*, London, Secker and Warburg.

FRASER, NANCY and BARTKY, SANDRA LEE (Eds) (1992) *Revaluing French Feminism*, Bloomington and Indianapolis, Indiana University Press.

FUSS, DIANA (1989) *Essentially Speaking: Feminism, Nature and Difference*, New York and London, Routledge.

FUSS, DIANA (1991) *Inside/Out: Lesbian Theories, Gay Theories*, New York, Routledge.

GATENS, MOIRA (1983) 'A Critique of the Sex/Gender Distinction', in ALLEN, J. and PATTON, P. (Eds) *Beyond Marxism? Interventions after Marx*, New South Wales, Intervention Publications, pp. 143–60.

GERGEN, MARY (1993) 'Unbundling our Binaries – Genders, Sexualities, Desires', in WILKINSON, SUE and KITZINGER, CELIA (Eds) *Heterosexuality*, London, Sage.

GUILLAUMIN, COLETTE (1981) 'The Practice of Power and Belief in Nature. Part 1: The Appropriation of Women', *Feminist Issues*, 1 (2), pp. 3–28.

GUILLAUMIN, COLETTE (1987) 'The Question of Difference', in DUCHEN, CLAIRE (Ed.) *French Connections*, London, Hutchinson, pp. 64–77.

HEARN, JEFF, SHEPPARD, DEBORAH L., TANCRED-SHERIFF, PETA and BURRELL, GIBSON (Eds) (1989) *The Sexuality of Organization*, London, Sage.

HOLLAND, JANET *et al.* (1994) 'Power and Desire: The Embodiment of Female Sexuality', *Feminist Review*, 46.

HOLLWAY, WENDY (1993) 'Theorizing Heterosexuality: A Response', *Feminism and Psychology*, 3 (3).

IRIGARAY, LUCE (1985) *This Sex Which is Not One*, trans. Catherine Porter with Carolyn Burke, Cornell University Press.

IRIGARAY, LUCE (1993) *Je, tu, nous: Toward a Culture of Difference*, trans. Alison Martin, London and New York, Routledge.

JACKSON, STEVI (1982) 'Masculinity, Femininity and Sexuality', in FRIEDMAN, S. and SARAH, E. (Eds) *On The Problem of Men*, London, The Women's Press.

JACKSON, STEVI (1992) 'The Amazing Deconstructing Woman: The Perils of Postmodern Feminism', *Trouble and Strife*, 25.

JACKSON, STEVI (1994) 'Theorizing Heterosexuality: Gender, Power and Pleasure', Strathclyde Papers on Sociology and Social Policy, University of Strathclyde.

JARDINE, ALICE and SMITH, PAUL (Eds) (1987) *Men in Feminism*, New York, Methuen.

JEFFREYS, SHEILA (1990) *Anticlimax: A Feminist Perspective on the Sexual Revolution*, London, The Women's Press.

KITZINGER, CELIA (1994) 'Problematizing Pleasure: Radical Feminist Deconstructions of Sexuality and Power', in RADTKE H.L. and STAM, H.J. (Eds) *Power/ Gender: Social Relations in Theory and Practice*, London, Sage.

KITZINGER, CELIA and WILKINSON, SUE (1993) 'Theorizing Heterosexuality', in WILKINSON, SUE and KITZINGER, CELIA (Eds) *Heterosexuality: A Feminism and Psychology Reader*, London, Sage.

LANDRY, DONNA and MACLEAN, GERALD (1993) *Materialist Feminisms*, Oxford, Blackwell.

MARKS, ELAINE and COURTIVRON, ISABELLE DE (Eds) (1981) *New French Feminisms: An Anthology*, Brighton, Harvester.

MATHIEU, NICOLE-CLAUDE (1977) *Ignored by Some, Denied by Others: The Social Sex Category in Sociology*, London, Women's Research and Resources Centre.

MITCHELL, JULIET (1982) 'Introduction I', in MITCHELL, JULIET and ROSE, JACQUELINE (Eds) *Feminine Sexuality: Jacques Lacan and the École Freudienne*, London, Macmillan, pp. 1–26.

OAKLEY, ANN (1984) *The Sociology of Housework*, 2nd ed., Oxford, Blackwell.

ONLYWOMEN PRESS (Eds) (1981) *Love Your Enemy: The Debate between Heterosexual Feminism and Political Lesbianism*, London, Onlywomen Press.

QUESTIONS FÉMINISTES COLLECTIVE (1981) 'Variations on a common theme', in MARKS, E. and DE COURTIVRON, I. (Eds) *New French Feminisms*, (originally published in *Questions Féministes*, 1977, no. 1), Brighton, Harvester.

RAMAZANOGLU, CAROLINE (1994) 'Theorising Heterosexuality: A Response to Wendy Hollway', *Feminism and Psychology*, 4 (2), pp. 320–1.

RICHARDSON, DIANE (1993) 'Sexuality and Male Dominance', in RICHARDSON, DIANE and ROBINSON, VICTORIA (Eds) *Introducing Women's Studies*, London, Macmillan.

RILEY, DENISE (1988) *'Am I That Name?' Feminism and the Category of 'Women' in History*, London, Macmillan.

ROBINSON, VICTORIA (1993) 'Heterosexuality: Beginnings and Connections', in

WILKINSON, SUE and KITZINGER, CELIA (Eds) *Heterosexuality: A Feminism and Psychology Reader*, London, Sage.

ROWLAND, ROBYN (1993) 'Radical Feminist Heterosexuality: The Personal and the Political', in WILKINSON, SUE and KITZINGER, CELIA (Eds) *Heterosexuality: A Feminism and Psychology Reader*, London, Sage.

SEGAL, LYNNE (1994) *Straight Sex: The Politics of Pleasure*, London, Virago.

SWINDELLS, JULIA (1993) 'A Straight Outing', *Trouble and Strife*, 26.

WEEDON, CHRIS (1987) *Feminist Practice and Poststructuralist Theory*, Oxford, Blackwell.

WESTWOOD, SALLIE (1984) *All Day, Every Day*, London, Pluto Press.

WITTIG, MONIQUE (1992) *The Straight Mind and Other Essays*, Hemel Hempstead, Harvester Wheatsheaf.

YOUNG, ALISON (1993) 'The Authority of the Name', in WILKINSON, SUE and KITZINGER, CELIA (Eds) *Heterosexuality: A Feminism and Psychology Reader*, London, Sage.

Chapter 2

Back to Basics: Heterosexuality, Biology and Why Men Stay on Top

Caroline Ramazanoglu

The philosopher Wittgenstein, in his search for the conditions for a logically perfect language, said that 'everything that can be put into words can be put clearly', and that 'what we cannot speak about we must consign to silence' (Wittgenstein, 1961). Feminists, in their various attempts to understand and improve human social relations, live with the human problem that what can be said about social relations can never be said very clearly, and what has been passed over in silence is what must be talked about. This has given feminists particular problems of specifying what it is that women have in common, and so whether Women's Studies and feminist politics can be addressed to anything more than local or specific interests. Feminists have argued that our visions of gender are not rooted in our bodies but in culture and meanings (see, for example, Keller and Grontkowski, 1983, p. 208). Since theory is not framed by our bodies, seeing social life as a feminist is not the same as seeing as a woman.

This chapter comes out of my concern that the current impact of some 'postmodern feminisms' on feminist theory is pushing towards a logical perfection of thought which may impede understandings of relations between women and men. The recent wave of Western feminism from the 1960s, with all its diversity, weaknesses and divisions, has been driven by a moral and political concern to identify, confront and change oppressive power relations. By feminism I mean a political commitment to working with women and against gendered power. This does not make gender the only or most important form of oppressive social relationship; it does not mean that all

27

women are always subordinated by their gender; it does not make men the enemies of women; it does not mean that all men are powerful: but feminism only makes sense as knowledge of gendered power and moral and political resistance to it.

If Women's Studies is international, some conception of what women have in common seems necessary, but it is clearer that many women lack common interests than that they have anything basic in common. Western feminists' claims, that what women have in common is male power over them, have led to waves of criticism and increasing clarification of the extent of political differences between women and the shared political interests between some women and some men. Even in the most patriarchal of societies, men are not simply oppressors, nor are women simply oppressed. An alternative suggestion, that what women have in common is their female bodies, raises a different but equally intractable set of problems. It is these problems, and the connections between them, that I want to consider here.

To suggest that women's bodies, the physical stuff of being female, are one aspect of a common female existence is not the same as saying that people's social existence as men or women is determined by a fixed, bodily make-up. I want to argue that it should be possible to take account of biological existence in understandings of social life, without having to assume that people's bodies rule their behaviour. In the 1990s, most of the population of the world are caught up in an international system in which war is normal; torture is routine; violence done to bodies is an everyday reality; the poor are left as the most exposed to storms, earthquakes, fires and floods; the chronically sick and the disabled struggle for basic human rights; and millions are malnourished or starving. Women have many different and opposed interests in harming bodies and keeping bodies from harm, but bodily matters are always also gendered.

What people do to each other around the world in terms of bodily contact, pleasure and pain, does not vary all that much, but what they think they are doing, and so what they experience, can vary considerably. Pleasurable heterosexual intercourse and horrific rape may not necessarily differ greatly in terms of bodily activity (and this is an argument used by some rapists in their own defence). But the social relationships of rape, the experiences and emotions it produces, and its social consequences are culturally distinct, but at the same time have some common features. The common features have been central to the identification of rape as an area of struggle in feminist politics and the identification of women's interests in opposing male power.

The idea that women have political interests in common has come both in theories of social construction (that relations between women and men are made in societies) and in those of biological determinism or essentialism (the view that we have some corporeal, essential identity as women or men which can explain behaviour). There is a difference, though, between saying that some essential femaleness makes women behave differently from men (a sociobiological position that has been extensively criticized), and suggesting that bodily differences may be one factor in enabling men to dominate women in particular social circumstances – which is the argument I want to make here. Feminists, however, have had enormous difficulty in addressing the possibility that bodily differences between men and women have some relevance to social relationships, without becoming entangled in biological determinism. From postmodern and poststructural perspectives the whole of feminist thought is increasingly being dubbed 'essentialist' and so dismissed. Opting for poststructuralist deconstructions seems to offer feminists an escape from the simplicities of an unwanted determinism.

Escaping from determinism, though, still leaves a problem of distinguishing between bodily differences that can and do make a material difference to human life and those that do not, or need not. In this respect, the natural bases of 'racial' difference are not the same as the natural bases of sex, illness or disability.

Bodily differences between men and women, between the well and the dying, or between the able-bodied and disabled, differ from bodily differences between 'races' or ethnic groups. The argument that 'race' is not an identifiable biological category is politically sensitive and still contested, but is now well established.[1] The 'racialized' body differs from the 'sexed' or 'disabled' body in the extent to which boundaries of racial differences can be shown to be socially constructed. In this country, questions of how 'white' you have to be before you are 'not black', how 'black' you have to be before you are 'not white', what constitutes 'Asian' and how ethnic boundaries are drawn, are ones of historical struggles around cultures, identities and subjectivities. Essential bodily differences have no bearing on how racial power is created and exercised.

'Sex', like 'disability', differs from 'race' in that there are material differences between male and female, able and disabled bodies, but they are comparable to 'race' in the sense that the boundaries between men and women, the able and disabled, are not simply natural. Recognizing sex, bodies and gender *as* social and cultural, however, does not logically entail that the differences between men and women are *only* social or cultural.

The possibility that women's political interests are in part grounded in differences between male and female material bodies is increasingly being written out of feminist theory. Asking questions in this area can arouse a good deal of emotion, if not outright contempt for the naivety of the questioner.

Nevertheless, I think that feminism has not adequately explained why men *have* been so successful in dominating women, and why women tend *not* to dominate men. It seems premature for the significance of bodily differences to be ruled out of feminist thought.

Male Domination, Material Existence and the Contradictions of Feminist Politics

Questions about biological natures and biological differences between women and men have been thought relevant to feminism, because the common sense of Western cultures, supported by considerable scientific expertise, declared women to be naturally subordinated to men, and designed by nature for a limited range of feminine capabilities (although these capabilities included hard physical labour for some women). Alison Jaggar (1992) notes that 'feminists have always been suspicious of talk about biology – and their suspicion has good historical grounds'.

Feminism countered both scientific and common-sense assumptions that differences between women and men are biological with accounts of sexuality and gender as socially constructed (e.g. Lieven, 1981; Sayers, 1982). But there are persistent problems of biological essentialism in feminist debates – both implicit and explicit. These debates, as Diana Fuss (1989) has argued, have been constrained by being caught in a framework of thought that defines bodies as *either* natural and essentially given, *or* socially constructed. This either/or framework inhibits a full voice for women's accounts of bodily experiences, risks and pleasures. Feminists, as a result, have often been divided, misunderstood and vilified over their various efforts to take account of both the natural, material differences which differentiate the sexes, and social constructions of sexuality and gender which produce variable notions of differentiation. Feminists can be both critical of essentialism, and also widely accused of essentialism. Diana Fuss (1989, p. 50) usefully points out that theories of the social construction of the body do not escape the pull of essentialism: one can talk of the body as matter without assuming that matter has a fixed essence.

More recent theories of deconstruction are increasingly turning the problem of how to understand bodies into an abstracted intellectual puzzle. Explanations of the relations between women and men define the possi-bilities of Women's Studies and feminist politics, and feminists have noted how poststructuralist and postmodern theories can put any general feminist politics in doubt (Braidotti, 1991; McNay, 1992; Ramazanoglu, 1993).

I do not think a feminist politics has to be uniform across differing social circumstances and political interests, but while feminism is dismissed as essentialist, and feminist theory increasingly shifts towards poststructuralism and postmodernism, the view that understandings of power need to continue to be grounded in the basic, embodied existence of material beings (people's everyday, gendered lives) slips away. While it has been productive to have a Foucauldian critique of feminism that insists on a history of the body (e.g. Gatens, 1992),[2] feminists have been producing their own histories and should be cautious about throwing real babies out with the poststructuralist bathwater.

Poststructuralist theory can work against feminism's requirement of both a clear identification of oppression/power, and a clear identification of men/ women, male/female. It is precisely in regard to these most basic elements of human life that political clarity is lacking. There is no clear connection between being a woman and being a feminist.

Most women reject any kind of feminist identity. For example, it is not fashionable for young women in Britain today to identify themselves as feminist. Although the conditions of their lives are deeply affected by recent feminist struggles, feminism has such a negative popular image that many young women associate it with a man-hating older generation that has nothing to offer them, or an able-bodied, white ethnicity that excludes them. Kate Figes, who describes herself as happily married, with two children and no problems as a working mother, has commented: 'Like many women I found certain aspects of feminism so tedious and discredited that the last thing it needed was to be handed down from generation to generation like some gruesome hereditary disease' (*The Guardian*, 6 July 1994).[3]

If women want close and loving relationships with men or identify politically with some men, and ask of feminism, 'what's in it for me?', they do not usually see a positive answer. Feminism has been splintered by the power relations between women, grounded in class, racism, ethnicity, nation, disability, sexuality and other social divisions which make any feminist politics problematic. If women feel that they are not *like* feminists, there is no popular basis for broad-based political movements for women. Feminist politics depends on women being, in at least some critical respects, like each other. But it is this basic 'likeness' that is difficult to establish.

Given the profound and persistent divisions between women, and the power that some women exercise over others, it is problematic to claim that women in a single country, let alone around the world, share common political interests as women. It is easier to see bodies, sex, and gender as cultural products, and women as having multiple identities. Yet in most societies today, male power is (with considerable variations) more or less effectively entrenched at all levels from private sexual relations to the political system, state and economy. This entrenched, and often violent, power is very hard to change. It is possible for both women and men to develop a critical consciousness and to resist male power, but such resistance is not general and is difficult to achieve and sustain.

Feminism needs to get back to basics, in order to be able to ask whether the enormous success of men's power over women is entirely cultural, or whether it is still worth considering whether it owes anything to the bodily differences between the sexes, and whether this question has any political significance. Women may claim that they do not need or want feminism; the mass media may pronounce the death of feminism, or transform it into sound bites from Camille Paglia; but feminism has identified male power over women as a problem to be explained, and this problem is widespread and persistent across women's differences.

Male dominance of women is not universal and is not a requirement for human social relations. But given the great variety of human social arrangements, and the great adaptability of people to differing social and environmental conditions, it does seem striking that male domination is so widespread, and female domination so absent, in so many different circumstances. It is the extent of the success and durability of male power that raises the question of whether male domination has anything to do with differences between male and female bodies. Understanding male power raises the question of how we know differences between women and men, but also whether differences 'really' exist. I approach this question through considering what a woman is.

What Is a Woman? Bodies and Boundaries

Feminist theorists as well as critics of feminism have convincingly argued that the assertion of 'woman' as a single social or political category is not tenable. 'Woman' with its assumption of a common political female condition has been deconstructed into varieties of historically and culturally specific women, each with their own relationships to power and their own political concerns. However, theorists who deny that 'woman' exists continue to talk about 'women', which suggests that there is something there to be talked about. Women are certainly intractably divided against other women in many different ways, but ceasing to take for granted that women are a common category raises the question, what is a woman? That is, what is a woman when she is a female body, but not in any general terms 'woman'? To whom is feminism addressed?[4]

The trend in feminist theory which is becoming academically dominant in this country is to accept the deconstruction of a common female identity, so that *being female* cannot be the basis of a common feminist politics. This rules out a common or essential female condition grounded in the female body, but it does not explain in what sense women continue to exist despite their differences. If women are not in some sense women, Women's Studies are left out on a limb.

The deconstruction of women is necessarily also a deconstruction of men. But it provides no explanation of why deconstructed men, despite their multiple cultures, identities and subjectivities, have so often so much power over women, nor of why women so often have so little power. If the simple dualism of determinism versus construction is abandoned, there is still no clear way out of the problem of explaining what a woman is, or why men so often dominate, because the boundaries of the physical cannot be clearly differentiated from those of the social. Our conception of the body itself is only accessible through ideas clouded by language and meanings, so the impact of anatomy and physiology on social arrangements (and vice versa) cannot be clearly measured (Benton, 1991; Sharp, 1992; Benton, 1992).

The most basic bodily experiences of pleasure and pain are never simply biological, since we can only experience them through the meanings they are given in cultures. There is also the problem that, even as adults, we may have bodily states and experiences for which we have no language. There is no simple conceptual dualism that allows us to distinguish the material, biological body from the social meanings, symbolism and social management of the socially constructed body. The corporeal body cannot be known in any neutral and clearly bounded fashion. The body we enter social life with, and its pleasures and pains, are given meaning through processes of social construction; ideas about the body are social, but are not entirely separable from bodily constraints and possibilities. Our bodies, after infancy, cannot be experienced independently of our ideas about them, but our ideas about them and, presumably, our desires, are not wholly independent of our biology. What then is the point of grappling with this issue?

I would answer in terms of feminist politics. If the boundaries between male and female bodies mark sites of political struggles, then what these struggles are about, and whether, or how, they can be resolved, matters. Lorena Bobbitt, in her distress, cut off her husband's penis, his bodily part which could enter her own body. She did not cut off a phallic signifier. While this was a social and symbolic as well as an emotional act, its physicality is inseparable from the act in its social context.

Reproduction is one obvious area of basic natural difference between women and men, but reproduction is never either simply biological or simply social. It is obvious that men cannot physically give birth to babies; they cannot reproduce without access to a woman's ovaries and womb (or an artificial substitute), and so without devising some sort of emotional/social relationship to a woman. They cannot claim a relationship with the child that results, without a cultural conception of this relationship. Most women can give birth, but none can do so without some social arrangement for insemination. Some women cannot conceive or bear children, or not without medical intervention. The physical capacity or incapacity to reproduce is lived socially, and emotionally. Men and women cannot have access to each other's bodies independently of their cultures and emotions. The reproductive and sexual functions of their bodies remain critically different, but the boundaries of gendered difference are not fixed.

First, human bodies are not as fixed and stable as popular scientific thought might suppose. While female bodies are characterized by the ability to reproduce the species, not all women have wombs or ovaries; not all are able to bear children; some can bear children but do not; some experience long painful labours; some die in childbirth, others have trouble-free pregnancies and give birth quickly and easily. Second, these differences are always socially framed and made meaningful, always emotional, and never simply physical, but it seems improbable that the extent of variation in reproductive experience can be explained simply as cultural or psychological.

It is possible that same-sex and opposite-sex sexual attraction and desire may have some bodily basis, as well as being constituted by social forces, but it does not follow that this is the same for everyone. It is possible to envisage heterosexuality, homosexuality and bisexuality as modern social categories in particular cultures, but it is also possible to think of these identity categories as more organically grounded for some people than for others.

There is no neutral way of identifying some people as 'women' from the evidence of particular understandings of the nature of their bodies, independently of culture. Only some biological beings are socially recognized as women, and femaleness is a cultural category. In different times and cultures the same body could be classified as female or male or allocated to other categories. Gender classification is a social process based on ideas of classification. However, the classification of 'men' and 'women' is not infinitely variable. Through history, very different societies have distinguished men from women in quite similar ways which are related to apparent genitalia and reproductive function. What they have differed considerably on is exactly how this is done, what identities are recognized, how boundaries are drawn and ambiguity regulated, and whether everyone has a fixed gender identity.

The current insistence in international sport that the bodies of women competitors must be proved by physical testing to be wholly female has not produced any clear anatomical basis for distinguishing 'more or less female' from 'not quite female', or 'not female' from 'really male'. The imposition of strict social categories of gender as if they were natural has created a social problem of gender ambiguity in sportswomen. This is an example of the rigidity with which complex and variable physical characteristics can be constructed as fixed biological categories. This supposedly scientific process of demanding a definitive gender identity takes no account of the social construction of bodily boundaries; nor does it take responsibility for the social and emotional consequences of labelling someone's body as 'not female'. The biological body can be seen to be being constructed in the social relations of male-dominated competition that dominate the regulation of international sport.

The boundaries between male and female are *simultaneously* both those of variable elements of bodily existence and also of variable cultural categories through which sameness and difference are specified. These boundaries cannot always be clearly drawn for each individual, and each culture has to deal with anatomical ambiguity (for example, through flexible or multiple categories, or by the rigid imposition of two categories in which a person must be declared either male or female). But the fact that bodily boundaries cannot be specified independently of cultural categories does not mean that they are not there.

It is not necessary to identify biology as a source of women's oppression in order to ask whether bodily differences play any part in the ways men so generally, persistently and successfully gain control of reproduction and sexuality, and of military prowess. Why was it that Genghis Khan, rather than his sister and her virgin hordes, struck fear into the mediaeval world? Since women can be violent and can be powerful, the reason why women have not simply countered male violence with force, ended rape, deconstructed heterosexuality, or taken control of reproduction, remains unclear unless we can account for the material basis of male and female bodies.

'What about the materiality of the body, *Judy*?'

Feminism has struggled to find useful ways of recognizing that social lives are lived in material bodies, and so to take a stand against theories which are abstracted from the everyday world of concealing menstrual flow, cleaning babies' bottoms, organizing food, controlling desires and so on. There is a constant tension in feminism between the potential abstractions of theory, and their grounding in women's experiences of daily life which inform theory as well as being coloured by it. One resolution of this tension has been a shift into poststructural and postmodern theories which acknowledge that the body has a material existence, but treat material existence as constituted by social forces.

Judith Butler, writing on the body as a philosopher, acknowledges this as a problem when she comments on the difficulty of writing about the body without doing so in a disembodied way (Butler, 1993, p. ix). She says that coming to the body from philosophy invites the question 'what about the materiality of the body?':

> Actually, in the recent past, the question was repeatedly formulated to me in this way: 'What about the materiality of the body, *Judy*?' I took it that the addition of 'Judy' was an effort to dislodge me from the more formal 'Judith' and to recall me to a bodily life that could not be theorized away. (Butler, 1993, p. ix)

Judith Butler (1993, p. xii) sets out to explore the 'workings of heterosexual hegemony in the crafting of matters sexual and political', and in doing so shows the weaknesses of feminist conceptions of gender as socially constructed that are less philosophically sophisticated and logically rigorous. She criticizes theories of social and cultural construction which rely on proposing a subject who is doing the constructing, and those (including misreadings of Foucault) that propose some other force, such as discourse, language or the social which acts like a subject in doing the constructing (1993, pp. 6–9). Her quarrel here is with theories that understand sex and gender as socially constructed in the sense of a 'unilateral process initiated by a prior subject' (1993, p. 9).

She rejects the view, though, that gender is so flexibly socially constructed that it is like something we can choose to put on when we get up in the morning. She approaches gender through a theory of performativity, in which gender is the practices that produce it, rather than what we are. This deconstruction of gender to its constituent practices sees gender performativity as practices produced through the operation of regulatory norms:

> construction is neither a subject nor its act, but a process of reiteration by which both 'subjects' and 'acts' come to appear at all. There is no power that acts, but only a reiterated acting that is power in its persistence and instability. (Butler, 1993, p. 9)

In this view, material bodies certainly exist, but the physical properties of bodies, their matter, are seen as '*a process of materialization that stabilizes over time to produce the effect of boundary, fixity, and surface we call matter*' (*ibid.*; Butler's emphasis).

In this way Butler acknowledges that bodies have a material existence, but argues that this does not tell us anything about how they are also social (1993, pp. x–xi). Bodies are matter, but not matter with some sort of independent existence. She says (1993, p. 10):

> Thus, the question is no longer, How is gender constituted as and through a certain interpretation of sex? (a question that leaves the 'matter' of sex untheorized), but rather, Through what regulatory norms is sex itself materialized? And how is it that treating the materiality of sex as a given presupposes and consolidates the normative conditions of its own emergence?

Sex, in Butler's theory, is produced through the reiteration of norms which both produce it and destabilize it. Through this process of reiteration, sex comes to appear to be natural and stable. Where the norms come from, and *why* norms so often produce 'heterosexual hegemony', male dominance, or any other imbalance of power does not appear to be an appropriate question to be asked within the logic of her theory.

The problem for Butler is to explain *how* the materiality of sex is socially produced: 'What are the constraints by which bodies are materialized as "sexed"?' (Butler, 1993, p. xi). Her explanation focuses on how 'heterosexual hegemony' in a particular culture shapes and constrains the ways in which we can exist as gendered, sexed beings; in particular how heterosexual hegemony acts to exclude some versions of gender. The question of *why* men so often come out on top then slides out of the picture.

Butler is frankly irritated by the rigidity and limitations of feminist theories of social construction. Although she acknowledges that sex is in some way material, that bodies are sexed (1993, pp. 10–11), she claims that referring to this is part of the process that is itself formative of the body. She seems to deny that there are bodies 'out there' that can exist independently of the processes of their production. If there was something outside discourses we would have to say what it was and specify its boundaries. But, in defining it, we would bring it into some discourse.[5] In this respect Butler seems to have some common ground with Wittgenstein. In pursuing the logical implications of her theory, women's bodily experiences for which we have no discourses (perhaps, for example, same-sex sexual desires in cultures that have no concept of same-sex desire), cannot be known. That which cannot be talked about must remain silent.

Most women do not come to the body through logic, philosophy or theory, but through bodily experiences, through their own feelings, pains and pleasures; through the possibilities and constraints of embodiment, and through making what sense they can of their experiences.[6] The idea of 'women' is an idea of a female gender and is clearly a variable social construction, produced and practised within cultures. But asking how one *knows* who is really a woman and who is not a woman indicates real confusion between 'knowing' as a political, culturally specific process, and the possibility of some bodily reality 'out there' which we may feel but have no language for knowing (Cain, 1993). Butler's decisive rejection of the possibility that bodies may be partly physically given and partly socially constructed leaves feminism with the problem of how unspoken bodily realities can be known and whether this matters.

I think we should be very cautious about giving up so decisively the possibility of some bodily reality which could be independent of how we know it. Feminist politics requires consideration of the consequences of making reality dependent on the logic of theory. How do we know that there is no way in which our given bodies shape our experience? Questions such as 'is a male-to-female transsexual a woman?', 'does M.E. really exist?' and 'am I disabled?' raise questions not only about how we categorize knowledge and create a social sense of boundary issues, but also about the validity of feelings and the complexity of bodily experience. Too little attention has been paid to considering experiences of disability in theories of the body. Butler's conception of the materiality of the body seems to suggest that feminists are fooled either by the social norms that produce the body as apparently natural, or by their inadequate theories that are less than logical.

Judith Butler does say (1993, p. ix) that she tried to focus on the materiality of the body 'only to find that the *thought* of materiality invariably moved me into other domains' (my emphasis). I have emphasized 'thought' here because Butler's theory does not allow the materiality of the body to be grounded in real matter. If there is no knowable reality 'out there', women's embodied experiences have no claim to be valid. This position appears to rule out the possibility of the common features of women's experiences as embodied females providing one source of feminist knowledge.[7]

This critique of Butler is intended to suggest that there does not have to be any simple correspondence between experience and reality for bodies and experience to be taken as aspects of gender. If we rule the grounded, material body out of knowledge of gender relations, and so out of theories of power, the wider problems of where power lies and why men exercise so much power over women remain.

Conclusion

When John Major campaigned in 1994 for British citizens to go 'back to basics' he was unable to specify the base to which he was referring. Feminists still have serious problems both in specifying the basics of any common interests between women, and in explaining the success and strength of male power. If feminist political concerns are to be organized around identification of women's interests and opposition to male domination, it is a political problem that women (and men) are simultaneously both the same and different.

The contribution of bodies to gendered existence remains particularly difficult to grasp. Human societies without male dominance are possible, but the part played by experiences of bodily differences has neither been adequately explained, nor explained away. If feminist politics have any future, they need to clarify the connections between lived experience, theories of gender and power, and the constraints and possibilities of our material bodies.

Notes

1   I do not have space to review this extensive literature here. The 'scientific' arguments for and against the idea that racial boundaries really exist are usefully reviewed by Liebermann (1970). See also Gilroy (1987); Fuss (1989).

2   Gatens (1992, p. 132) argues, following Foucault:

> Significantly, the sexed body can no longer be conceived as the unproblematic biological and factual base upon which gender is inscribed, but must itself be recognized as constructed by discourses and practices that take the body both as their target and their vehicle of expression. Power is not then reducible to what is imposed from above, on naturally differentiated male and female bodies, but is also constitutive of those bodies, in so far as they are constituted as male and female.

3   Kate Figes has not wholly rejected feminism, and has exposed the persistent inequalities between men and women at work in the UK.

4   This question is considered by Teresa de Lauretis (1986, p. 13) in asking how feminism can have a female subject when women are politically divided:

> If the goal of feminist theory is to define sexual differences for women, to understand how one becomes a woman, and what gives femaleness

(rather than femininity) its meaning as the experience of a female subject, then the starting point can be neither 'man' nor 'woman': neither the Man with the capital M of humanism, or the lower-case man of modernism; nor, on the other hand, woman as the opposite or the complement of man: Woman as Nature, Mother, Body, and Matter, or woman as style, figure, or metaphor of man's femininity.

De Lauretis deals with how feminism might survive the political differences between women by suggesting that a feminist frame of reference should be built 'from women's own experience of difference ... [and that] ... the female subject is always constructed and defined in gender, starting from gender' (*ibid.* p. 14). But she does not say how she knows that the female subject can start from gender and not from body or matter. This is because she assumes that to define the female subject of feminism from the body denies social differences between women.

5   The problems of knowing the extra-discursive – how it is possible to postulate structures and processes that exist independently of the ways they can be known – have been raised by Marxism and developed by Bhaskar (1979). This issue has been taken up in feminist appraisals of Foucault (see, for example, Cain, 1993; Soper, 1993).

6   This claim is implicitly or explicitly a claim that women – people with 'female' bodies – share common experiences. The problems with this claim open up the debates over both the morality of theory and whether experience can be a source of knowledge (see, for example, Haraway, 1990; Ransom, 1993).

7   This is not to claim that expressions of women's (or men's) experience simply constitute valid knowledge. Personal experience is always limited. It is only known through cultural categories, and only generalized through theory. But there is *a priori* no reason for experience to be ignored in the grounding of theory.

References

BENTON, TED (1991) 'Biology and Social Science: Why the Return of the Repressed Should Be Given a (Cautious) Welcome', *Sociology*, 25 (1), pp. 1–29.

BENTON, TED (1992) 'Why the Welcome Needs To Be Cautious: A Reply to Keith Sharp', *Sociology*, 26 (2), pp. 225–32.

BHASKAR, ROY (1979) *The Possibility of Naturalism*, Brighton, Harvester.

BRAIDOTTI, ROSI (1991) *Patterns of Dissonance: A Study of Women in Contemporary Philosophy*, Cambridge, Polity.

BUTLER, JUDITH (1993) *Bodies that Matter: On the Discursive Limits of 'Sex'*, London and New York, Routledge.

CAIN, MAUREEN (1993) 'Foucault, Feminism and Feeling: What Foucault Can and Cannot Contribute to Feminist Epistemology', in RAMAZANOGLU, CAROLINE

(Ed.) *Up Against Foucault*, London, Routledge.

DE LAURETIS, TERESA (1986) 'Feminist Studies/Critical Studies: Issues, Terms and Contexts', in DE LAURETIS, TERESA (Ed.) *Feminist Studies/Critical Studies*, Bloomington, Indiana University Press/Basingstoke, Macmillan.

FUSS, DIANA (1989) *Essentially Speaking*, London, Routledge.

GATENS, MOIRA (1992) 'Power, Bodies, Difference', in BARRETT, MICHELE and PHILLIPS, ANNE (Eds) *Destabilizing Theory: Contemporary Feminist Debates*, Cambridge, Polity.

GILROY, PAUL (1987) *There Ain't no Black in the Union Jack: The Cultural Politics of Race and Nation*, London, Hutchinson.

HARAWAY, DONNA (1990) 'A Manifesto for Cyborgs: Science, Technology and Socialist Feminism in the 1980s', in NICHOLSON, LINDA J. (Ed.) *Feminism/Postmodernism*, London, Routledge.

JAGGAR, ALISON (1992) 'Human Biology in Feminist Theory: Sexual Equality Reconsidered', in CROWLEY, HELEN and HIMMELWEIT, SUSAN (Eds) *Knowing Women: Feminism and Knowledge*, Cambridge, Polity Press in association with the Open University.

KELLER, EVELYN FOX and GRONTKOWSKI, CHRISTINE R. (1983) 'The Mind's Eye', in HARDING, SANDRA and HINTIKKA, MERRILL B. (Eds) *Discovering Reality: Feminist Perspectives on Epistemology, Metaphysics, Methodology and Philosophy of Science*, Dordrecht, Reidel.

LIEBERMAN, LEONARD (1970) 'The Debate over Race', in CURTIS, JAMES E. and PETRAS, JOHN W. (Eds) *The Sociology of Knowledge: A Reader*, London, Duckworth.

LIEVEN, ELENA (1981) 'If It's Natural, We Can't Change It', in CAMBRIDGE WOMEN'S STUDIES GROUP (Eds) *Women in Society*, London, Virago.

MCNAY, LOIS (1992) *Foucault and Feminism: Power, Gender and the Self*, Cambridge, Polity.

RAMAZANOGLU, CAROLINE (Ed.) (1993) *Up Against Foucault: Explorations of Some Tensions Between Foucault and Feminism*, London, Routledge.

RANSOM, JANET (1993) 'Feminism, Difference and Discourse: The Limits of Discursive Analysis for Feminism', in RAMAZANOGLU, CAROLINE (Ed.) *Up Against Foucault*, London, Routledge.

SAYERS, JANET (1982) *Biological Politics: Feminist and Anti-Feminist Perspectives*, London, Tavistock.

SHARP, KEITH (1992) 'Biology and Social Science: A Reply to Ted Benton', *Sociology*, 26 (2), pp. 219–24.

SOPER, KATE (1993) 'Productive Contradictions', in RAMAZANOGLU, CAROLINE (Ed.) *Up Against Foucault*, London, Routledge.

WITTGENSTEIN, LUDWIG (1961) *Tractatus Logico-Philosophicus* (trans. D.F. Pears and B.F. McGuinness), London, Routledge and Kegan Paul.

Chapter 3

British Sex Tourists in Thailand

Julia O'Connell Davidson

I just get turned on very much by Orientals ... They're completely different ... You ... take a girl from a bar, and it might be eleven or twelve at night, and you have a shower and get in bed and have sex, and then most guys go sleep till next morning. Then they'll have a bit more in the morning and then she'll go. I've had them in the morning tidy up the room, fold me clothes up, even wash me socks, stuff like that. I was quite amazed to see it. I think they might've been after an extra tip on top ... You should never fall in love, or you'll be heartbroken when you leave. They might be heartbroken too. Because quite a few of them have got cuts on their arms here. They cut themselves with a knife. They get drunk and just slash themselves. I find that terrible. When I see a girl, when I'm looking to buy her, I always look at her arms to see what she's been doing to herself. ('Dick' – British sex tourist to Thailand)

The term 'sex tourism' is widely associated with organized sex tours, often conjuring up images of groups of middle-aged businessmen being shepherded into state-sanctioned brothels in South Korea or Go Go bars in the Philippines and Thailand. But if sex tourism is defined as consisting of people from economically developed nations travelling to underdeveloped countries 'specifically to purchase the sexual services of local women [and men]' (Enloe, 1989, p. 36), it embraces a far broader range of people, activities and locations. Male sex tourists of all ages travel to Brazil and some African and Caribbean countries as well as to South East Asia; Bali, the Gambia and the Caribbean are popular destinations for female sex tourists. The nature and terms of the exchanges between sex tourists and local people vary enormously, as does the degree to which any third party, including the state, is involved.

A number of authors have discussed the economic, social, political, institutional and ideological factors which underpin the growth of sex tourism in South East Asia (Barry, 1979, 1984; Mitter, 1986; Heyzer, 1986; Enloe, 1989; Lee, 1991). In this chapter, I do not set out to contribute to debate in this area, but will merely refer the reader to Truong's (1990) detailed and scholarly analysis of the phenomenon. Instead, my primary aim here is to provide some empirical data on the attitudes, motivations and activities of male, British sex tourists in Thailand. For between 1980 and 1986, Britain supplied over a million of the 15.8 million tourists who visited Thailand, 73 per cent of whom were male (Truong, 1990, pp. 173–4), and it is important to ask what kind of people the hundred thousand or so British men who annually visit are, and why so many of them are prepared to travel so far in order to pay for sex.

Preliminary data from an on-going piece of research[1] suggests that British sex tourists are not an entirely homogeneous group – they can be subdivided into three broad types – but that for all these men, sex tourism in Thailand has three main attractions which, to varying degrees, shape their decision to travel for sex. The paper begins by developing a typology of sex tourists, then goes on to look at what they get out of sex tourism.

Varieties of Sex Tourists

Of the British tourists I interviewed and observed who had chosen Thailand as a holiday destination specifically for sexual purposes, one clearly identifiable subgroup was made up of 'Macho Lads'. These men were typically skilled, semi and unskilled manual workers in their early twenties. Not all are package tourists, in fact, those that I interviewed had all made their own travel arrangements. For most, this was at least their second or third visit to Pattaya (Thailand's premier sex resort), and all had first travelled to Thailand on the personal recommendation of another sex tourist. Macho Lads often travel in groups of three or four, and those who arrive alone seem to quickly team up with others with whom they sunbathe, drink and visit clubs. For these young men, Pattaya is a kind of macho theme park with beer, motorbikes, Go Go bars, kick boxing, live sex shows, pool tables in English-style pubs, and guaranteed access to dolly birds to posture with and fuck. Most of the Macho Lads interviewed said that they use prostitutes in England either regularly or occasionally, though some claimed never to have purchased sexual services anywhere except in Thailand.

As well as the Macho Lads, there are large numbers of men to whom I shall refer as 'Mr Averages'. Though most of these men were on second or third trips to Thailand, all of those I spoke to had originally come to Pattaya on package tours, some specifically targeted at 'single men'. Mr Average is usually, but not always, older than the Macho Lad, and he is often divorced or widowed. He may be a skilled manual worker, self employed or in a junior or middle management position, but he prides himself on being a respectable, 'ordinary bloke'. He is primarily (though not exclusively) interested in simulating some kind of emotional or romantic relationship with either one woman or a series of women, rather than pursuing large numbers of anonymous sexual encounters. These men describe Pattaya as 'Fantasy Island', and, except for the early evening period when they tend to sit round the hotel bar engaging in manly conversation with each other, they have a Thai woman on their arm at all times. Most claim never to visit prostitutes in Britain and do not consider themselves as punters even in Thailand.

Many people would, no doubt, explain the behaviour of Mr Average and the Macho Lads through reference to their class position and their lack of formal education. But sex tourism is also practised by more bourgeois men. Numerous 'Cosmopolitan Men', well off, well read and well travelled, also buy sexual services in Thailand. These men are keen to differentiate themselves from their compatriots – 'I'm not a sex tourist', 'I'm not a package tourist', 'I am spending a few months travelling South East Asia', 'I'm here on business really'. They visit more remote and less developed spots, they spend more time in Bangkok, but they also go to Pattaya for a few days in order to 'relax'. They are worldly-wise but they do not see themselves as the kind of men who frequent prostitutes. Several said that they would never use a prostitute anywhere else in the world.

In short, then, sex tourists do not constitute an entirely homogeneous group. They vary in terms of age and social class, and there are differences in terms of their willingness to see themselves as punters.[2] However, to a greater or lesser degree, all the three types described above are drawn to Thailand as sex tourists for three sets of reasons. First, commoditized sex is cheap in Thailand and the degree of 'consumer' choice is immense. Second, the nature and terms of exchange between prostitute and client in Thailand are very different to those between prostitute and client in Britain or any other European country. In Thailand, the exchange is far less contractual, and this makes it far more attractive to British men for a number of reasons. Finally, all three types of men find sex tourism affirmative of a particular 'racialized' and sexualized masculine identity. The following sections discuss these issues in detail.

Price Advantages and Sovereign Consumers

Any analysis of sex tourism which fails to consider its economics is doomed to provide only a partial explanation of the phenomenon, for without the obscene disparity in average per capita incomes between the countries which host sex tourists and those which supply them, sex tourism would be a marginal activity of a very different character. Feminists, socialists and policy makers may not all be entirely happy about the tourists who visit Amsterdam in order to buy sexual services from local people, for example, but because the power relations and economics involved here are of a very different order to those involved in sex tourism in underdeveloped countries, it does not excite the same moral and political repugnance. Throughout the following discussion, it must be borne in mind that whatever the complexity of British men's motivations, the bottom line in terms of explaining why they are in Thailand is cost. In Thailand, a prostitute can be rented for almost twenty-four hours for as little as 500 Baht (around £18), a sum of money that would barely secure a man a ten-minute blow job in Britain. The cheapness of sexual services (as well as of accommodation, food, drinks, travel and other services) furnishes a single, working-class British man with a level of economic power that he could never enjoy at home, or in any other European country, and all the sex tourists I interviewed commented on the fact that, in Thailand, they 'live like kings' or 'playboys'.

These men not only find themselves with untold economic power, they also find themselves 'spoilt for choice', for, in Thailand, the relationship between the tourist and the sex industry is so complex and multifaceted that the array of different forms of commoditized sex on offer to tourists is quite staggering. Truong (1990, p. 199) explains that the historical roots of this diversity lie in the fact that

> The legal persecution of prostitutes occurred almost simultaneously with the legal formalization of the entertainment industry, owing to an investment policy skewed towards capturing the 'Rest and Recreation' market during the Indochina conflict. The duality between the recognition and denial of prostitution, coupled with a massive arrival of US military servicemen, led to a proliferation of forms of prostitution disguised within the entertainment industry. Ad-hoc practices of hosting prostitution gradually became systemic as a result of the high rate of capital accumulation. (Truong, 1990, p. 199)

Today this proliferation means that female, male and transsexual prostitutes are to be found working from a huge variety of settings (including brothels, bars, massage parlours, escort agencies, discos, hotels, streets, beaches), and a range of more diffusely sexualized entertainment and personal services are also widely available in Bangkok and most major Thai resorts (for example, cabarets which are mildly erotic rather than overtly sexual; beachside masseuses who caress feet, hands and backs but provide no direct, genital stimulation). Moreover, there is both a formal market for mail order brides and marriage bureaux catering almost exclusively to Western men, and an informal market consisting of women who independently seek Western men for long-term relationships, so that, in essence, tourists are provided with a continuum of opportunities to purchase sexual pleasure and rights of sexual access in Thailand. This continuum runs through from the mere pleasure of looking at sexually available women (and men and children) at one pole to the satisfaction of complete sexual possession at the other.

Thailand's sex industry has become a tourist attraction in itself, and reputable guide books recommend a visit to red light districts (see Kusy, 1991). In these areas, tourists (even those who never go on to become punters) are provided with opportunities of voyeurism and mild titillation, pleasures which are generally paid for indirectly through the inflated prices of drinks, or directly through a cover charge made upon entering or leaving bars or live sex shows. For those tourists who do go on to purchase the services of a prostitute, the extent and visibility of 'vice' in these areas doubtless enhances their pleasure, for as Hoigard and Finstad (1992, p. 88) found in their study of punters in Oslo, 'some men find sexual value in peeping as a prelude to the act of prostitution'.

For tourists who want more than titillation, it is possible to purchase what is known as 'short time' with a prostitute. This service is generally on offer in massage parlours as well as at the Go Go and live sex show bars/brothels mentioned above. The tourist pays the parlour or bar owner a fee, which varies between 300 and 1,000 Baht (£10–£25),[3] then takes the prostitute of his choice to an upstairs room where he enjoys one or two hours of sexual access to her. A variation on this arrangement is found in bars which make a cover charge of around 500 Baht, in exchange for which the customer receives one drink and the sexual attentions of a woman as they consume it. In Pattaya, for example, there is a bar known as the 'No Hands Bar' where prostitutes crawl under the tables in order to fellate the customers.

Men can also rent bar prostitutes for around twenty-four hours at a time. The punter pays what is known as a 'bar fine' of 200 to 500 Baht to the bar plus a sum that is negotiated with the prostitute directly to her. Having paid the fine, the punter is free to take the prostitute back to his hotel room for the whole night and most of the following day. The formal rationale for this is as follows. Bar owners employ people to work the bar (selling drinks, cleaning up, chatting to customers) or as dancers. If a customer wants to take one of the workers away from the bar for the night, he must pay the bar owner a 'fine' in compensation for the loss of that person's labour. In reality, however, these workers are rarely paid a regular wage by the bar owner,[4] and there are always far more women or men attached to any one bar than is necessary to run it, so that the 'fine' system is actually a source of income for the bar owner who is effectively operating a 'take-away' brothel. He gets his cut without having to support the overheads associated with providing rooms and facilities for clients, who use their own hotel rooms.

Overnight deals can also be negotiated with freelance prostitutes who solicit outside bars and discos as well as from a variety of other settings, and it is worth noting that these twenty-four-hour deals underline the extent to which the tourist and the sex industries are interwoven. Such arrangements would be impossible without the active collusion of hoteliers. Some hotels charge customers a fee for bringing a prostitute back for the night, others simply profit by the extra drinks and breakfasts sold and the custom won through not making a charge. Many Western package tour operators negotiate with hoteliers over these fees, for their absence is a major selling point – indeed, seasoned sex tourists state that this is the one real advantage of buying a package holiday rather than travelling independently.

Sex tourists can also enter into transactions of more extended duration with prostitutes, keeping the same woman with them for several days or weeks. This kind of arrangement is generally made with bar or freelance prostitutes following a twenty-four-hour deal which has proved satisfactory to the punter, but can also sometimes be made with women who do not work full-time as prostitutes. For those white men who want more than just this kind of 'long haul' deal, there is often the option of complete sexual possession through marriage. This can be arranged through one of the many agencies operating in Bangkok, or informally with the woman and/or her relatives.

Thailand thus offers an abundance of choice and diversity in terms of the sexual pleasures that can be bought and the kind of transactions involved, all at knock-down prices. The sheer numbers of prostitutes working in Bangkok and Pattaya mean that it also offers choice in terms of the prostitutes themselves. As one man put it, 'You can go with a different girl every night. It's every man's dream come true'. It is also possible for men to 'experiment' with troilism, and, for those who are so inclined, with transsexuals and/or under-age girls and boys.[5] Finally, it should be noted (and this overlaps with points that will be made in the following section) that British men believe that their money buys them sexual access to a 'better class' of women in

Thailand – 'You can take your pick of thousands of the most beautiful women in the world and they're nice girls too. A lot of them are very respectable.'

The Non-contractual Nature of Transactions

Although it is the low price of sexual services in Thailand which makes sex tourism a viable activity for so many British men, there is more to their motivation than simply cost considerations. No doubt £200 would buy sexual access to almost as many junkies and homeless teenagers in Kings Cross as it does to Thai women, but few British sex tourists would consider spending a fortnight in London for that purpose. This is partly because the setting would be colder and not in the least 'exotic', and the accommodation and food more expensive, and partly because British street prostitutes are considered to be 'low life' by these men. But it is also because transactions between punter and prostitute in Britain and in Thailand have a very different character.

In Britain, sexual services are generally sold by the piece and the transaction is modelled on the lines of other commercial exchanges. Like contractual labour in modern, capitalist societies (Little, 1985), the exchange normally involves an explicit agreement to perform a specified and limited service or task. Obviously, formal contracts are not drawn up, but each party's rights and duties are implicitly defined, and generally speaking, in Britain the exchange is so highly focused that the prostitute has fulfilled her side of the contract once the punter has ejaculated. An important skill is therefore to be able to bring men to orgasm as quickly as possible (see O'Connell Davidson, 1994; Hoigard and Finstad, 1992). The narrow and commercial nature of the exchange is more than evident to punter as well as prostitute and a man would no more expect a prostitute to cuddle or stroke him or act as his companion after sex than he would expect a plumber to do so after fixing a leaking pipe.

There are men who find sexual value in such anonymous and instrumental encounters, but one of the more curious findings of research on prostitution (at least for those who are surprised by the extent of human hypocrisy and capacity for self deceit) is that many punters in European countries bemoan the impersonal approach of prostitutes. De Graaf *et al.* (1992, p. 9), for example, quote some clients in Amsterdam as saying that they really want comfort, contact and a 'nice chat' from prostitutes and complaining that 'You don't get the warmth and attention that you are looking for'. Hoigard and Finstad (1992, p. 95) found that although a majority of clients in their Oslo study 'say that they go to a prostitute among other reasons because it is non-committal, they also say that they want warm girls, increased intimacy, and understanding'.

In other words, many punters want to buy sex as a commodity, but do not want the exchange to be simply a contractual, market one. Just as capitalist employers would ideally like employees who are disposable at will, yet wholly devoted, bound to them by pre-market codes of loyalty and allegiance and willing to do more than just stick rigidly to a job description, nirvana for many punters would be access on demand to the full range of sexual, emotional and other services from women in exchange for nothing more than a pre-set sum of money. That European prostitutes are often able to use the rational, economic principles of a free market society to limit and control how much of their sexual and other labour is alienated in exchange for a given fee is a sign of their relative social and economic strength, and this becomes clear when their experience is compared to that of most Thai prostitutes.

In Thailand, transactions between punters and prostitutes are far less explicitly contractual. Although men can and do buy 'short time' with prostitutes, giving a predetermined sum of money for a more or less set period of time, the exchange between prostitutes and clients is typically far more diffuse and open-ended than that which takes place in Britain. So far as overnight deals are concerned, the sum of money which the man will pay directly to the prostitute is not always negotiated in advance and the services which the prostitute will provide are rarely explicitly stated. Moreover, these deals are seldom a simple, focused exchange of *sexual* services for money. Prostitutes also provide other forms of labour. They often act as companion and interpreter, shop, carry luggage, tidy and clean the punter's room, wash and fold his clothes, for example, as well as providing personal services such as massages and manicures. With 'long haul' deals, women are likewise expected to provide both sexual and non-sexual services but the terms of the exchange are usually even more varied, vague and ill-specified than those associated with twenty-four-hour deals. One sex tourist described his three-week arrangement as follows:

> I started off going a bit crazy, but then I thought I'd just settle with this one girl. I liked her so I told her how much money I'd got left for me holiday and I said to her I could give her 350 Baht a day, and she could do all my shopping, sort out the hotels and laundry and that, and then any money I've got left over at the end of my stay, she can keep it. She was dead pleased with that, and she's really got some bargains, so I'll be able to leave her quite a bit extra.

Another man explained how he had spent two weeks with a woman the previous year, during which time he covered all expenses, bought her several gifts and gave her 'pocket money'. Once back in England, he sent her £50. She then wrote to tell him that she had given up bar prostitution and moved back to the countryside, and asked him to pay for a buffalo for her family. Before parting with the necessary £200, the man asked a friend of his who was about to visit Pattaya to check that she had really left the Pattaya bar and was no longer working as a prostitute. When his friend confirmed her story, he paid for the buffalo, and arranged to spend the whole three weeks of his next holiday with her, again on terms that were essentially left to his discretion rather than negotiated in advance. Walker and Ehrlich's (1992) collection of 'love' letters to Bangkok bar prostitutes from Western men reveals that such stories are by no means uncommon.

Three points need to be made about all this. First of all, the fact that sex tourists exercise so much control over how much they pay a prostitute and get so much more for what they do pay than they would from British prostitutes is obviously, in itself, very pleasing to them. A Macho Lad commented:

> It's up to you what you give the girl, I've give 300, I've give 1,000.
> It's up to you. It depends how much you've had to drink . . . They say
> 'you give me what you want'. I don't think there's ever a set price
> for it.

His friend also observed that 'getting the girl' for a whole night made the experience very different from 'going with English prostitutes':

> There's no pressure, you can take your time, you don't have to do
> it straight away and you can do it as much as you like. With some
> of the girls anyway. It depends a bit. But they're all much more
> friendly, they really want to please you.

Second, the punter experiences his power over the prostitute in a different way in Thailand. The reality is that in Thailand as much as in Britain, the punter, like all individuals in capitalist societies, 'carries his social power, as also his connection with society, in his pocket' (Marx, 1973, p. 94). But because he does not have to explicitly agree a price for every service the Thai prostitute provides, she appears to him as acquiescent and subordinate to his whims and desires in a way that a British prostitute never could. The third point follows from this, and is that the non-contractual nature of the prostitute–client exchange in Thailand serves to conceal its commercial nature from the punter. This aspect of Thai prostitution is absolutely central to most sex tourists, for it makes it possible for them to pay for sexual services without having to see themselves as the kind of men who use prostitutes. I have no empirical data to support this claim, but nonetheless, I would suggest that though hundreds of thousands of men do use prostitutes, very few willingly and happily embrace the identity of a punter. To visit a prostitute on occasion may be a sign of machismo, but to be dependent on the services of prostitutes because you are unable to 'pull' women is a sign of failure, and the line between the two is a dangerously fine one, especially for men who do not conform to their society's ideals of physical attractiveness.

Certainly, the Mr Average type does not wish to see himself as a punter. Pattaya is 'fantasy island' precisely because when a 22-year-old woman approaches him and puts a slim arm around the rolls of fat bulging over the waistband of his trousers or strokes his balding head and tells him that he is 'a sexy man', he can convince himself that it is true. He can suspend his disbelief. In the mirror of the 'beautiful Oriental girl' he sees himself reflected back not twice as large, as Virginia Woolf had it, but half his size and half his age. But it is not just Mr Averages who are keen to avoid acknowledging the commercial nature of transactions. Macho Lads and Cosmopolitan Men also stress the fact that Thai prostitutes are not like prostitutes, and, therefore, the fact that they themselves are not like punters:

Over here they're not low life like English prostitutes ... You don't really think of them as prostitutes.

You don't feel as if you're going with a prostitute, it's not like that.

They're more like girlfriends really. You do everything with them. It isn't just sex, they're not like prostitutes.

They really look after you. They make you feel special. You don't feel like a, I don't know how to put it, you don't feel like a customer. They're very natural, very genuine, you can tell that they do really like you.

Because sex tourists do not have to enter into explicit agreements on the terms and conditions of the exchange, and because Thai prostitutes make gestures and provide services which are interpreted as demonstrations of genuine affection, it is relatively easy for men to forget that they are engaged in an economic transaction. This in turn helps them to delude themselves into thinking that they have really 'scored', that their personal charms and not their wallets have attracted the woman in question. Given that the vast majority of British (in fact of all European) sex tourists are less than appealing in terms of European cultural norms of male beauty, it is not difficult to see that sex tourism can do something more for these men's self image than simply make them feel all right about using prostitutes. The following sections examine the ways in which sex tourism helps British men to reinforce and construct a powerful and positive image of themselves as a particular kind of white heterosexual man.

Sex Tourism and Masculinity

Segal (1990, p. 123) has observed that 'masculinity is not some type of single essence, innate or acquired', rather there are competing and contradictory representations of masculinity in Western culture. She continues:

> 'masculinity' is a quality of being which is always incomplete, and which is equally based on a social as on a psychic reality. It exists in the various forms of power men ideally possess: the power to assert control over women, over other men, over their own bodies, over machines and technology.

I want to argue that, if the words 'machines and technology' are substituted with 'material objects', then British sex tourists find in their sex tourism the opportunity to become truly 'masculine'. Because the economic power of British men of all social classes is far greater in Thailand than it is in Britain, sex tourists (like all tourists) obtain control over the material world in ways that are not open to them at home. They can buy rounds of drinks carelessly, eat in smart restaurants and stay in smart hotels, they can indulge in Dallas and Dynasty fantasies as they sit by swimming pools, waited on hand and foot, they can rent big motorbikes, travel to and from the airport in air-conditioned limousines, they can buy cheap silk shirts and fancy leather boots. The lifestyle that, at home, is reserved only for rich and powerful men, is temporarily within their grasp, and, as a British observer, you cannot help but be struck by the strutting, swaggering confidence of men who, in their own country, exhibit so little of it. And obviously these men obtain power over women as well as over the material world (because, of course, women have been reduced to material objects). As one sex tourist put it:

> There's no pressure on you there, you don't have to worry about going out and getting someone, because you know any time, day or night, you can have anyone you want within seconds. You feel so

powerful, you feel you're in control of your sex life.

Unless it is assumed that all men have some kind of biological drive to sexually possess as many women as possible (a view which sex tourists, along with sociobiologists, adhere to) then it is necessary to explain why these particular men have such a strong desire for this kind of control. Almost all the sex tourists interviewed spoke with great bitterness about white women's power to deny them sexual access. Macho Lads complained that English women are 'hard work', that going to discos in England is 'a waste of time'; Mr Averages bemoaned the fact that 'pretty' English women know they are pretty and demand the world (they want to marry you then soak you for every penny when they divorce you); a Cosmopolitan Man told me: 'I'm 48, I'm balding, I'm not as trim as I was. Would a charming, beautiful, young woman want me in England? No. I'd have to accept a big, fat, ugly woman. That's all I could get.'

In short, sex tourists express a kind of misogynistic rage against women who have the power to demand anything at all, whether it is the right to have a say over who they have sex with and when, or the right to maintenance payments for their children. Psychodynamic theories which view all eroticism as an expression of infantile rage, revenge and hostility (see, for example, Stoller, 1979) might explain these men's particular passion for women who are perceived as powerless and sexually available through reference to childhood experiences of rejection and humiliation. However, one could equally well argue that there is nothing very individual or distinctive about these particular men's attitudes and desires, it is just that they are less well equipped (in terms of economic power, physical appearance and/or social skills) to achieve the degree of access to British women that they would like.

As well as attaining power over the material world and over women, these men experience a greater sense of power over their own bodies in Thailand, certainly so far as their sexuality is concerned. The sex tourist quoted above said that he was 'in control of his sex life', and told me he needed penetrative sex to 'get me sex drive out for the night'. In fact, all the sex tourists I interviewed imagined themselves to be at the mercy of a biological imperative to regularly ejaculate inside a woman's vagina, and the fact that they enjoy sexual access on demand in Thailand is thus interpreted as a form of power over their own bodies. Sex tourism also frees men from other aspects of the body's control over them. Cultural definitions of beauty turn many people's bodies into prisons, making their sexual desires unattainable, and it is certainly the case that large numbers of sex tourists are either physically repellent by European standards (I have never seen so many enormously overweight men together in one place before), or disfigured or disabled in some way, or too old to be considered sexually attractive.

Finally, sex tourism gives sex tourists a sense of power over other men. The fact that they are in a position to fuck as many 'beautiful' women as they want makes them feel 'one up' on the men who stay at home. They also engage in a kind of 'ranking' process in relation to other male sex tourists, one which, as the following section shows, allows them to place themselves on the top of a sexualized and 'racialized' scale.

The Construction of a White Heterosexual Identity

One of the more unexpected characteristics of the sex tourist is that he appears to be obsessed by the morality of other sex tourists. At first this appears to be simply an extreme form of hypocrisy. It is acceptable for them, as heterosexual men, to exploit the economic misfortunes of Thai women, but homosexual men who do the same thing to Thai men are 'sick'. It is acceptable for them to pay a bar fine and take a 16-year-old girl back to their hotel for the night, but they expressed a desire to do physical violence to men who pay pimps to take 14- or 15-year-old boys back to their rooms. Their own observations of paedophiles, 'gays' and 'perverts' form an endlessly diverting topic for conversation between themselves and serve as a platform from which to assert their own moral superiority.

In practice this obsession with morality is, I would argue, an obsession with defining and preserving a particular masculine, heterosexual identity, for the moral issue at the heart of their conversations is not whether there can be genuine consent between people who are unequal in terms of age or economic power, but whether sex tourists' actions transgress rules about 'normal' male sexuality. This is well illustrated by the following story told to me by a sex tourist from Newcastle:

> When I was in Ko Chang there was this old Austrian bloke, must have been 70 at least, and he was enticing the dogs into his beach hut, tempting stray dogs in there with food. It was fucking disgusting. Anyway, someone told the police and they had words with him, but I was telling this bloke at the bar one night and I pointed the bloke out to him and he just walked over to the Austrian bloke and punched him in the face. He said 'You dirty fucking poofter' and he floored him. He says to me after, 'He comes to paradise and what does he do? Fucks dogs'.

The 'natural' and morally proper thing to do in 'paradise' is, of course, to fuck a debt bonded 16-year-old girl in a room above the bar where night after night she must pull strings of razor blades from her vagina in front of an audience of leering men.

But the construction of moral hierarchies by British sex tourists is not only about reinforcing a particular kind of male heterosexual identity. It is also about reinforcing and constructing a specifically white identity. The most powerful venom and moral condemnation is directed towards sex tourists from the Gulf States. Every sex tourist I spoke to, with the exception of a couple of 'Cosmopolitan Men', told me that Thai women hate 'the Arabs' and avoid 'going with them'. This is because 'Arabs', unlike European men, rape them, cheat them, refuse to pay them, do 'depraved things' to them, insist on anal intercourse, and because 'Arabs' are 'dirty', 'smelly', 'do it with boys and girls', 'hold hands with each other in the streets' and are unattractive to Thai women because they are not white-skinned. In Pattaya, I was even confronted by the extraordinary sight of a British skinhead sitting at a bar with one arm around a Thai woman and the other raised in a Sieg Heil salute at a passing citizen of the Arab Emirates. There is also a British-owned bar which proudly displays a poster of a pig wearing a yashmak above which is written 'We respect your religion – that's why we refuse to serve you'.

Colonial ideologies did and still do express complex and variable forms of racism (see Thomas, 1994), and British sex tourists construct a positive image of themselves as white men not only through the denigration of 'Arabs' but also through their exoticization and idealization of Thai women. For these men, Thai women are definitely 'Other', but not the same kind of Other as 'Arab' men or even African Caribbean women (see Collins, 1990; hooks, 1981; Kovel, 1988; Beckles, 1989). Thai women are believed to think differently and to have different values and expectations to white women. 'They' are also held to be more affectionate, loyal, innocent and natural than white women. Thai women are also uniformly held to be great beauties. 'They're all like film stars or models, aren't they? It's the hair and the skin, and they're mostly always petite, you know, slim and small'. The destructive consequences of 'racist' constructions of Thai women as Other are most immediate and most terrifying around issues of safer sex.[6] All the men I interviewed commented on how clean Thai women are, noting things like the frequency with which 'they' wash, 'their' neat and tidy appearance, 'their' scrupulously clean and manicured nails and so on. The implications of this were spelled out clearly by one man:

> I don't know why people always go on about AIDS in Thailand. Thai women are the cleanest women in the world. They don't shower once

a day, they don't shower twice a day. They shower four times a day.

His friend, who also appeared to believe that frequent washing is a prophylactic against AIDS, told me that 'most of the girls will do it without a condom if you pay them enough', but that he would never have unprotected sex with a bar girl, only with freelances who seemed new to the work.

Romanticized views of Thai women as 'innocent', 'natural', 'clean' and so on exist alongside an implicit denigration of Thai men, for British sex tourists are convinced that, despite their own 'exotic' charm and beauty, Thai women recognize the superiority of whites. Sex tourists continually assert that Thai women prefer white men (white skin 'turns them on', white men 'treat them better than Arabs and their own kind') and that Thai women would actually like to be white themselves ('they admire white skin', 'they won't sunbathe because they want to be white', 'basically, they all want to get married to a European'). There are some interesting parallels between contemporary British sex tourists' beliefs about Thai women and nineteenth-century Britons' beliefs about black women in the Caribbean. Beckles (1989, p. 148) quotes a visitor to Barbados in the 1820s:

> Generally speaking, the [coloured women] look down ... with a feeling of contempt on men of their own color ... and rather than live with them a virtuous and inoffensive life, they prefer dwelling with a white man in a state of moral degradation. ...

So far as sex tourists today are concerned, such beliefs help them to explain to themselves why young and beautiful Thai women find them so irresistible without having to refer to the commercial side of their relationship, and thus to further deflect attention from their identity as punter. But they also link into other self serving stereotypes, especially those surrounding the supposed subservient, passive and accommodating nature of Thai and other 'oriental' women. For as well as attributing the characteristics already mentioned to Thai women, sex tourists are of the opinion that Thai women are genetically and culturally predisposed towards subordination and self denial.

Through the lens of their 'racism', these men interpret virtually everything that Thai women do as a mark of their desire to serve. If a British man holds a door open for a British woman, it is not interpreted as a mark of his subjugation to her. But when Thai women observe certain formal codes governing respect for and the care of others (for instance, speaking in a low voice, paying attention to a companion's physical comfort and so on), it is taken to be a mark of their willing subjection. British sex tourists tell you that 'it's in their nature to be subservient' or that 'it's part of their culture', and this is why prostitutes will carry their bags and suitcases, clean their combs, pour their drinks, plump up their pillows and so on. They also view Thai women as sexually passive, using terms like 'innocent' and 'natural' to describe their sexuality. 'They aren't into anything kinky' one man told me, and those who use prostitutes in Britain claim that Thai prostitutes seem inexperienced; 'English prostitutes know all the tricks, they take the lead, they suggest things. But Thai girls are very innocent, they're very natural and affectionate'. These qualities are described as 'a big turn on' to British men, and it is also conveniently assumed that 'innocent' Thai women thoroughly enjoy straight, penetrative sex with them (which is, of course, partly why they don't like 'perverted Arabs').

All variants of 'racism' serve to deny the subjectivity and humanity of those defined as Other, and Ward (1988, p. xxviii) points out that this denial can 'be constituted through a process of idealization' as much as through one of denigration. Certainly the idealized 'innocence' of Thai women appears to serve the same purpose as the attribution of 'voracious' sexual appetites to Brazilian women by sex tourists in São Paulo (and the attribution of 'libidinous' and 'animalistic' sexuality to black women by whites in slave societies of the Caribbean). For whether she is constructed as passive and innocent or active and depraved, the Other is imagined to relish the white man's sexual attentions.

But it is also important to note that, even so far as any one 'racialized' group is concerned, there is a certain plasticity about these processes of denial, and the 'racialized' world view of British sex tourists in Thailand can serve ends other than those described so far. For although a majority of the sex tourists I interviewed were primarily interested in penetrating the vaginas of 'beautiful' and subservient women, there were some, particularly Macho Lads, whose sexual interests were more wide-ranging. Again, their 'racism' helped them to feel all right about their desires and activities. It has already been observed that sex tourists draw very sharp boundaries between the 'natural' and 'unnatural', the 'normal' and the 'perverse', and that these boundaries also mark off masculinity. Men who transgress them are not 'real men'. Yet several Macho Lads admitted to engaging in sexual practices in Thailand that they would normally define as 'perverse', for example, 'sharing' a Thai prostitute with male friends, allowing male friends to video them having sex with a prostitute, and having sexual contact with transsexual prostitutes. Patterson (1982, p. 51) has observed that where caste relations 'demarcate impassable boundaries', the essence of slavery is that 'the slave, in his social death, lives on the margins between . . . life and death, the sacred and the secular. Already dead, he lives outside the manna of the gods and can cross the boundaries with social and supernatural impunity', and for some

British sex tourists, it appears that Thai sex workers, as 'racialized' Others, have this kind of liminal status. They have so little social worth that it is possible for the sex tourist to transgress boundaries and do things which, if done with a white person, would bring dishonour. As one Macho Lad said:

> I was in this bar, a no hands bar, and this girl, well except she was a fella, a Lady Boy, come up and did a blow job . . . I knew she was a he, you can always tell by the Adam's apple. But I didn't really care. It's all right here. But I'd slit my throat if that happened in England.

Contradictions in the World View of the Sex Tourist

It should be evident from the above discussion that the world view of the British sex tourist is not wholly internally consistent, and that his desires are often self contradictory. He wants Thai women to be both sexually available and sexually innocent, and although sex tourists say that they like the 'subservience' of Thai women, they also complain about their 'passivity'. Several men told me that they often 'got sick of' the compliance of the women whose bodies and labour they purchase. As one said:

> It gets on your nerves after a while, whatever you ask, they say 'It's up to you'. 'Do you want the telly on?', 'Up to you'. 'Do you want something to eat?', 'Up to you'. 'Shall we stop at this bar?', 'Up to you'. 'Do you want to make love?'. 'Up to you'. It drives you mad.

Meanwhile, a general complaint about 'long-haul' deals is that it is very difficult to build a relationship with the woman because of language problems and the absence of a shared culture. In fact, many sex tourists say that they get lonely for their 'own kind' whilst on holiday in Thailand. As one Cosmopolitan Man explained:

> I could never be happy in a relationship with a Thai woman. They aren't intellectual, they don't read, they've nothing to say. Life's always a compromise. You can talk to Western women, but they don't look good. With Thai girls it's the other way round, so you always have to take the rough with the smooth. Life's never perfect.

Oddly enough, many sex tourists are actually also troubled by moral issues surrounding consent. These men generally know that Thailand is a 'poor country' and that many women are forced to prostitute themselves in order to support their families. On the one hand, this helps them to sustain the notion that Thai prostitutes are not *really* prostitutes (and thus that *they* are not *really* punters). These women do not conform to their stereotypes of prostitutes and can be considered as 'decent' and 'respectable' women who just unfortunately happen to live in a country where poverty drives them to sell their bodies. But in recognizing this, their own actions come to seem morally reprehensible. It looks dangerously as though they are taking advantage of the misfortunes of these damsels in distress. Now Macho Lads are not much troubled by this. They tend to view sex tourism almost as a form of welfare provision by the West for an economically 'backward' nation – 'If these blokes stopped coming out here, I'd hate to think what would happen to these girls', as one remarked. But for Mr Average, who wants so much to see himself as a 'decent' bloke, it is a real dilemma.

The easiest way to resolve it is to tell himself that the 'beautiful girl' in his bed is there because she finds him so desirable, not because her poverty has forced her there. But such a fiction is hard to maintain when Mr Average is daily confronted by the sight of 'beautiful girls', perhaps his own former sexual partners, telling other, often still less attractive, Europeans that they too are 'sexy men'. Thus there is always a tension for Mr Average between seeing himself as truly desired and so feeling good about himself, and seeing himself as exploiting 'nice, respectable girls' and feeling bad about himself. Some men become defensive in response to this. A number of Mr Averages expressed great ambivalence towards prostitutes, lurching irrationally from paternalistic sympathy – 'They do it for their families' – to malevolent hostility – 'They're hard bitches really' in the space of only a few minutes' conversation. I was assured that despite all appearances to the contrary, most of the bar girls in Pattaya were actually earning huge sums of money and frittering it away instead of 'saving for a rainy day'. 'You buy them gold and the moment you leave, they just sell it and spend the money', one complained, 'You must never fall in love, or they'll skin you alive', another warned. Perhaps the most unpleasant Mr Average of all was the one who sat down with me in the hotel lobby one morning, still drunk from the night before, three days' growth of stubble on his face, his shirt and trousers stained with food, and said:

It's all changed here. You never saw a girl drink or smoke when I first came to Thailand. All the business with whisky and cigarettes is totally new. They were nice girls then. They were soft, very soft. Now it's all changed. It's commercialism. They're hard and they're after money.

Some Conclusions

I have set out in this chapter to provide some empirical data on the attitudes, motivations and activities of male, British sex tourists, rather than to develop a theoretical analysis, either of these men or of the phenomenon of sex tourism. However, I will end with some brief comments on theoretical issues. In particular, I wish to take issue with those analyses which give primacy to the concept of patriarchy in discussions of sex tourism and prostitution, for it seems to me that this concept alone is not enough to explain the attitudes, motivations and activities of British male sex tourists. Radical feminists hold that 'sexuality is gendered as gender is sexualized ... the eroticization of dominance and submission creates gender. ... Thus, the sex difference and the dominance-submission dynamic define each other' (MacKinnon, 1988, p. 107; see also Jeffreys, 1990). Although I believe that British sex tourists provide a very clear example of how a masculine identity can be expressed, reinforced and constructed through a given sexual practice, I think it would be wrong to conclude that the power these men exercise is simply or even primarily patriarchal. Their power is also 'racialized' and its currency is economic, and it is only if we recognize this that we can develop analyses of sex tourism that can accommodate the unpalatable fact that not all sex tourists are heterosexual and not all sex tourists are men.

It is also clear that male sex tourists are not the only group of people to derive benefits from sex tourism. Its economic benefits for national and international capital are equally if not more striking. As well as being part of the planned economic development of a number of South East Asian countries, providing a vital source of foreign exchange and substantial profits for local entrepreneurs, national and international travel, tourist and leisure companies, I would argue that sex tourism plays a broader economic role, contributing to an on-going process of primitive accumulation.[7] A number of Marxist theorists have argued that non-capitalist modes of production have been artificially preserved in underdeveloped countries, and that these household economies supply cheap labour to the capitalist system. Potts (1990, p. 188) summarizes as follows:

> According to the requirements of capitalism, [the worker] is either incorporated – in various ways – into the capitalist productive process or thrown back into the household. This household feeds the worker during unproductive periods, and thus reproduces the worker's labour power.

In this way, reproduction takes place at no cost to capital. In Thailand, it seems that a prostitution economy serves precisely this same function, for not only are women thrown into this economy whenever their labour is surplus to capital's requirements, but also, women's sexual labour often wholly or partly supports the households that furnish both national and international capital with a cheap, disposable workforce. To argue that sex tourism, or indeed any other form of prostitution, exists in order to ensure that men can buy 'the sex act' and so exercise patriarchal rights of access to women's bodies (see Pateman, 1988, p. 199) deflects attention from these economic and social relations, yet it is precisely upon these relations that the power men like Dick (quoted at the start of this chapter) exercise over Thai prostitutes rests.

Analyses which view patriarchy as *the* locus of social power also create political problems when applied to sex tourism. If prostitution is seen as a form of sexual oppression rather than of economic exploitation, it follows that 'Free prostitution does not exist, whatever the means of exercising it ... prostitution of women [is] always by force ... it is a violation of human rights and an outrage to the dignity of women' (Barry, 1991, quoted in van der Gaag, 1994). As well as drawing radical feminists into direct conflict with most grass roots prostitute organizations campaigning to develop, extend and protect the rights of sex workers (a project which necessarily involves a view of prostitution as a form of paid work and also, therefore, a recognition of women's individual freedom to choose this route to economic survival), such a position obscures all distinctions between prostitutes and the very different social relations which govern their work (see Truong, 1990). In reality, the term 'prostitution' embraces an enormous range of activities undertaken on very different terms and under very different conditions, and for reasons of political strategy it is vital to distinguish between them.

My own view is that while sex tourism must be recognized as first and foremost a form of economic exploitation, it should also be seen as a unique and distinctive form of exploitation. There are fundamental differences between capitalist employers and punters which must be borne in mind in any programme of political resistance. The relationship between capital and labour is characterized by a mutual dependence as well as antagonism. Without a class of wage workers, capital accumulation cannot take place. But though sex tourists exercise economic power over prostitutes, there is no mutual economic dependency between the two groups. Thai prostitutes need sex tourists in order to subsist, but sex tourists would not actually starve, wither or die without Thai prostitutes. Since sex tourists as a collective group are not locked into a dialectical relationship with these women, it would be extremely difficult for prostitutes to win concessions through struggle with these men, who can, after all, simply move their custom elsewhere.[8] It is not

punters, but governments, international travel companies, hoteliers, local
business people and so on, who have an economic interest in maintaining the
flow of sex tourists, and thus to engage in direct action against sex tourists
(as some feminist and guerrilla organizations do – see Lee, 1991), satisfying
as it may be, will not necessarily improve the lot of the women who sell their
sexual labour to them.

The phenomenon of sex tourism reveals all too graphically the nature of
the relationship between underdeveloped countries at the periphery of
'regional political economies' (Cohen, 1987) and those at their centre. It also
rests upon the articulation of structures, ideologies and sexualities that are
simultaneously gendered and 'racialized'. Sex tourism thus represents an
immense theoretical challenge for both feminists and Marxists, as well as an
urgent political one.

Notes

I am grateful to the Social Science Faculty Research Board of Leicester University
for funding the fieldwork in Thailand upon which this paper is based.

1 Thus far, this research has involved interviews with a snowball sample of sex
   tourists to Thailand and the manager of a travel company specializing in sex
   tours to Pattaya; in January 1994, twenty-five sex tourists in Thailand were
   interviewed and hundreds more observed on a field trip to Bangkok and Pattaya
   funded by the research board of the Faculty of Social Sciences, Leicester
   University. Documentary evidence in the form of publicity and advertising
   material from travel companies and mail order bride agencies is also being
   collected.
2 It should also be noted that sex tourists vary in terms of sex (although
   uncommon, it is not unknown for women to engage in commercial sex with Thai
   women and men) and in terms of sexual orientation. There are male homosexual
   sex tourists and a distinct group of paedophiles, both hetero and homosexual.
   Since none of these groups formed the focus of my research, I am unable to enter
   into any analysis of them.
3 For male prostitutes it is generally at the upper end of this scale.
4 I have focused in this chapter on sex tourists, not sex workers, but it is important
   to note that the social relations which govern the work of prostitutes who supply
   these services vary enormously. Some bar/brothel prostitutes are debt bonded,
   some are directly employed by the owner, but many women and men work from
   bars or brothels on a self employed basis, paying the owner a portion of their
   takings. There are also freelance prostitutes who solicit on beaches and street
   corners, or from hotel bars. Clearly, the amount of money (if any) that a
   prostitute who works for a third party receives in exchange for providing 'short-

time' or twenty-four-hour deals will depend upon the terms that have been negotiated with that party.

5   It is estimated that there are around 200,000 prostitutes under the age of 16 in Thailand (Anderson, 1991), many of whom are debt bonded. Children aged between 9 and 14 in the Chiang Mai region have been identified as at the greatest risk from the brothel owners and pimps who will offer their parents between 20,000 and 30,000 Baht (US $800–$1,200) as a loan to be paid off through the forced prostitution of the child (DEP, 1993).

6   Thailand has a population of 59 million. Of those people who had been tested by 1990, half a million were HIV positive, and this figure is currently rising by 1,400 per day (Illman, 1993).

7   I use the term primitive accumulation to refer to any process through which capital acquires something (whether raw materials or labour power) without covering the cost of its reproduction.

8   Indeed, a number of sex tourists told me that they would be visiting Vietnam next year, where the 'girls' are reputed to be 'less commercial' than Thai prostitutes now are – 'They're like the Thai girls used to be, a few years back'. Some British travel agents are currently setting up sex tours to Vietnam. Meanwhile, for the hardened sex tourist in search of real bargains, in Cuba, the economic situation is so bad that women are presently offering oral sex for $1 and penetrative sex for $2 (Gerard, 1994).

References

ANDERSON, S. (1991) 'Sex Tourism in Thailand', *WRI Women*, No. 10, 55 Dawes Street, London SE17 1EL.

BARRY, K. (1979) *Female Sexual Slavery*, New Jersey, Prentice Hall.

BARRY, K. (Ed.) (1984) *International Feminism: Networking Against Female Sexual Slavery*, New York, International Women's Tribune Center.

BARRY, K. (1991) *The Penn State Report on Sexual Exploitation, Violence and Prostitution*, UNESCO/Coalition Against Trafficking in Women.

BECKLES, H. (1989) *Natural Rebels: A Social History of Enslaved Black Women in Barbados*, London, Zed Books.

COHEN, R. (1987) *The New Helots*, Aldershot, Gower.

COLLINS, P. HILL (1990) *Black Feminist Thought*, Boston and London, Unwin Hyman.

DEP (1993) 'Thai Women Face Greater Opportunity', *DEP Newsletter*, March, Daughter's Education Programme, PO Box 10 Mae Sai, Chiang Rai 57130, Thailand.

ENLOE, C. (1989) *Bananas, Beaches and Bases*, London, Pandora.

GERARD, L. (1994) 'Game for a Fistful of Dollars', *Observer*, 26 June.

GRAAF, R. DE VANWESENBEECK, I., ZESSEN, G., STRAVER, C. and VISSER, J. (1992) 'Prostitution and the Spread of 'HIV', in *Safe Sex in Prostitution in the*

Netherlands, Mr A. de Graaf Institute, Westermarkt 4, 1016 DK Amsterdam.

HEYZER, N. (1986) *Working Women in South-East Asia*, Milton Keynes, Open University Press.

HOIGARD, C. and FINSTAD, L. (1992) *Backstreets: Prostitution, Money and Love*, Cambridge, Polity.

hOOKS, b. (1981) *Ain't I a Woman: Black Women and Feminism*, Boston, South End Press.

ILLMAN, J. (1993) 'The Carnal Cabaret', *Guardian*, 30 November.

JEFFREYS, S. (1990) *Anticlimax: A Feminist Perspective on the Sexual Revolution*, London, The Women's Press.

KOVEL, J. (1988) *White Racism: A Psychohistory*, London, Free Association Books.

KUSY, F. (1991) *Thailand*, London, Cadogan.

LEE, W. (1991) 'Prostitution and Tourism in South-East Asia', in REDCLIFT, N. and SINCLAIR, M. THEA (Eds) *Working Women: International Perspectives on Labour and Gender Ideology*, London, Routledge.

LITTLER, C. (1985) 'Work in Traditional and Modern Societies', in LITTLER, C. (Ed.) *The Experience of Work*, Milton Keynes, Open University Press.

MACKINNON, C. (1988) 'Desire and Power: A Feminist Perspective', in NELSON, C. and GROSSBERG, L. (Eds) *Marxism and the Interpretation of Culture*, Houndmills, Macmillan Education.

MARX, K. (1973) *Grundrisse*, Harmondsworth, Penguin.

MITTER, S. (1986) *Common Fate, Common Bond*, London, Pluto.

O'CONNELL DAVIDSON, J. (1994) 'The Anatomy of Self Employed Prostitution'

PATEMAN, C. (1988) *The Sexual Contract*, Cambridge, Polity.

PATTERSON, O. (1982) *Slavery and Social Death*, Cambridge, Mass., Harvard University Press.

POTTS, L. (1990) *The World Market for Labour*, London, Zed Books.

SEGAL, L. (1990) *Slow Motion: Changing Masculinities, Changing Men*, London, Virago.

STOLLER, R. (1979) *Sexual Excitement: Dynamics of Erotic Life*, New York, Pantheon.

THOMAS, N. (1994) *Colonialism's Culture*, Cambridge, Polity.

TRUONG, T. (1990) *Sex, Money and Morality: Prostitution and Tourism in Southeast Asia*, London, Zed Books.

VAN DER GAAG, N. (1994) 'Prostitution: Soliciting for Change', *New Internationalist*, 252 (February), pp. 4–7.

WALKER, D. and EHRLICH, R. (1992) *'Hello My Big Big Honey!': Love Letters to Bangkok Bar Girls and Their Revealing Interviews*, Bangkok, Dragon Dance Publications.

WARD, I. (1988) Introduction to KOVEL, J. *White Racism: A Psychohistory*, London, Free Association Books.

Chapter 4

Prostitution: Problematizing the Definition

Jo Phoenix

Introduction

Feminist and non-feminist research into prostitution has a very long history both within the UK and abroad. In feminist literature, discussions typically centre on issues of control, consent and coercion as they exist or are made manifest in the lives and experiences of prostitute women. The focus tends to be not only on the 'conditions of entry' into sex work, but also on the conditions of work and more generally on whether prostitution is an expression of violence against women or whether it is a form of 'legitimate' work structured and conditioned by women's general economic dis-advantages. Moreover, these discussions are trying to understand how the nexus of individual biographies, institutional practices and formal and informal social relationships that prostitute women find themselves in, circumscribe or control the individual and collective lives of prostitute women.

However, what I seek to demonstrate here is that issues of power and politics, as expressed in the lives of prostitute women, cannot be fully appreciated or understood until they are examined in their full diversity, multiplicity and complexity. In this sense, this chapter is not about challenging the conclusions of existing literature, nor is it about providing a new definition of prostitution, rather it is a 'prologue' to the discussions focused on the lives of prostitute women.

Existing Definitions

In much of the established research on prostitution, authors have typically defined and conceived of prostitution as a singular activity (i.e. selling sex) which involves a limited set of relationships (i.e. worker/punter, worker/ pimp and occasionally worker/police). Examples of this abound in the literature which defines prostitution as being 'the provision of sexual services in exchange for some form of payment, such as money, drink, drugs or other consumer goods' (Plant, 1990, p. xiv); 'buying and selling sexual services for cash payment' (Hoigard and Finstad, 1992, p. 8); 'a business transaction understood as such by the parties involved and in the nature of a short term contract in which one or more people pay an agreed price to one or more of the people for helping them to attain sexual gratification by various methods' (Bennett and Perkins, 1985, p. 4). Alternatively, authors do not provide a definition but rely on an assumed common-sense notion of what prostitution is (see McLeod, 1982; Delacoste and Alexander, 1988; Roberts, 1992).

The primary difficulty of defining and conceptualizing prostitution in the above fashion is that it creates 'closure'. It limits the relationships which come under the heading 'prostitution' to worker/punter and worker/pimp at the same time as narrowly circumscribing the activities involved in prostitution to the actual exchange of money for sexual activity.

With this in mind, the next two sections tease out the different relationships and activities that occur in two well-known forms of prostitution: street work and parlour work. In order to achieve this, I take these two familiar labels and deconstruct the social phenomena that lie behind those labels in terms of place of work, mode of client contact, employment status, peripheral activities, formal relationships entered into and negotiation of risks and protection. By each of these I specifically mean:

- place of work: where does the work take place?
- mode of client contact: how do clients and workers get into contact with each other?
- employment status: is the worker full-time, part-time, regular or casual?
- peripheral activities: are there any other activities commercialized in the prostitution exchange?
- exchange practices: how are monies from the prostitution exchange collected and distributed? What type of economic relationships does the worker enter into?
- formal relationships with others: what are the formal relationships that the worker is involved in, apart from with her client?
- risks and protection: what risks to the worker are involved? What

protection is offered to the worker? What strategies and relationships does she enter into to obtain protection and who is she needing protection from?

This is a largely descriptive section, but one which, I hope, will enable the reader to appreciate the nexus of activities and relationships that prostitute women are involved in, particularly in terms of diversity and complexity.

Street Workers

Place of Work

A street worker's place of work is the street. However, even here we can begin to see diversity of the activity which is collapsed when conceptualizing prostitution in narrow terms of sex for money. Initial contact may be on the street, but business may be conducted on the streets, or in cars, hotel rooms or other accommodating indoor locations (Overs, 1994, p. 27; Matthews, 1993; Hoigard and Finstad, 1992; Roberts, 1992; Delacoste and Alexander, 1988; Bennett and Perkins, 1985; McLeod, 1982). Business may also be initiated from doorways or front windows in houses (McLeod, 1982, p. 5). These latter places tend to be unpopular choices because they do not afford the women the 'freedom' of the street (such as escape from potentially violent punters) and can incur 'rent' expenses.

Mode of Client Contact

Although the stereotype of the street worker portrays client contact as being initiated by the worker, research shows that it is the client who tends to initiate contact (Delacoste and Alexander, 1988).

> If you see somebody you know then it's alright, otherwise you just stroll about and a car will pull up. If he stops, you know that if he's passed you once he's looking for business. Some people say, 'Are you doing business love?' or you say, 'Do you want business?' (Kathy, in McLeod, 1982, p. 5)

Employment Status

The employment status of street workers also shows the diversity of arrangements and activities encompassed under the familiar label. There is no singular employment status: women may work regular hours or casually. Furthermore, they may be 'away-day' women who have arrived from another locality, specifically to work (Delacoste and Alexander, 1988). Alternatively, street workers may be runaways who are trying to obtain either cash or lodgings for the night (Summers, 1988, p. 117), or they may simply work on an irregular, part-time or casual basis (Delacoste and Alexander, 1988; McLeod, 1982; Roberts, 1992; Bennett and Perkins, 1985).

Peripheral Activities

Street work has no formally associated peripheral activities (Delacoste and Alexander, 1988; McLeod, 1982; Roberts, 1992; Bennett and Perkins, 1985).

Exchange Practice

There are at least two layers of exchange practices in street prostitution. The first layer is the exchange practice between the client and the worker. This tends to be simple and direct, with clients paying the workers directly, in advance, a pre-arranged price for services (McLeod, 1982, p. 5; Delacoste and Alexander, 1988). A second layer may be the exchange practice between worker and pimp/ponce. The ponce may take a percentage cut of the worker's earnings or may take a flat rate; this may be all but a small sum so that the worker can cover her expenses (i.e. condoms, taxis etc.) (Roberts, 1992). Alternatively, the ponce may be a man that the worker is having a relationship with. In this instance, the exchange practice may not be so strictly demarcated.

Formal Relationships with Others

The degree to which the stereotype of a street walker is over-simplified becomes apparent when the issue of a street worker's formal relationships with others is focused upon. Furthermore, the complexity and diversity of these relationships is similarly exposed. A street worker is involved primarily in six sets of formal relationships, each of which have several different permutations.

Firstly, there is a formal relationship that the street worker may or may not have with a ponce. Legally, a ponce is a man who benefits directly from and is able to exercise a degree of control over the woman's prostitution activities. In reality there are several 'types' of ponces which will involve women in qualitatively different types of relationships. There may be the ponce who has no relationship with the woman, other than a strictly business relationship. He may or may not exercise coercion over her through the use of threats and violence (Hoigard and Finstad, 1992, p. 142). Moreover, the ponce may be the woman's boyfriend, husband or partner who similarly may or may not use threats and violence to gain her compliance (Hoigard and Finstad, 1992, p. 142).

Secondly, there is a formal relationship that the street worker may or may not have with other street workers. Whether the street worker is independent or not does not preclude her forming relationships with her 'co-workers'. Often this may be 'teaming up' with others for company, protection or the provision of 'specialist services' (Matthews, 1993, p. 11). Street workers may also work collaboratively in order to provide child care for each other (Lawrinson, 1994).

Thirdly, there is a formal relationship that the women have with the police. In many cases, the relationship is characterized by a 'functional camaraderie' with both the police and women knowing that each other are 'just doing their job' (Dunhill, 1989, p. 206). This may include the police coming to an arrangement with the street worker about when to arrest her so that she may be able to arrange child care, raise the money for the fine, etc. (Dunhill, 1989, p. 206). This is not to imply, however, that the relationship does not include the exercise of power. The police will often use the women to obtain information about drug deals, have sex with them in lieu of arrest or harass them (Dunhill, 1989, p. 207; Overs, 1994, p. 26).

Fourthly, there is the relationship that the street worker has with residents. This again has several different permutations ranging from open hostility to placid acceptance. Locally organized residents' committees focusing on 'cleaning up the street' (occasionally manifesting in vigilante groups) are not unheard of. In other cases, residents may form good 'working' relationships with the women.

Fifthly, because of police targeting of street work, most street workers are by necessity involved in negotiating relationships with the courts and the officials working there, such as court team probation officers, court clerks and the magistrates (see Kinnell, 1993, p. 37). These, too, can range from the coldly indifferent whereby the courts 'process' the women as quickly as possible, operating a 'revolving door' policy, to the sympathetic.

Sixthly, many street workers find themselves negotiating relationships with non-statutory outreach agencies, such as the SAFE project in Birmingham. Many use the projects in a strictly utilitarian fashion, obtaining free condoms and medical advice in a 'non-judgmental' atmosphere.

Protection

Protection is an issue which involves street workers in three further layers of relationships. This is most easily understood in terms of: protection from whom and who is used to develop which strategies offering protection? An obvious and important issue is protection from client violence. The women will use each other to develop strategies offering them some modicum of protection, such as another worker ostentatiously noting down the car registration number of the client when her co-worker gets business (Dunhill, 1989, p. 204). Alternatively, co-workers may 'spread the word' about a potentially dangerous client, or develop a street 'folklore' about which types of clients are more likely to be dangerous. A further strategy may simply be to walk together (Matthews, 1993, p. 11; Dunhill, 1989, p. 204).

Secondly, there is the threat of ponce violence, which comes in two forms: either violence from a ponce whom the woman is currently connected with, or violence from a man who wishes to ponce the woman. Each of these needs to be treated separately. The strategies that are developed to deal with violence from a woman's ponce are as diffuse and divergent as the strategies employed by women who are experiencing domestic violence. They range from 'tea and sympathy' from friends and co-workers to involving outside agencies such as outreach workers, probation officers etc. However, it needs to be noted that some Battered Women's Refuges operate unofficial policies of excluding prostitute women. Regarding violence from potential ponces, women may avoid or hide from these men or invoke the threat of counter-violence from existing ponces.

Lastly, there is the issue of protection from the police. Most street workers 'tailor' their behaviour in such a way as to afford them a modicum of protection from arrest or harassment: 'then you'll probably get in the car because if you've got the car door open and you're standing outside, you're liable to be spotted by the vice squad' (Kathy, in McLeod, 1982,p. 5). Alternatively, street workers will accept the deals proposed by police officers in order to protect themselves from harassment:

However, the woman who reported that she never made deals with the police also said that she was not able to make working arrangements with them, and so did the woman who said that the police arrested her nearly every night. She said her face 'didn't fit'. (Dunhill, 1989, p. 207)

Distinguishing Features

The distinguishing features of street work lie in not only where the work takes place (i.e. on the streets) but also in the issues of risk, protection and control. In no other type of prostitution is the risk of police harassment or ponce control so high. With these risks, protection strategies and control mechanisms come a unique set of relationships between the parties involved that is not mirrored by any other type of prostitution. Hence, what is originally portrayed, in the stereotype, as an unproblematic prostitution exchange which takes place in a different location from other types of prostitution, is in fact a unique combination of a multiplicity of relationships (i.e. ponce, worker, other workers and police) and activities which can be enacted in several different ways.

Parlour Work

Place of Work

In terms of place of work, parlours are more specific than other avenues of prostitution. Parlour work is conducted in established locations that offer legitimate services, such as massages, saunas or health consultations (Edelstein, 1988, pp. 62–9; Delacoste and Alexander, 1988). Business is conducted in private rooms arranged for the purpose of the legitimate business.

Mode of Client Contact

The mode of client contact in parlours differs from that of street work in one significant way. Parlours are not legally restricted from advertising, as long as it is their legitimate business which is advertised (Smith and Hogan, 1983). That is to say, parlours are able to establish client contact much more openly than other forms of prostitution. Adverts, which direct the potential customer to an address or phone number in which initial personal contact is made, are typically placed in local papers and contact magazines (Roberts, 1992).

However, client contact may also be established in other ways. Parlours will typically be located in areas well known for prostitution and will hope to establish contact with passers-by. Moreover, just as street workers will dress in a symbolic fashion, so parlours make use of symbolic codes, such as an open front doorway, to alert potential customers to their business (Alexander, 1988).

Employee Status

Employment status in parlour work consists of a number of dimensions. There is, for example, the issue of whether or not the worker is full-time or part-time, casual or regular. Any of these statuses is possible, but because parlour work involves a legitimate business, the conditions in which women are hired or contracted tend to be less flexible than those experienced by women working from the streets. In short, although parlour workers may work shifts and be part- or full-time workers, the incidence of casual or 'away-day' working is much lower (Velarde, 1975).

Employment status will also relate to the organizational structure of the parlour and how it manages the collection and distribution of monies, a feature that is particularly influenced by the worker's position as either an employee or self employed (Velarde, 1975; Delacoste and Alexander, 1988; Roberts, 1992). The distinction between these two categories will be explored when the exchange practices within parlours are explored (see below).

Peripheral Activities

When the issue of peripheral activities is examined, the distinctiveness of parlour work from other types of prostitution can be demonstrated. With street work, peripheral activities were non-existent. Furthermore, the stereo-type of parlour work portrays the peripheral activities of massages etc. as being a thin disguise for the prostitution exchange. However, it is possible to argue that the prostitution exchange is, in fact, the peripheral activity of parlour work. The women are legitimately contracted to perform massages etc. (Velarde, 1975). These legitimate and licit activities comprise the 'core' of parlour work. Any prostitution exchange that may take place is extra to this contract; it is negotiated privately between the worker and the client. In short, parlour workers, although typically engaging in a prostitution exchange with the customers, do not necessarily need to do so.

Exchange Practice

When focusing on the exchange practices of parlour work it is possible to see the diversity of activities encompassed under the label as well as gain a degree of insight into the complex web of relationships that comprise parlour work. Typically, money collection and distribution in parlours follows a pattern whereby the receptionist will collect a flat fee from the punter, any prostitution exchange which takes place is negotiated and paid for directly from punter to worker and, finally, the management will expect a pay-back from the worker. The first dimension of exchange practices (between punter and management) typically acts as protection for the management from charges of brothel running. The second dimension of exchange practices (between punter and worker) emulates the exchange practice in street work. It is a simple and direct exchange. However, another aspect of exchange departs radically from what was shown to exist on the streets, and may reveal several different permutations. The management can charge 'shift' money whereby there is a fee incurred by the worker for every shift she works. Alternatively, the management can demand a percentage of the women's overall taking per shift. In other cases, however, a flat fee may be taken from the worker for every client she has, regardless of her overall earnings.

A second layer of exchange practices is discernible for parlour workers. Working in a parlour does not preclude the possibility of a woman having a ponce and as such some workers may also have to pay their ponce. These exchange practices are similar to those outlined for street workers.

Formal Relationships with Others

This feature of parlour work also departs from the formal relationships entered into by street workers, in a number of ways. Firstly, the workers may be self employed or may be employees (Velarde, 1975). The distinction between the categories is a function of the distribution of money and does not affect in any substantive way the formal relationships the worker has with the parlour. The worker will still be in a position of 'employee' with the management setting the working hours, conditions of service, fees charged, etc. regardless of whether the worker is technically self employed. In short, the relationship the worker has with the parlour management in both cases is a relationship of control.

Parlour workers also enter into formal relationships with other workers in the parlour. This relationship is a business one and each woman stands as a co-worker in relation to the other women. It is common for there to be a hierarchy amongst the workers, with one or two of the women being favoured by management or used by the management as shift managers. In addition, as mentioned previously, the worker may or may not have a ponce. The different permutations of this are the same as for street workers. It is important to note also that, although the frequency of contact is greatly reduced, the worker will still have to negotiate a relationship with the police. As with the relationship with ponces, this mirrors the relationship between the street worker and the police.

Protection

The issue of protection involves parlour workers in a very different set of relationships and strategies from those of street workers, in particular a decreased risk of client violence (Delacoste and Alexander, 1988). This will be a function of the work being conducted in less isolated environments. Furthermore, parlours may employ bouncers or maids to deal with potentially violent customers (Hoigard and Finstad, 1992; Roberts, 1992; van der Gaag, 1994; Bennett and Perkins, 1985).

Parlour workers may also experience a decreased risk of police harassment as compared to street work, attributable, perhaps, to the less visible nature of the prostitution exchange in parlour work, the lack of police policies targeting parlour work, or because the inherently legal and legitimate nature of parlour work affords both management and the workers protection.

However, unlike street workers, parlour workers experience the risk of management exploitation. This may be expressed in overly long shifts, high (if not extortionate) shift fees and poor working conditions, which may or may not include excessive control measures on the part of the management. These control mechanisms, which may include not allowing a worker to have more than one condom in her possession at any one time, or even extend to watching, through a 'peephole', the prostitution exchange taking place, function to stop the women 'cheating' the management. The workers, in order to protect themselves from the risk of management exploitation, develop similar strategies to those adopted by brothel workers, such as devising elaborate 'cheat' schemes like hiding condoms, 'back-talking' the management or developing an informal trade union.

As mentioned above, parlour work does not preclude poncing. A parlour worker, therefore, may or may not experience the risk of ponce violence or violence from potential ponces. The strategies employed by parlour workers to deal with both these risks are similar to those employed by street workers.

Distinguishing Features

Parlour work is not distinct from other types of prostitution by virtue of the place in which it is conducted. The features that make parlour work distinctive are a combination of place, peripheral activity, mode of client contact and the relationships involving protection and control that the workers find themselves in. No other type of prostitution, except escort work, involves the women in a complex web of relationships that have a legitimate and illegitimate side. This two-sided nature of the work affects all the relationships that a worker finds herself involved in. Similarly, in no other type of prostitution, except escort work, is the prostitution exchange a second dimension in the overall exchange practices.

Conclusion

This rather descriptive deconstruction of two avenues of prostitution shows that prostitution needs much more careful definition and conceptualizing than in much of the existing literature. Under each type of prostitution I have tried to map out some of the array of activities and the nexus of relationships in which working women find themselves. However, by way of conclusion, a few further comments need to be made.

I have discussed only two of the many different avenues of prostitution. Others include brothel work, call and home work, escort work, and hotel and bar prostitution. In a similar fashion to the two types of prostitution discussed here, each of these will also have many different activities and relationships associated with them, some in common with other avenues of prostitution and some unique. What this potentially means is that the diversity of activities and relationships involved in prostitution grows accordingly. If this is the case, then to define and conceptualize prostitution as merely the exchange of sex for money is surely short-sighted and narrow. If feminist research aims to produce a valid insight into issues of control, coercion and consent as expressed in the lives of prostitute women, then the conceptualization of prostitution needs to incorporate the full constellation of activities and relationships experienced by working women.

As I stated in the introduction to this chapter, much of the current debate in prostitution is about control, consent and coercion (or, put another way, the power and politics of prostitution). It is my opinion that these issues can be at least partly understood only after each form of prostitution has been mapped out and the distinguishing and similar features then examined and analysed systematically. This can be seen in debate over whether prostitution is 'work', in which some authors compare prostitution to service work (see Pateman, 1983; McIntosh, 1994) and examine the working conditions of legitimately employed women in gendered jobs, attempting to draw parallels or divergences with prostitution. However, if one is to examine the activities and relationships of prostitution as previously suggested then it may be possible to draw more comprehensive parallels or to highlight the differences.

The exercise of gendered power, although happening at a social level in terms of realistic options and alternatives, institutional controls, and so on, is also exercised in the personal lives and individual relationships that working women enter into. For example, it needs to be established just how street workers can negotiate issues of 'protection' or 'control' particularly around violent ponces. Similarly, it needs to be established what the gendered nature of the relationship between parlour workers and management is.

I have attempted to demonstrate that prostitution is not just the exchange of sex for money. While this exchange is certainly a necessary part of prostitution, it takes place amidst a plethora of relationships and a multitude of activities, each of which will be made sense of, structured and influenced by issues of gender, class and race. To understand the politics of prostitution and to permit 'openness' rather than 'closure' of analysis, it is necessary to reconceptualize and redefine 'prostitution'.

References

ALEXANDER, P. (1988) 'Prostitution: A Difficult Issue for Feminists', in DELACOSTE, F. and ALEXANDER, P. (Eds) *Sex Work*, London, Virago, pp. 184–214.

BENNETT, G. and PERKINS, R. (1985) *Being a Prostitute*, Hemel Hempstead, George Allen and Unwin.

DELACOSTE, F. and ALEXANDER, P. (Eds) (1988) *Sex Work: Writings by Women in the Sex Industry*, London, Virago.

DUNHILL, C. (1989) *The Boys in Blue*, London, Virago.

EDELSTEIN, J. (1988) 'In the Massage Parlor', in DELACOSTE, F. and ALEXANDER, P. (Eds) *Sex Work*, London, Virago, pp. 62–9.

HOIGARD, C. and FINSTAD, L. (1992) *Backstreets: Prostitution, Money and Love*, Cambridge, Polity.

KINNELL, H. (1993) *Wolverhampton Sex Workers Survey Report*, Birmingham, SAFE Project.

LAWRINSON, S. (1994) unpublished thesis, Staffordshire University.

MCINTOSH, M. (1994) 'The Feminist Debate on Prostitution', presented to the BSA Conference (Preston), March.

MCLEOD, E. (1982) *Working Women: Prostitution Now*, Beckenham, Croom Helm.

MATTHEWS, R. (1993) 'Streetwise: A Critical Review of the Recent Criminal Law Revision Committee's Report on Prostitution', *Critical Social Policy*, Issue 12, Vol. 4, No. 3.

OVERS, S. (1994) 'Prostitution', *New Internationalist*, 252 (February).

PATEMAN, C. (1983) 'Defending Prostitution: Charges against Ericcson', *Ethics*, 93 (April).

PLANT, M. (1990) *Aids, Drugs and Prostitution*, London, Routledge.

ROBERTS, N. (1992) *Whores in History*, London, HarperCollins.

SMITH, J.C. and HOGAN, B. (1983) *Criminal Law*, London, Butterworth.

SUMMERS, R. (1988) 'Prostitution', in DELACOSTE, F. and ALEXANDER, P. (Eds) *Sex Work*, London, Virago, pp. 113–18.

VAN DER GAAG, N. (1994) 'Prostitution: Soliciting for Change', *New Internationalist*, 252 (February).

VELARDE, A. (1975) 'Becoming Prostituted', *British Journal of Criminology*, Vol. 15, No. 3 (July).

Media Discourses of Sexuality

Chapter 5

'Freedom From' or 'Freedom to' ...? Contemporary Identities in Women's Magazines

Esther Sonnet and Imelda Whelehan

'Post-feminist' is a descriptive term which has gained currency since the mid eighties, a term favoured by the mass media to suggest that we have moved beyond the bad old days of 'women's lib' to a period when women can be both sexy *and* powerful. It is also a term that might, albeit problematically, be applied to a number of contemporary feminist critics who identify tyrannical or even puritanical streaks in what they characterize as seventies feminism – particularly in its applications to popular culture. In one collection of cultural criticism, *The Female Gaze* (Gamman and Marshment, 1988), feminism of the 'old school' is consistently cast as boring, or prescriptive:

> To put it bluntly, having grown old while fighting many a bitter battle
> in the name of feminist politics, veteran campaigners now have to
> come to terms with the fact that to most young women their vision
> of a feminist future is a big yawn. (Young, 1988, pp. 173–4)

Like an older relative, old-style feminism putatively gazes on a younger generation and disapproves of their love of Madonna, their addiction to soaps, or their enthusiasm for high fashion – the 'women who dare to dress up' (Young, 1988, p. 179). In another context, Janice Winship notes that her students' reluctance to identify themselves as feminist 'seemed to me to be not just a sign of an as-yet-unformed feminist consciousness but a sign that the style of seventies feminism felt inappropriate to them' (Winship, 1985, p. 44).

In contrast to the association of feminism with 'alternative puritanism' (Young, 1988, p. 178), today's 'post-feminists' have bravely cut through the perimeter fence of feminist orthodoxy in order to freely indulge in the pleasures of the popular text – whether it be TV, pulp fiction or magazines. It is hardly surprising, then, that 'post-feminism' is described in the language and imagery of bravery and daring. Feminism, it is argued, has developed a particular hegemonic discourse which actively *oppresses* women – espe-cially by virtue of being primarily identified with white, middle-class, heterosexual women; and one might be forgiven for thinking that feminism itself, cast as static and inflexible, is the *dominant* oppressor of women. What is curious about this demonization of feminism in the late eighties and nineties is that, in popular culture, politically reactionary positions are, as Tania Modleski has pointed out, adopted in the name of feminism (Modleski, 1991, p. ix). The controversies generated by the term 'post-feminism' are nowhere more keenly registered than in the field of cultural productions, where issues of female imagery and the politics of appearance have become troubled and fraught with contradiction. As important (because popular) sites of the negotiation of 'post-feminist' identity, these contradictions are most powerfully coded in women's glossy magazines of the nineties. In these, the discourse of feminism is turned against itself and mobilized to often anti-feminist ends, so that oft-used terms associated with feminism – such as 'liberation' – are hijacked for quite other purposes.

The young woman of the nineties is exhorted to take pleasure in the 'feminine' things in life, as it is the construction of a *new* femininity which supposedly allows her to be liberated from the dour uniformity of feminist dogma by taking pleasure in the gaze. These magazines have reached beyond the idea that such images are merely 'playful'; the 'new' femininity represents power – even when the most obvious interpretation of pose or dress is of an abdication of power. This freedom of 'self determination' is a backhanded tribute to the success of feminism in politicizing popular awareness of the dominant ideological power invested in the female image as object of the look. But while acknowledging that the freedom for women to determine their own standards of desire and pleasure is 'a measure of the force of feminism's impact on contemporary forms and practices' (Young, in Gamman and Marshment 1988, p. 174), it does not provide any means for engaging with the consequences of occupying a space beyond the conven-tional 'feminine' (where 'men' define the meanings of the image configur-ation). Rather than taking the politics of the spectacle on the terrain of the male gaze, 'post-feminism' signally refuses to engage with feminism's concern with the power of the look under patriarchy. Instead these magazines invest in the fantasy of a cultural vacuum devoid of any male gaze, thus ensuring that patriarchal givens remain unchallenged. What the mainstream glossies are out to sell is a feminine power which can be located in both the escapist and pragmatic elements of the magazine; and this particular notion of 'power' seems to reside in the female body and the female heterosexual response. As Janet Lee has remarked:

> *Cosmo* exhorts the female reader to construct herself through self-discipline, and the reward for this is physical pleasure – or, more specifically, sexual pleasure.... The 'new woman' *Cosmo* version is the sexy woman. Sex equals not only fun, but independence and success. And *Cosmo* claims to have the knowledge that will tell you how to have it all – sex, success and liberation. (Lee, 1988, p. 169)

The co-option of 'post-feminist' as a positive term in women's magazines facilitates the elision of some harder material realities foregrounded by feminists. Issues such as sexual harassment, domestic violence, the continuing sexual division of labour, and the increasing poverty among women are sporadically acknowledged in the true life stories, or self-help pages – physically consigned to the margins of the magazine itself. The rosier picture, of the successful individual woman as capitalist 'post-feminist', takes centre stage, and fashion, beauty, health and money features emphasize that things are getting better all the time – and if women are not basking in material and sexual success, they must take a long hard look at themselves. The collective transformational political feminist response is deftly supplanted by an older liberal humanist rhetoric of self help and personal responsibility. Issues of racial difference and sexual orientation are almost wholly ignored in such magazines, so that beneath the facade of the infinitely various, totally individual 'new woman', lies the ideologically homogenized ideal-type white, middle-class, heterosexual, politically moderate, size 10–14 woman. Of course it is by no means novel to point out that women's magazines operate on such ideological versus material contradictions; Janice Winship has pointed out the crucial operation of such contradictions, particularly in relation to the appearance of pluralism that this offers (Winship, 1987, pp. 63, 106). What has changed, however, is the means by which an idea of second-wave feminism – as tyrannical, judgmental, anti-pleasure, and anti-sex – is quite categorically situated as the enemy of 'post-feminist' 'new' women, in ways that patriarchy, capitalism and New Right pro-family legislation are not.

Women's magazines, whilst relying on the woman reader's working knowledge of and investment in the normative aspects of femininity, are constantly reinventing old tried and trusted and even pre-feminist themes, with the result that 'skilfully, ingeniously, and sometimes brilliantly, the old becomes the new' (Ferguson, 1983, p. 7). The new woman of 'post-feminism', then, may have close associations with the 'woman' constructed by magazines of earlier periods in the ritual reinvention of femininity. A 'new' diet, fashion, health or beauty product does not necessarily rupture the conventional relationship of woman to specific roles and identities, nor the timeless wisdom that 'being "good" at being a woman involves doing womanly things at regular and appointed times' (Ferguson, 1983, p. 7). One of the consistent functions of women's glossies has been to reassure women that the dominant ideological life-choices offered by society at large (heterosexual monogamy, pro-capitalist democracy, aspirational individualism, a high value placed upon physical beauty, familial norms, etc.) are indeed the right ones. The 'rightness' of these choices is 'proved' when articles – 'Fat thighs and the men who love them' (*Company*, March 1994); 'Do real women have hairy armpits?' (*Company*, June 1994) – appear to transgress perceived norms, then conclude by reinforcing the original normative position.[1] Beneath the rhetoric of constantly shifting 'newness', women's magazines show a marked reluctance to endorse any form of social change which threatens to radically alter current social/sexual relations, and this reluctance sets them in opposition both to radical and socialist feminist politics. 'Post-feminism', then, is equated with an extremely dilute form of liberal feminism – a position more compatible with the needs of publications which depend wholeheartedly on advertising and the cult of individualism. The 'post-feminism' of magazines such as *Cosmopolitan*, *Company* and *Elle* is therefore a pronouncement of female power emptied of any feminist political resonance; the personal is publicized as *the* crucial site of women's power in an inversion of feminism's designation of the family and the home as the central site of women's oppression.

Having established that 'post-feminism' in this context may actually work against the interests of feminism, it is important to note that any period or stance described as 'post' must carry with it a concept of what is supplanted. The means by which the shift from feminist to 'post-feminist' is achieved in women's magazines is by casting the 'new' in terms of a 'revolution'. This effects a transformation in which the new state of affairs is constructed as a qualitative improvement on the old. Women's magazines accomplish this effect by constantly historicizing the moment, associating all things currently deemed to inhibit women's freedom of self expression with the 'bad old days' of the past; whereas the 'new' present can usually only be made intelligible by referring to the past. Significantly, the language used is nominally appropriated from feminist politics, and the conflict between past (often taken to mean last month/season) and present (always threatened with consignment to the annals of magazine 'history') is played out as a contest between feminists (an amorphous group of 'unfeminines' who wish to rob women of their 'liberty' to enjoy themselves) and post-feminists (any woman who feels uncomfortable with the epithet 'feminist' – something all readers of glossies are encouraged to be).

An example of the present being defined as a resistance to the past would be *Elle*'s definition and defence of the 1994 Schoolgirl look:

> By reclaiming styles of dress that have fallen from grace, playing up their connotations and revelling in their allure, women are wiggling in the face of anyone who spoils their fun or misconstrues the message. ('The Big Sleaze', *Elle*, February 1994)

The new look is quickly revealed as a reclamation of the old; but on this occasion the article argues that the meanings of the images are transformed by women's independent appropriation of them – 'This one, says the look, is for us – by invitation only.' Yet as the previous quotation indicates, its 'allure' remains intact – although to whom it is *now* alluring is unstated. The use of the term 'the look' to describe a fashion statement is itself ambiguous; and what this article attempts to deny is the position of others who look on, as well as whose gaze defines 'the look' in the above terms. Those whose look is unauthorized will be confronted by the women who 'own' 'the look' 'wiggling in the face of anyone who spoils their fun' – the overall tenor of the piece suggests a challenge to the voyeur or prude (still undefined); but the image of the woman 'wiggling' in their face returns us to a past register of meanings associated with feminine allure. There is a 'message' contained within this look, we are informed; that it emanates from the woman who wears it, and therefore she exerts some control over its meanings:

> The look has taken the two polar opposites of sexual fantasy – the schoolgirl and the slut – and produced a style that is positive and invigorating. Saucy stereotypes have been plundered for their most evocative elements: the hold-up (part-stocking, part-over-knee sock – part-hooker, part-hockey); the lace ankle sock (sweetheart style in seductress form). Basic messages are mixed and stirred to create something exciting and liberating. ('The Big Sleaze', *Elle*, February 1994)

The heterosexual register is unmistakable. However, another aspect of the look is that it is worn with the intention 'to shock, to tease, to provoke and then sit back and watch – with a girlfriend': presumably those who are shocked, teased or provoked comprise different interest groups, and somewhere among the implied spectators sits the feminist, so often characterized in these magazines as the entity who denies 'us' the right to dress as we please. The whole article adopts a tone which anticipates a feminist criticism of the celebration of a look which fetishizes the pubescent girl as the model of ideal-type femininity. The images which accompany the text are disturbing because the models themselves adopt poses and expressions which suggest sexual naivety and are a world away from the 'in your face' challenge that the text assures us is part of the look. The inference at the end that this look is best shared 'with a girlfriend' offers a homoerotic reading which strikes a discordant note, and reminds us that the glossies continually offer us the contradiction of celebrating woman for a specifically female audience, and yet never articulating the relationship of desire or pleasure to the image of woman in anything but displaced heterosexual terms. One of the most popularly mythologized elements of feminist politics is its supposed obsession with controlling the way women look and behave in sexual relationships. However, it is difficult – if not impossible – to find instances where feminists *prohibit* personal adornment, or specific modes of dress, as part of a political agenda. Rather, the reconstruction of feminism as a prohibitive and homogenizing discourse is due largely to the fact that second-wave feminist interventions into the politics of appearance were strategic, local and *historically specific* resistances to the undeniable social fact that certain forms of dress and make-up had come to connote an ideal-type femininity: that is, feminists of the seventies could only show their resistance by dressing and looking *different*. It is probably inevitable that an anti-dress code would become a discrete code of its own.[2]

In general, sex is one of the major delineations of female freedom in the glossies, and 'new' revelations are constantly being promised on the front covers, only to deteriorate into old received wisdoms in the text. Given that feminism is generally characterized as the villain of the piece, it is common for the glossies to displace feminist ideas by reinventing, or repositioning, them as 'post-feminist' responses. Consider, for example, the following:

> We still forget how long the female sex drive was misunderstood. Only when Masters and Johnson presented their ground-breaking work in the 60's did anyone begin to grasp the importance of the clitoris. And it wasn't until the 1976 publication of Shere Hite's *The Hite Report* that we had the first real *mandate* for equal sexual pleasure. ('Sexually Assertive Women', *Cosmopolitan*, February 1994)

This serves as a clear example of how feminist critiques are re-presented as contemporary 'post-feminist' knowledge, in that in 1994 it is still being postulated that the discovery of the clitoris is the key to equal sexual pleasure with its concomitant of women's liberation. It is interesting that the 'new' 'discovery' of the clitoris is presented in such a way that textual authority for its existence is taken to be correlative with its absence in actual sexual practice. Similarly:

> Until now, we have tended to conform to male standards of sexual behaviour bowing to the greatest ego, faking the odd orgasm and pretending to enjoy one-night stands. But we've got tired having to pretend that men's penises are a constant source of excitement. The cover has been blown on heterosexual penetrative sex as the be-all-and-end-all. ('What's sexy now?', *Elle*, November 1993)

The sentiments expressed here are remarkably similar to those in Anne Koedt's famous pamphlet, 'The Myth of the Vaginal Orgasm'. The impression that *Elle*'s discovery is in any way new or revolutionary is undermined by the fact that Koedt's observations were first circulated in 1968.[3] Just as Koedt concluded that 'Lesbian sexuality could make an excellent case ... for the irrelevancy of the male organ' (1991, p. 333), so *Elle* seems to toy with at least the prospect of a redefinition of heterosexuality with the uncompromising assertion that 'we don't miss what we were doing before' (November 1993).

Adrienne Rich was one of the first commentators to observe that 'a feminist critique of compulsory heterosexual orientation for women is long overdue' (Rich, 1986, p. 27); and contemporary magazines still reflect a high degree of anxiety about defining heterosexuality, apart from by virtue of what it is not. The recurring articles in such magazines (on orgasms, impotence, improving performance) expose the inadequacies of normative views of heterosexual response, as well as demonstrating that responsibility for success in sex lies with the woman.[4] Yet sex remains the single most important preoccupation of the heterosexual women's glossies, itself a comment on feminism's traditional avoidance of questions of desire, sexual identity, licit and illicit pleasures. The March 1994 edition of *Company* asks 'Should You Sleep with Him?' bringing us full circle and implicitly uniting the features on health, hygiene and beauty directly to heterosexual desire:

> Any man worth his salt won't care whether you've shaved under your arms or not, but if the fact that you haven't is going to inhibit your fun, then give it a miss. We know it's politically correct to let it all hang out and for both of you to take it or leave it but we also

know how hard it is to put into practice.

If you don't feel attractive, you won't be attractive. No girl ever enjoyed sex after she spent ten minutes pointing out her fat bits. If you feel you can't bear him to see your white knickers that got lost in the red wash, then put it off until next time.

Any reader prepared to 'let it all hang out' before *Company* is more likely to feel the weight of someone's disapproval afterwards – but whose? The 'post-feminist' 'we' of the world of the glossies addresses the individual 'you' of the reader, and the result – in extracts such as the above – is to expose the homogenizing effect of this first-person-plural narrative voice which abnegates any responsibility for its utterances, by laying the blame for any prescriptive tendencies at the door of a predecessor – usually feminism. Sometimes it becomes impossible to determine who (in terms of their sexual identity) is being addressed; an article which treads the well-worn path to the old chestnut of whether 'we' should shave 'our' collective armpits suggests:

> ... the odd thing is, somehow this hairy rebellion can make a woman seem even sexier. She looks spirited and independent, comfortable with her body and the pleasure it can bring. It's amazing how one hairy armpit can give us so much information, perhaps it's because even in the liberated Nineties there's still something a bit shocking about the sight of those delicate curls. It's almost like we've caught a glimpse of another, more secret, hairy place on a woman's body . . . and we all know how titillating even the thought of that can be. ('Do real women have hairy armpits?', *Company*, June 1994)

Are we, then, being offered the 'freedom' to homoerotically identify with the sexualized others in the 'we' of the readership? How else can one interpret the insinuated image of genital hair? Nonetheless, the promise of lesbian possibilities is immediately foreclosed.

This collective editorial persona adopted by the glossies (symbolized perfectly by *Cosmopolitan*'s 'Our Cosmo World') has previously been examined by Janice Winship who notes that

> On the one hand the various 'we's' of magazines are fictional collectivities only some women are invited into; others are excluded or left on the margins: black women, lesbian women, women who are not able-bodied, older women. On the other hand it is the magazines who set the terms of friendship. (Winship, 1987, p. 75)

This sets up the framework in which there are implicit penalties for failing to conform to this 'friend's' wisdom, in a curious perversion of peer group pressure, particularly pertinent when we turn to the new 'lesbian lifestyle' magazine, *Diva*, where analogous processes can be observed. Launched in April 1994, *Diva* overtly addresses a lesbian audience, which can be contrasted with the fact that mainstream glosses never feel the need to define themselves as 'heterosexual'. While wholeheartedly supporting the emergence of magazines which offer a new cultural visibility and point of identification for lesbians, we are concerned to assess how the new lesbian 'lifestyle' magazines (if we include the gay and lesbian *Phase*, launched in March 1994) visually codify their political relationships to feminism and 'post-feminism'. *Diva* targets a group of women on the grounds of their sexual identity, and in doing so rehearses some of the well-trodden debates of lesbian feminism. For example, in recent years, debates on the politics of role-playing have again figured prominently in lesbian feminist circles, where the split is between two main camps – those who see role-playing as empowering and transgressive, and those who maintain that it results in the inevitable return to patriarchally defined mechanisms of power. Again, the spectre of 'post-feminism' emerges behind the editorial voice and lesbians, in *Diva*'s terms, are engaged in an embittered struggle to free themselves from feminism's past atrocities. For example, a feature on the perceived tensions between young and older lesbians, which operates on the assumption that the identities of older lesbians are intimately tied to second-wave feminist politics in a way that a younger generation are not, quickly deteriorates into collective censure of feminism:

> Has butch and femme ever been away? It only went out of fashion because those feminists made such a fuss about it. If I think about all the lesbian couples I've known, there's always one partner who's a fair bit butcher than t'other. We've always polarized. I've been butch since the day I was born. (Mon, 70, retired dogbreeder, in 'Generation Gaps', *Diva*, June 1994)

and

> A lot of dykes who were around in the '70's, who are very dogmatic about their version of feminism think that younger women do not care about feminism. It's as though we are the 'bad daughters' to their 'good mothers', kind of like a teenage rebellion thing. But we are just as feminist as they are. We just don't want to label ourselves with a word that conjures up such ugly images. Why should we have

to be frumpy or bitter and twisted just to be a feminist? (Cath, 21, student, in 'Generation Gaps', *Diva*, June 1994)

Just as *Cosmo* might deem feminism responsible for not allowing straight women to have a good time, it is feminism which has allegedly narrowed the available identities for lesbians by denying them the 'right' to identify as butch and femme, or to enjoy S/M sex. Feminism is surreptitiously implicated as the homogenizing discourse of the same, and in response to this *Diva* opens up the possibility of multiple ways of identifying with lesbian lifestyles. The ideal-type lesbian addressed in *Diva*, in common with the post-feminist of the straight glossies, is the 'reclaimed' dyke of the fifties and sixties with a twist – the butch/femme configuration has been 'liberated' from the feminist dictates which prescribed an 'inauthentic' politicization of lesbian identity. An interview with Lois Weaver (actress and writer) produced the following:

> Being so overtly femme has not always met with the approval of Big Sister. She remembers appearing at a show at the Oval House in the late 70's in which she wore a push-up bra, high heels and a blonde wig, only to be cornered by a well-known lesbian photographer afterwards who asked: 'don't you realize that you're titillating the men in the audience?' 'What I thought I was doing,' she explains, 'was reclaiming some idea of what it meant to be feminine; reclaiming these images of myself . . . but what I can't stand is when that kind of oppression is aimed at other lesbians, or other women.' ('Femme feminist – a profile of Lois Weaver', *Diva*, June 1994)

This dramatization of an incident in the 'feminist past' neatly encapsulates how 'post-feminism' pillories the lesbian feminist, here, for appropriating the male 'right' to determine the meaning of the feminine image. What is also at stake here is the gap between the 'right' of self-determination for lesbian signification of feminine identity and the articulation of a politics which can address the inescapable wider cultural codes constructing the plurality of meanings of femininity.

In considering the construction of lesbian identities in *Diva* it must be observed that the relations of 'looking' set up by the magazine demand recognition of its governing assumption of a totally woman-identified gaze – both subject and object of visual pleasure are female, which therefore facilitates a space which allows exploration of a non-heterosexual structure of looking and desire. Jackie Stacey has asked, 'are women constructed differently as objects of other women's desire, or do the same conventions of looking and desiring merely get mapped on to ... representations of lesbianism?' Gamman and Marshment (1988, p. 113). As we have illustrated, there are moments in straight magazines where infractions of the dominant codes of 'compulsory heterosexuality' are offered, if not fully articulated. The gazer in straight glossies may then be indeterminate or contradictory; but are we offered a 'lesbian' gaze in *Diva* which encompasses all the possible meanings and images generated by the term 'lesbian'? If we consider *Diva*'s centre spread (June 1994), we are offered a highly polyvalent image of one black and one white woman dressed in floor-length diaphanous shift dresses; the black woman's dress is transparent enough for her body to be clearly visible and both women have stylized devil's horns bound into their hair. The captain reads, 'NAUGHTY ...' and we are prepared for what follows overleaf – the caption of the double page 'but nice ...!' The same models have escaped their fantasy scenario (shot against a blank pink background), into the monochrome world of the 'street' – they could almost be wearing their everyday clothes (seventies retro), and now they are embracing with a clear sexual message for the lesbian viewers. Whatever the sexual orientation or even gender of the actual spectator, in the context of the 'new' 'post-feminism', lesbian pleasure in looking is purchased at the cost of any feminist intervention into the fantasy vacuum. In other words, are we again looking at a refusal to engage with patriarchal definitions of femininity, even though the only way these images resist such readings is by their statement that they just *are* different? There is a risk of believing that the fantasy space – free from the everyday manifestations of patriarchal power – is a space of empowerment.

Intrinsic to the playful visual imagery of a lesbian 'lifestyle' is the perpetuation of a shared knowledge about 'proper' lesbian sex. While straight feminists are welcoming 'release' from the tyranny of penetrative sex (*Elle*, November 1993), lesbians are celebrating penetration as a pleasing antidote to the feminist conspiracy of sex devoid of powerplay. Within the interstices of these images that counterpoise butch/femme, S/M, top/bottom with the vanilla icons of Brookside, EastEnders and Emmerdale, there is a clear sense of license to escape from the putative tyranny of feminist puritan 'vanilla' sex, to an equally unwritten, but possibly coercive, normalizing of role-play sex as 'new' standard. The imagery of butch and femme in the nineties is seemingly welded to that of S/M – if not in terms of practice, then in terms of paraphernalia. But just as one expectantly seeks the last word on lesbian sex there is a notable slippage between promise and delivery – instead the 'old' tyranny of vanilla sex (with all the connotations of cuddly 'nice' worthy political lesbians) is set against the freedom to express oneself in pure style terms, which is reflexively acknowledged in the magazine itself:

'realistically speaking, clubbing and shopping still seem a teeny-weeny bit inadequate as a bid for female sexual autonomy' (Paula Grayham, *Diva*, April 1994). Indeed it would be a difficult decision to choose between the two identities facetiously on offer in the following:

> They – the media and the heterosoc at large – could only perceive one kind of dyke: a crop haired, cosmetic free, dungaree clad, bollockstomper whose main fashion accessory [sic] were labryses from Lesbos, patriarch-free canvas bags and non leather shoes made in the Welsh valleys by worshippers of the goddess Clenchbuttock Spiritwombyn. Now we're in the dead-from-the-neck-up Nineties and the rallying cry of the gay community appears to be 'we're here, we're queer, we're going shopping...' (Rose Collis, *Diva*, April 1994)

Whichever is posed, after the promise of difference, of securing the space to invent the self and of multiplying the 'ways of being' (straight/gay) female, it would appear that the 'new' of both straight and lesbian identities that the 'post-feminist' moment offers is inescapably predicated on the same techniques of homogenization.

Winship offers the following, rather charitable, interpretation of 'post-feminism':

> the mid-80's marks the appearance of post-feminism, or of a social and political context which no longer requires either such clear demarcations between those who are, and those who are not, feminists, or, as a consequence, such disparity between feminist magazines and those more geared towards commercialism. (Winship, 1987, p. 15)

The 'political context' for feminism, however, seems at best ephemeral and at worst positively denied, if the only currently 'permissible' form of feminism is founded upon an acceptance of a politics based on style and the myth of the transcendental individual. There may be some appeal in accepting the postmodern terms of the inevitability of the surface appearance of self and the eschewal of the possibility of truth claims based on 'what it is to be a woman'. But all that is on offer to compensate for the contraction of the sphere of the political in favour of the space of play, contradiction and indeterminacy as modes of pleasure is *faux*-heterogeneity which is exclusionary, unidimensional and entirely compatible with unreconstructed patriarchal notions of 'the feminine' – despite repeated disclaimers to the contrary.

Hopefully, we have made clear our opposition to assertions, such as Winship's, that it is feminism which needs to 'be strong enough to acknowledge that our politics have to shift in order to take account of these changes' (Winship, 1985, p. 46). Firstly, it is a shortcoming of contemporary feminists that they have not successfully put paid to the myth that a feminist catechism exists in the hands of Big Sister. Secondly, asking feminists to consider accommodating 'these changes' perpetuates another myth – that 'post-feminism' is a position coherent enough to destabilize feminism; this works to obscure the fact that 'post-feminism' actually *evacuates* the territory upon which feminism has made its greatest impact. If feminism's biggest crime is to try to release women from a broader range of epistemological givens than are addressed by 'post-feminism' in order to create a space for the negotiation of identity beyond abstract individualism, then to argue that feminism crushes 'the individual' and individual 'rights' of self-expression is to miss a rather large historical point.

Notes

1   In the case of 'Do real women have hairy armpits', a textual insert considers the pros and cons of various means by which 'unsightly' hair might be removed.
2   Consider for instance Germaine Greer's observation that 'The women who dare not go out without their false eyelashes are in serious psychic trouble' (Greer, 1971, p. 324). This kind of statement is intended to raise consciousness rather than proscribe; it is of course the case that close links between early second-wave feminism and left-wing politics meant that many feminists felt that consumerism should itself be challenged (Greer, for instance, goes on to give cheap beauty tips).
3   Koedt's piece has recently been reprinted in Sneja Gunew (Ed.) *A Reader in Feminist Knowledge*, London, Routledge, 1991, pp. 326–34.
4   July 1994 *Cosmopolitan* carries a 'woman's guide to impotence'; May 1994 *Company* discusses what you can learn from bad sex; June 1994 *Company* has 'The orgasm work-out'.

References

FERGUSON, M. (1983) *Forever Feminine: Women's Magazines and the Cult of Femininity*, London, Heinemann.
GAMMAN, LORRAINE and MARSHMENT, MARGARET (Eds) (1988) *The Female Gaze: Women as Viewers of Popular Culture*, London, The Women's Press.
GREER, GERMAINE (1971) *The Female Eunuch*, London, Paladin.
GUNEW, SNEJA (Ed.) (1991) *A Reader in Feminist Knowledge*, London, Routledge.

KOEDT, ANNE (1991) 'The Myth of the Vaginal Orgasm', in GUNEW, SNEJA (Ed.) *A Reader in Feminist Knowledge*, London, Routledge.

LEE, JANET (1988) 'Care to Join me in an Upwardly Mobile Tango?: Postmodernism and the "New Woman"', in GAMMAN, LORRAINE and MARSHMENT, MARGARET (Eds) *The Female Gaze*, London, The Women's Press.

MODLESKI, TANIA (1991) *Feminism Without Women: Culture and Criticism in a 'Postfeminist' Age*, London, Routledge.

RICH, ADRIENNE (1986) *Blood, Bread and Poetry: Selected Prose 1979–1985*, London, Virago.

STACEY, JACKIE (1988) 'Desperately Seeking Difference', in GAMMAN, LORRAINE and MARSHMENT, MARGARET (Eds) *The Female Gaze*, London, The Women's Press.

WINSHIP, JANICE (1985) 'A Girl Needs To Get Streetwise: Magazines for the 1980s', *Feminist Review*, 21 (Winter), pp. 25–46.

WINSHIP, JANICE (1987) *Inside Women's Magazines*, London, Pandora.

YOUNG, SHELAGH (1988) 'Feminism and the Politics of Power: Whose Gaze Is It Anyway?' in GAMMON, LORRAINE and MARSHMENT, MARGARET (Eds) *The Female Gaze*, London, The Women's Press.

Chapter 6

Hetero-sensibilities on *The Oprah Winfrey Show*

Debbie Epstein and Deborah Lynn Steinberg

Mention *The Oprah Winfrey Show* to almost anyone and, in our experience, she or he will have an opinion, indeed a considered opinion, to offer. The appeal of both the show and of Oprah herself seems to reach an unusually diverse range of audiences and seems to stimulate distinctively thought-out reactions to the issues and politics of the show. 'Oh that's interesting, I've been thinking about Oprah and ...' is a typical response when either of us mentions that we have been carrying out an analysis of the programme.[1] In the light of this, we have been struck by the fact that there has been, as yet, so little feminist and other critical writing about it. Notable exceptions include recent articles by Janice Peck (1994) and Corinne Squire (1994). Because of its focus on the gender politics and feminist potential of the show, we shall, for the purposes of this chapter, refer extensively to Squire's article, 'Empowering Women? The *Oprah Winfrey Show*'. This article was published at a point when we had completed a substantial portion of our research on *The Oprah Winfrey Show* and, interestingly, on first reading we felt that we were substantively in agreement with points Squire made about the gender politics of the show and with her optimism about its potential to empower women. However, our estimation of the empowerment potential of *The Oprah Winfrey Show* diverged significantly from Squire's when we considered not only the gender agenda of the show, but also its politics around sexuality.

Squire notes a number of factors which constitute *The Oprah Winfrey Show* as a distinctive televisual phenomenon in feminist terms and which, we would suggest, account, at least in part, for the appeal of the show. Central to these are the ways in which Oprah positions herself explicitly with reference to feminism and anti-racist struggle and constructs the show as a forum for the empowerment of women and other marginalized groups. Squire forwards several key arguments about how to understand *The Oprah Winfrey Show* as a specifically feminist project. Firstly, she suggests that, despite its apparent endorsement, at times, of conventional femininities, the show nevertheless has a feminist dynamic arising from the ways in which it deals with gender. For example, Oprah makes the taboo speakable, a way of making the personal political, and much of the content of the programme addresses problems which arise from gender inequality (ranging from women's lower economic status to physical and sexual abuse by men). Moreover, as Squire illustrates in her opening quotation, Oprah explicitly states that 'we do program these shows to empower women' (quoted in Squire, 1994, p. 63). Secondly, Squire sees Oprah as presenting a kind of black feminist politics in her and the show's explicit anti-racist agenda and in Oprah's personal association with some well-known black feminists. Thirdly, Squire argues that Oprah also problematizes class and indeed that she is 'at times better able to recognize the shifting and intersecting agendas of class, gender and "race" than is much feminist theory' (*ibid.*, p. 72). Squire concludes that while *The Oprah Winfrey Show* is characterized by a number of contradictory elements (e.g. 'fluff and gravity; psychology, social analysis and emotions; realism and super-realism' (*ibid.*, p. 76)), it emerges, precisely through this mixture, as an important and complex black feminist challenge to dominant common senses.

We share with Squire an interest in *The Oprah Winfrey Show* for its feminist potential. As feminist viewers, we find ourselves particularly attracted by its many stranded objectives for the empowerment of marginalized groups and for the liberal anti-discriminatory education of the viewing public. Furthermore, we think it is important not to underestimate the importance of the incorporation of an agenda for social justice, albeit a liberal one, in a context (both of popular culture generally and of most chat shows) which is characterized by the absence of, indeed hostility towards, any kind of oppositional politics.[2] However, throughout our research, we have also experienced frustration at the ways in which this potential is not realized or indeed is, at times, actively subverted in and through the dynamic of the programme. In the remainder of this chapter we will examine two particular frameworks underpinning the show which we believe significantly disrupt Oprah's black feminist project – the presumption of heterosexuality and therapy.

Straight Talking

> In common with the rest of television, the *Oprah Winfrey Show* is heterosexist. (Squire, 1994, p. 71)

Squire points out that *The Oprah Winfrey Show* is, at best, ambivalent about lesbian, gay and bisexualities, and that while the programme does promote a kind of liberal, lifestyle pluralism around sexual preference, it is nonetheless a distinctly uncomfortable forum if not a silent (silencing) space for non-straight issues, perspectives, audiences and guests. However, while Squire sees the heterosexism of the show as a problem, she does not seem to see it as one which substantively detracts from the show's potential to empower women.[3] We differ from Squire in her estimation of the importance of this issue. Indeed, we would suggest that the heterosexism noted by Squire is crucial to a consideration of the show's potential to challenge conventional gender relations. We would suggest, furthermore, that such a consideration necessarily entails an exploration of the ways in which heterosexuality is institutionalized and of the interconnections between gender and compulsory heterosexuality.

One of the key ways in which heterosexuality is made compulsory is through the unquestioned presumption that everyone is heterosexual unless otherwise stated (Epstein and Johnson, 1994).[4] This presumption, as Squire indicates, is amply demonstrated on *The Oprah Winfrey Show*. For example, in the general run of programmes dealing with relationships, it would be virtually impossible for a guest or studio audience member to introduce the possibility of anything other than a straight relationship. Imagine, for example, trying to offer a gay date for one of Oprah's 'Alaskan Men',[5] talking from the perspective of being a lesbian mother in programmes discussing 'giving mothers a break';[6] or trying to talk about lesbian and gay relationships in programmes about elopement or marriage. Secondly, when lesbian and gay issues *are* included, they are invariably ghettoized as 'special'[8] and almost invariably framed in ways which force lesbian and gay guests to defend their '(ab)normality' against normative heterosexuality.

A case in point is 'Lesbian and Gay Baby Boom' (10 May 1993) where Oprah framed the programme by asking her guests to answer the question, which she identified as being on 'everybody's' mind, of whether children would be damaged by having lesbian or gay parents.[8] In this context, 'everybody' clearly did not and could not include lesbians or gays. Oprah made it clear that her intention in this programme was to dispel fears and negative stereotypes about lesbian and gay people and to show that lesbian and gay parenting could be as good as heterosexual parenting. Thus the programme was to be an anti-homophobic educational forum for assumed heterosexual audiences. However, by beginning with the homophobe's putative question, the programme (albeit not intentionally) colluded in reinscribing the marginality of lesbians and gays. Firstly, Oprah's opening question immediately introduced homophobia as the framing reference for the rest of the programme. It was in this context that lesbian and gay parents were required to defend themselves against the implicit allegation of being dangerous to (their) children. In so doing, there was a reproduction of the very marginality which the programme was attempting to challenge. Not only were lesbians and gay men expected to bear the primary burden of educating those who oppress them, but, perhaps even more disturbingly, were asked to prove themselves to be as good as those who were/are so bad to them. Significantly, this programme stands in contrast to the notable absence of such questioning of heterosexual parents or about heterosexual parenting, despite the large proportion of Oprah's programmes which portray problematic heterosexual family relationships. Thus, with 'Lesbian and Gay Baby Boom', while it can be said that homophobia is, albeit problematically, challenged, heterosexism is taken for granted and reinforced. We witness this in the ways that the legitimacy of lesbian and gay lives can only be gained through demonstrating their approximation to putatively problem-free heterosexual relations. In this way, the inherent heterosexism of the framing of the programme subtly reinforces the very homophobia it is attempting to challenge. And, as graphically illustrated by the verbal abuse hurled at the guests by many members of the studio audience, heterosexism is a dangerous context through which to challenge homophobia.[9]

The presumption of heterosexuality is also demonstrated in the predominant subject-matter of *The Oprah Winfrey Show*. Nearly all programmes involve kinship work of one kind or another and nearly all of that work is about heterosexual kinship. It is in this context that one of the main contradictions of the show emerges. We see, on the one hand, the regular exposure of serious problems, particularly for women and children, within heterosexual relationships. Indeed *The Oprah Winfrey Show* seems almost like a showcase for the prevalence of male sexual and/or violent abuse and for a continuum of problems which reflect the fundamental (gender, age and other) inequalities inhering in heterosexual kinship relations. Yet, on the other hand, at the same time that *The Oprah Winfrey Show* recognizes the casualities of normative heterosexuality, it also idealizes its institutions, such as dating, marriage and (nuclear) family values, all of which have been celebrated in numerous shows. Notwithstanding the evidence shown on the show that normative heterosexuality is very frequently injurious (particularly to women and children), there is never any questioning of the presumptions, either that everyone is heterosexual or that heterosexuality is 'normal', 'benign' and 'desirable'.

At the heart of these programmes are significant assumptions about the importance of and necessity for heterosexual relationships, particularly in the case of families with children. These include the idea that you have to work on your relationships and the idea that heterosexuality works if you work on it. However, what happens in the context of *The Oprah Winfrey Show* is that it becomes clear that it is primarily women who are expected to do this work.[10] The contradictions around this are exhibited in 'When Divorce Gets Ugly' (7 May 1993). One part of the programme began by spending a great deal of time expressing disapproval and a rather disingenuous shock at one male guest who had failed to pay child support until a court order of enforcement was placed on his wages. Oprah herself conducted a searching interrogation of his motives. Yet, in the end, the audience's initial sympathy for the woman and her anger was rejected. This was accomplished partly by the 'expert' therapist's interjection that men felt powerless and angry when they were the non-custodial parent. She said this even though, clearly, this was the choice of this father and, in fact, the choice of a multitude of men who refuse to pay child support. Her comment created the space for a shift in emphasis away from the non-payment of child support and, indeed, the failure of the father to share in the work of child-rearing even before the divorce. Suddenly, the question became whether the mother (and, by implication, other women) was (were) doing enough work to mitigate the man's anger and empower him to take responsibility for his own actions and for his children. This switch was then punched home by bringing the children on and allowing them to end the programme with an unchallenged and very emotional statement by the older girl that she did not care about child support. She just wanted her dad.[11] Now the situation appeared as if the mother had wilfully deprived her children of their father through the selfish and venal motive of wanting money. In an instant, the man and the children became the wronged parties.

Programmes such as this can be seen as a testament to the gendered inequalities constitutive of compulsory heterosexuality. The imbalances of power and position amongst Oprah's guests are strikingly apparent and yet at the same time obscured by the programme's emphasis on the accessibility of resolution through the ostensibly 'rational' and 'egalitarian' dialogue it promotes and displays. In this context the therapy discourse serves to reinforce the notion of equal responsibility in any and all relationships. Yet, to expect and demand equal responsibility by people who do not have equal power, as we have seen, effectively places an unequal burden on the less powerful. That this is so is painfully revealed in the characteristic displacement of primary obligations for work on heterosexual relationships on to women. Here, then, we find continually reinforced and often applauded power without responsibility for men and responsibility without power for women. Again, it is clearly not Oprah's intention to reinforce or celebrate the disempowerment of women in heterosexual relationships. Yet the dominant discourses which inform the programme, and in which Oprah herself is an active participant, undermine the quest for happiness in heterosexuality, 'rational' marriages and 'civilized' divorces.

In sum, while *The Oprah Winfrey Show* could be said to provide a critique of modes of heterosexual relating, it does so without problematizing the institution of heterosexuality. In turn, the assumption of heterosexuality as an unproblematic institution substantively weakens, if, indeed, it does not reverse, the programme's critique of particular heterosexual relationships.

On the Analyst's Couch

Squire points out that the therapy mode of the programme creates space for the airing of relationship problems and indeed, for testimony about forms of abuse women pervasively experience in heterosexual relationships. This should not be underestimated. It is, indeed, a key way in which the programme makes speakable the unspeakable and in so doing seeks to empower women (among others).[12] However, we would suggest that the therapy discourse also circumscribes the speakable and the analysable in much the same ways as the programme's presumption of heterosexuality. Indeed, as illustrated above with regard to 'Acrimonious Divorces' both heterosexuality and gender are often reinscribed precisely through the programme's therapy framework. This is brought about partly through the ways in which this framework understands problems which arise in (heterosexual) relationships and partly by the particular burden it places on women to undertake the labour of making (heterosexual) relationships work.

Psychoanalytic theory and practice has always been characterized by a focus on the individual and on individual problems rather than on the social. Feminist and other radical therapists and psychoanalytic theorists have worked to challenge precisely the individualizing (and pathologizing) tendencies within psychoanalytic discourses. However, a tension remains between the assumptions underpinning the range of approaches to therapy and analyses which are interested in explaining the personal through an interrogation of social/political contexts (see, for example, Mitchell 1974; Frosh 1989).[13] Although there is no acknowledgment of this tension within the popular, programmatic, '12 step' styled approach to therapy which appears on *The Oprah Winfrey Show*, Squire argues that the relentless frequency with which abuse within heterosexual relationships is investigated on the show 'seems to go beyond psychological understanding to become facts about gender relationships that demand explanation in other, social terms' (pp. 75–6). We would suggest, in contrast, that the consistent airing of oppressive heterosexual relationships does, indeed, *suggest* a social explanation, but more often than not, the therapy discourses in play in the show obviate rather than demand it.

For example, there is a series of therapeutic catch-phrases consistently reinvoked by 'experts', other guests, audiences and Oprah herself on *The Oprah Winfrey Show*. Notions of 'dysfunctional family', 'cycle of abuse' and 'patterns we repeat' seem to have become *the* signifiers of unhappiness within familial/intimate relations. It seems likely that the investment in these phrases derives, in part, from the ways in which they make unhappiness speakable and encapsulate a framework that both explains it and promises rescue in relatively straight(*sic*!)-forward terms. Whatever the individual intent behind the use of these terms, however, they are part of a medicalized discourse which implies individual pathology (rather than social process) and they (re)construct a set of assumptions which have the effect both of erasing gender and of reaffirming gender inequalities.

The apparent gender neutrality of 'dysfunctional family', 'cycle of abuse' and of the 'we' in 'patterns we repeat' masks the gendered inequalities of normative heterosexuality and the predominant gender profiles of abusers and abused. Hence, in this context, we see women on the show not only held responsible but interrogated, sometimes with considerable hostility, both for their own behaviour and for the behaviour of abusive men. This is illustrated painfully in the frequency with which women who have been subjected to violence by their male partners are asked to explain why they do not or did not leave. That these concepts construct 'victims/ survivors'[14] as responsible for abuse while exonerating the perpetrators was exemplified in the programme 'How to Make Love Last' (18 January 1993). In this programme Oprah, who has often stated that children should not be blamed for being abused, described her own experience of having been abused as a child, and then subsequently by men in her early adult relationships, as a pattern *she herself* had set up.[15]

Furthermore, the connotation of a notion like 'dysfunctional relationship' is that 'functional' (heterosexual) relationships exist. Thus, the pervasive unhappiness and oppression within heterosexual relationships displayed on the show are implicitly defined as abnormal. That is, they are the rule which are taken to prove the exception. This has obvious implications for the show's project to empower women. Exhortations to 'work on ourselves' or to 'break our negative patterns' displace both social critique and possibilities for collective social action and effectively marginalize organized feminist critique and action. Moreover, as with the diagnostic terms discussed above, these notions of healing erase the gender politics of the patterns that need to be broken; they assume that the work of healing needs to be done by the people who are wounded (because it is the wounded who need to heal); and, as a result, they assume an unequal burden of work for women. It is women who are expected to undertake the labour of making heterosexuality work, a conventional gender role if ever there was one.[16]

In addition to the language of therapy through which problems in heterosexual relationships are usually analysed, *The Oprah Winfrey Show* almost invariably features a therapist to provide 'expert' advice, explanations and counselling.[17] The use of these 'experts' provides a scientifically validating point of reference for the programme. Expertise is a framing notion underpinning the show and experts are used to provide both a commentary and often a format (through their books) for the show. However, experts and expertise are seldom interrogated themselves. Indeed, the only programmes we have seen which challenged the infallibility of expertise were ones in which there were three 'experts' with different opinions (in 'Agony Aunts and Uncles', 7 April 1993) and one which dealt with sexual abuse of women patients by therapists ('Sex and Psychotherapy', 7 May 1992).

'Sex and Psychotherapy' was notable for its particular juxtaposition of the institutions of therapy and heterosexuality. The programme featured a number of women who had been abused by their male therapists, a telephone link with a male therapist having abused patients and a representative of the American Psychiatric Association's Ethical Board. The programme was framed by what may be described as a 'use/abuse' model of therapy. That is, the programme explicitly problematized 'bad' therapists while not exploring the ways in which the (gendered) power relations inherent in therapy might have the potential, in themselves, to facilitate abuse of clients by therapists. Moreover, it was clear that the kinds of abuse discussed in this programme resonated with discussions in other programmes about men's abuse of women and children within heterosexual and family relationships. Yet this link was not explored – that is, the ways in which professional power might reproduce and/or exacerbate other social inequalities, particularly those inhering in dominant heterosexual gender relations, was ignored.

Most extraordinarily, it was argued by the 'good' therapist that therapists who abuse as well as women who had been abused by therapists could be rehabilitated by therapy! However, by showcasing therapists who abuse, Oprah created a space to make some challenges to the profession. For example, she completely rejected the idea that any therapist who had abused a patient should be allowed to continue to practise, even if 'rehabilitated' by subsequent therapy. She also spent a great deal of time interrogating the therapist who, by his own admission, had abused patients and yet continued to practise. In this context, the programme was on the verge of questioning the power dynamics of professional therapy, not least because of what the testimonies were revealing about normative professional practices.[18] Yet this potential for radical critique was not fulfilled as the programme reverted to deference for the expertise of 'good' therapists who, in fact, advised that 'responsible patients' will select therapists who are licensed by a professional body, and who are in therapy themselves. While this may well be good advice, it nevertheless shifts the responsibility for good practice on to the patients, neglects the possibility that therapists might themselves experience abuse within the therapeutic relationship, and fails to provide any real safeguards for patients.

The characteristic deference to expertise and the view of therapy as an object of desire and a magic bullet thus resembled and reproduced the show's relationship to the normalization of compulsory heterosexuality. Oprah's scepticism notwithstanding, therapy, like heterosexuality, was assumed to be a benign and desirable institution. Here the critique of 'bad' therapists resonated with comparable critiques of particular 'bad' relationships or 'bad' men. In both cases, an investment in notions of 'abnormality' have the effect of recuperating the institutions. Moreover, 'Sex and Psychotherapy' illustrates the ways in which the institutions of therapy and heterosexuality can both be mutually reinforcing and leave women primarily responsible for the work of healing (in) both.

Healing Heterosexuality?

There are clearly a number of paradoxes about *The Oprah Winfrey Show*. As we have discussed here, there are tensions between the objective to empower women and the use of frameworks which have the effect of disempowering them and of avoiding consideration either of power or of gender. Thus, while the programme may be read as providing a sustained illustration of forms of gender inequality, the terms in which problems are discussed on the show characteristically resist that analysis. Secondly, there are tensions between the creation of a forum for testimony about the hazards of normative heterosexuality and the analysis of those hazards in terms which reinvest in or recuperate the institution. Thus we see how therapy opens up a possibility of talking about problems with particular heterosexual relationships but not about problems inherent in the politics, specifically the gender politics, of heterosexuality. And finally, there are tensions between the show's explicit participation in a form of feminist struggle and its investment in individualized explanations and solutions as well as in institutional forms of expertise. It seems to struggle for women's equality by assuming that this already exists, at least in the 'private' interpersonal context. At the same time, it reinforces the unequal burden of work which women conventionally bear both in relation to kinship and to healing and caring.

Thus, in common with Squire, we see a radicalizing potential and radical elements in *The Oprah Winfrey Show*. However, we would suggest that, more often than not, what takes ascendancy is the reinscription of common senses, often the very ones that Oprah wishes to challenge.

Notes

This chapter is a longer version of an 'Observations and Commentary' article forthcoming in *Feminism and Psychology*. Some of the issues discussed in it were raised in a paper we presented at the Women's Studies Network Conference, Portsmouth, July 1994. They are also explored more fully in Epstein and Steinberg (forthcoming, b and c).

1 We have been working on developing an analysis of *The Oprah Winfrey Show* for the past eighteen months as part of our contribution to the work of the Politics of Sexuality Group (forthcoming).
2 This point has been sharply brought home to us by the deluge in the autumn of 1994 of so-called competitors to *The Oprah Winfrey Show* on British television (hosted by both British and American women). Already, in October 1994, we have noted that despite certain similarities of format and even style in these new programmes, there is a notable absence of a political or educative agenda.
3 This comes through both in the very brief treatment of this issue within the article and also in the way her discussion of heterosexism is used to introduce her argument that the show challenges dominant notions of sexuality by 'marking differences within heterosexuality' (p. 71).
4 In linguistic terms, heterosexuality is, like 'white' and 'male', the unmarked form.
5 Indeed, this is reinforced in the title of the first 'Alaskan Men' programme: 'Desperate Women Meet Alaskan Men' (17 February 1989; N.B.: all transmission dates and titles are from the USA).
6 For example, one of the programmes we saw during the period in which we have

been viewing the show for this project involved the nomination of women by their husbands to receive an award of a special break for being a 'wonderful mother'. Given this format, there was no possibility for single mothers or lesbian mothers to be nominated.

7 This is to a certain extent in contrast to the presentation of other guests from marginalized groups. For example, black guests often appear as 'just guests' doing whatever the other guests are doing as well as in special programmes about the lives of black people. Both singling out and assimilation have been associated with positions of liberal tolerance.

8 The only exception we have seen to this pattern of putting lesbians and gays on the defensive has been one programme about the employment rights of lesbian and gay workers. In that context, the programme was framed within a liberal equal opportunities approach which put discriminating employers on the defensive.

9 To paraphrase Audre Lorde (1984), this seemed to be a case in point of the problem of trying to build the master's house with the master's tools.

10 The phrase 'working on your heterosexuality' was, in part, suggested in a course on *Gender in Contemporary Britain* taught by Maureen McNeil during 1991–2 at the Department of Cultural Studies, University of Birmingham, when she discussed femininity as 'work, working on your sexuality'.

11 This statement was greeted by a sigh of sympathy from the audience. While this would be understandable because she was a child and because she was obviously in pain, we felt that the sigh signified not just a sadness for her pain but, in fact, an unconsidered acceptance of the terms in which she put it. Both of us felt, watching this programme, an unutterable sadness for both the mother and the daughter. With respect to the mother, we felt despair at the way in which her work, her care of and for her children and her words were, in that moment, entirely erased. Her awareness of that erasure was reflected in her face when the audience sighed. We also felt deeply sad for the daughter. There was an unintended callousness in her statement, with its rejection, and yet taking for granted, of her mother's care and sole burden of work. We felt that she might, at some future time, come to regret bitterly that she had done this so publicly, or indeed at all, just as she might come to understand, and perhaps share, the sexual politics of the conditions of her mother's life.

12 It seems to us that this would be particularly effective in the US context where therapeutic language constitutes part of common sense (indeed can be seen as a kind of lingua franca for the expression of difficult feelings) and the experience of therapy in all its forms is much more widespread than in the UK.

13 Kitzinger and Perkins (1993) argue that this tension is not resolvable.

14 We use the term 'victims/survivors' with considerable discomfort as neither seems to adequately describe the experience of having been subjected to abuse. See also Kelly *et al.* (1994).

15 For a fuller treatment of this example, see Epstein and Steinberg (forthcoming, a).

16 This is regularly illustrated within the programme where female guests are consistently asked both to explain their role in precipitating what has gone wrong in their relationships and to do the work of repair both on themselves and on their male partners. For further discussion of this point see Epstein and Steinberg (forthcoming, a).

17 There is a promotional aspect to their presence on the programme, in that nearly all have PhDs and are there because they have written a book on the subject under discussion. Indeed, there seems to be a mutual feedback cycle between the books promoting certain programme choices and certain programme choices promoting the appropriate book. There is also a marked parallel between the formulaity of the books and that of the show.

18 In this respect, the profession of therapy is no different from other professions.

References

BUTLER, J. (1990) *Gender Trouble: Feminism and the Subversion of Identity*, London, Routledge.

EPSTEIN, D. and JOHNSON, R. (1994) 'On the Straight and the Narrow: The Heterosexual Presumption, Homophobias and Schools', in EPSTEIN, D. (Ed.) *Challenging Lesbian and Gay Inequalities in Education*, Buckingham, Open University Press.

EPSTEIN, D. and STEINBERG, D.L. (forthcoming, a) '12 Steps to Heterosexuality? Common-sensibilities on the *Oprah Winfrey Show*', *Feminism and Psychology*.

EPSTEIN, D. and STEINBERG, D.L. (forthcoming, b) 'All Het Up!': Rescuing Heterosexuality on the *Oprah Winfrey Show*', (submitted to) *Feminist Review*.

EPSTEIN D. and STEINBERG, D.L. (forthcoming, c) 'Straight Talking on the Oprah Winfrey Show', in Politics of Sexuality Group *Border Patrols: Policing Sexual Boundaries*, London, Cassell.

FROSH, S. (1987) *The Politics of Psychoanalysis*, London, Macmillan.

KELLY, L., REGAN, S. and BURTON, L. (1994) 'The Victim/Survivor Dichotomy: Beyond an Identity Defined by Violation', paper given at the British Sociological Association Conference, University of Central Lancashire.

KITZINGER, C. and PERKINS, R. (1993) *Changing Our Minds: Lesbian Feminism and Psychology*, London, Onlywomen.

LORDE, A. (1984) *Sister Outsider*, Freedom, California, The Crossing Press.

MITCHELL, J. (1974) *Psychoanalysis and Feminism: A Radical Reassessment of Freudian Psychoanalysis*, Harmondsworth, Penguin.

PECK, J. (1994) 'Talk about Racism: Framing a Popular Discourse of Race on Oprah', *Cultural Critique* 27.

POLITICS OF SEXUALITY GROUP (forthcoming) *Border Patrols: Policing Sexual Boundaries*, London, Cassell.

SQUIRE, C. (1994) 'Empowering Women? The *Oprah Winfrey Show*', *Feminism and Psychology* 4(1) *Shifting Identities: Shifting Racisms (Special Issue)*, pp. 63–79.

The Oprah Winfrey Show
(Dates of first USA transmission of programmes referred to in this paper)
'Desperate Women meet Alaskan Men', 17 February 1989.
'Sex and Psychotherapy', 7 May 1992.
'How to Make Love Last', 8 January 1993.
'Agony Aunts and Uncles', 9 April 1993.
'When Divorce Gets Ugly', 7 May 1993.
'Lesbian and Gay Baby Boom', 10 May 1993.

Chapter 7

'Women Warriors':
Representations of Women Soldiers in British Daily Newspaper Reports of the Gulf War (January to March 1991)

Christine Forde

Women Soldiers in the Gulf War

The Persian Gulf War saw the deployment of a substantial number of women soldiers. As part of the first phase, 'Operation Desert Shield', 15,000 female soldiers were included in the Western Alliance military forces; their number reached approximately 30,000 out of a total force of 500,000 during the war itself. Women soldiers made up over 11 per cent of the US forces (Micheletti and Debay, 1991) and 4 per cent of the British forces (Muir, 1992). In the US armed forces women are forbidden by law to be part of 'routine engagement in direct combat' (Micheletti and Debay, 1991, p. 10). However, female soldiers, in both the US and the British armed services, are trained in the use of weapons which, coupled with greater use of electronic technology in modern warfare, has led to a blurring of combat and non-combat zones. In the Gulf War, women soldiers in the US forces were posted as members of 'near-combat' units, and so could be engaged in 'defensive combat'. In these circumstances, then, female soldiers had the potential to be combatants: to kill or be killed. In the event, two women from the US Armed Forces were taken as prisoners-of-war and eleven were killed.

Combat and Ideologies of Masculinity and Femininity

Representations in popular culture such as film, television and popular literature continue to inscribe combat as masculine,[1] thus reconstructing the traditional dichotomy: masculine/feminine, active/passive, aggressive/ nurturing. The cultural focus on men at war, whether in literature or film, is, in Huston's (1982) view, an essential aspect of the social phenomenon of war. She argues that war and war storymaking are two entwined and mutually dependent processes. Mythmaking is a fundamental part of the social construction of war which in turn is an essential aspect of manhood in contemporary society. As Thompson argues:

> participation in war has affected the way men see themselves and the values and virtues they see as truly masculine. The proliferation of films and literature portraying the behaviour of men in war shows how central to our culture are ideas about the masculine virtues they celebrate. (Thompson, 1991, p. 65)

At the present time, great efforts are made by the army to ensure that female soldiers remain 'women' both in their dress and duties, and a fundamental sexual division exists in the notion of combat/non-combat. Even in armies where women have fought alongside men, notably in the wars of liberation in Israel, Zimbabwe and Nicaragua, where women formed a substantial part of the armed forces, once stability has been achieved there seems to be a need to reaffirm women's rightful non-combatant role. In the Chen (the Women's Army in Israel), which is often cited as an example of an army where women participated in combat roles, women now tend to carry out clerical and support duties. Within contemporary standing armies there remains the notion that combat is a male activity.

War is constructed as a male arena and women are placed on the margins. Woman's role, traditionally, has been that of either victim or comforter of the warrior. Nevertheless, war has a substantial impact on the position of women in patriarchal society. Stiemh (1982) claims that the construction of men as the protectors and women as the protected is central to maintaining the unequal gender relationships within patriarchy. Now women's changing role in war – the possibility of women participating as combatants – questions the 'master fictions' of war (Warner, 1985, p. 55) which are based upon traditional ideologies of masculinity and femininity. The presence of a substantial number of women soldiers prepared for combat challenges traditional notions of femininity within Western society. Women, who historically have been presented as being incapable, both physically and psychologically, of being combatants, were now ready to act in this role in the Gulf War. What, then, has been the impact of what is now a considerable number of women soldiers prepared for combat – albeit in 'near-combat positions' – on the construction of femininity and masculinity?

Representations of Women Soldiers in Newspaper Reports

Traditional notions of masculinity and femininity are inscribed upon and circulated through various cultural forms and practices in patriarchal society, including the news media. Newspaper texts, along with other news media, provide the cultural codes and frames of reference for members of the culture. In both written and visual texts, representations of women and war are ideologically determined. The involvement of women soldiers in the Gulf War posed questions about the traditional and polarized constructs of masculinity and femininity. To examine how this challenge was met, newspaper reports of women soldiers were analysed.

The analysis is based on a selection of British daily newspapers,[2] matched in terms firstly of political alignment (right/left) and secondly of target audience (quality/popular), both critical factors in the reporting on the war. The reports were published between the beginning of January and the middle of March 1991, a period covering the final two weeks of 'Operation Desert Shield', the duration of the Gulf War itself, and the return of the armed forces to Great Britain and the USA.

The involvement of a substantial number of female soldiers potentially posed a challenge to traditional notions of femininity within the male hegemonic order of patriarchy. At the same time the presence of these women, prepared for combat, endorsed the patriarchal values that underpinned the Western Allies' military campaign. This paradox was dealt with in two contrasting ways. At this point I will simply map out these two responses but, because this is a significant issue, I will return to it later in this chapter. The first response was to ignore this topic as in the case of the *Guardian*,[3] in which there were very few references to the presence of women soldiers in the Gulf in the news reports and no photographs of women in military roles. The second response, in contrast, was to treat the presence of women soldiers as a newsworthy item. Thus, women soldiers were fairly regularly featured in reports on the war in the other newspapers in the sample. In these representations of women soldiers, the paradox was dealt with by prioritizing alternatively the notions of femininity and militarism. Indeed the newsworthiness of women soldiers lay within the contradictions embedded in this construct 'woman soldier' for the male hegemonic order.

Hall (1978) suggests that the news value of an item 'is frequently augmented by counterposing in the headline, two apparently contrasting or oppositional themes' (p. 84). In the representations of women soldiers the codes of meaning played on the paradox embedded in the term 'woman soldier'.

The paradox is illustrated even in the use of apparently inclusive terminology; 'servicemen and women' was a phrase used repeatedly in news reports of the war. The rightness of the Allied campaign was endorsed by regular references to the willing and selfless contribution of those involved in the armed services. In this the contribution of women was explicitly acknowledged rather than being subsumed under the generic 'he'; the references to 'our servicemen and women' were especially noticeable in reports quoting official sources such as political or military leaders. The collectivist ethic of wartime, captured in 'our', also signified the legitimacy of women in the armed services. Yet within this apparent move towards greater acknowledgment of women's contribution, evident even within the idiom of the *Daily Record* – 'our lads and lasses' – the minor or unusual position of women was also stressed, as in the following two examples: 'They are a marvellous bunch especially the women';[4] and 'More than 27,000 American women are serving in Desert Storm and are outnumbered by almost 20 to 1'[5] – that is, outnumbered by soldiers, male soldiers.

Newspaper reports on women soldiers dealt with the paradox of woman/soldier in various ways, with the following codes of meaning emerging as the dominant themes.

'Girl soldier'

Women are traditionally portrayed as vulnerable in war, and this appears to be an even more critical feature in representations of women as soldiers. Frequent stress is laid on women's emotional behaviour, in contrast to the stoic behaviour of male soldiers. Hence, in the news story headlined 'TEARS AS GIRLS HEAD FOR GULF',[6] the female soldiers are shown crying and being comforted by family members, whereas the male soldiers are shown comforting their tearful wives and mothers. The vulnerability and immaturity of the female soldiers – these are 'girl soldiers' – is heightened by frequent contràst with male soldiers. This sense was often further intensified by the use of reported speech to represent women's feelings, especially of their vulnerability, as in this example: '"She was upset about going. She's only 20 and she was just scared," said her father',[7] and by the descriptions of the women's size and lack of strength: '"I didn't think I was going into the combat zone," said Pte Amy Deever, a diminutive 20 year old from Alabama, as she trudged off to the communications area where she works, weighed down with pack and flak jacket'.[8]

In contrast, male soldiers are presented as cheerful, determined and, even at these moments, the supporters of their families, especially of their tearful wives: 'Hugs and prayers as families see their brave boys set off'.[9] For male soldiers war is a challenge, an adventure, an association with bravery rather than fear. Those who 'worry' and 'anguish' are women, the wives and mothers of the soldiers.

In these reports men and women were positioned differently in the context of war, for in many instances representations of women soldiers were inscribed with traditional notions of femininity, in sharp contrast to the representations of male soldiers. Women are traditionally portrayed as vulnerable in a war situation, and this appears to be even more critical when the woman is a soldier. A special feature in the *Daily Express* illustrates this well: 'TENDER SIDE OF LIFE IN THE KILLING FIELDS'.[10] In this feature a male soldier is presented as protector, the female soldier as potential victim. Two photographs were placed together as part of the same feature. The poles of passivity and activity are aptly expressed by the juxtaposition of these two photographs: the first of a sleeping woman holding a teddy bear, the second of a male soldier in full battle gear protecting a young boy. The vulnerability of the female soldier, her immaturity and her need for protection are all emphasized:

> Army nurse Amy Short sleeps on a make shift bed, her helmet within easy reach. She has been trained for what she might see – chemical injuries, burns, lost limbs. But asleep she looks how she must have looked to her parents as a child, still comforted by teddy. Thank goodness for teddy bears . . .[11]

In this feature this soldier's role as a nurse is negated: she can only 'see', not be actively involved.

Some women soldiers are presented in non-stereotypical terms; the second woman to be taken as a prisoner-of-war is described as a 36-year-old Major who was 'as tough as nails' and 'a go-getter'.[12] There are a number of special features on individual women soldiers doing a range of jobs, both traditional (nurse, paramedic, ancillary worker) and non-traditional (doctor, pilot, gunnery, guard), in the war zone, including several reports of female soldiers guarding the Patriot missiles. However, the unusual position of these women, their essential difference, is constantly reiterated because, even when fulfilling a military role, women's important sexual role within war is embedded. 'They wear floppy hats, heavy boots, baggy camouflaged Army gear. But yesterday Jackie Chambers and Peggy Yi became the pin-up girls of the Gulf War.'[13]

The singular status of the individual woman among her male colleagues is also often stressed. In a feature on a woman soldier who had been on the frontline for three weeks leading a communications unit of forty-one men, the emphasis is laid upon her exceptional status: 'Nikki's commander Lt Col. John Kirby said she was our only girl so far forward'.[14] The informality of the address used – the shortened first name rather than her rank of lieutenant – and the reference to her as the only 'girl' create a sense of youthfulness and potential vulnerability rather than giving an indication of the level of responsibility and competence this soldier was demonstrating as leader of this unit. Other aspects included in this report signify her traditional feminine attributes: 'Nikki, 22 . . . who has a boyfriend at home'; 'Nikki's commander Lt Col. John Kirby said she was our only girl so far forward'.[15]

Thus, in this theme, any challenge posed to traditional ideologies of femininity by the women soldiers is accommodated by stressing their vulnerability and their traditional feminine qualities; this is then often combined with an emphasis on the exceptional position of these women.

'Maternal instincts'

This war was dubbed 'mom's war' (Greenberg, 1991), and the idea of mothers leaving young children to go off to war is a potent challenge to traditional ideologies of femininity. However, again the challenge was accommodated by presenting the role of mother as the primary and 'natural' role for these women and one that might be incompatible with a military role. The innocence of the young children is used to intensify the problematic position of women soldiers who are also mothers. The poignant photograph of Captain Joanne Conley[16] was reproduced in a number of publications. This photograph shows a woman in full combat gear wearing a badge containing a photograph of her infant daughter.

At one and the same time the ideologies of equal rights are being used to seemingly support the wider range of opportunities for women but ultimately to highlight their 'deficiencies' and maintain the notion that the military is male. 'It was women who demanded the right. It was women who insisted there was no differences between the sexes as far as competence in the job is concerned.'[17]

'Pin-up girl'

In this theme a different set of ideas found within traditional ideologies of femininity is drawn upon. In a number of reports women soldiers are constructed as sexual objects. The trappings of war are included but the guns, helmet and uniform serve only to enhance the sexual role of these women. In a feature entitled 'Made up and dressed to kill'[18] the stress is on the sexual nature of women in terms of their physical appearance; in terms of their potential deadliness, the echo of the film title leaves us in no doubt. The 'natural' aggression of male soldiers is reconstructed as sexual aggression in women soldiers and the sexual role of women is intensified by their military persona.

Women were presented in military roles but the challenge to traditional notions is anchored not only by stressing women as potential victims of war – 'But they've got to be able to handle that Uzi in case the unthinkable happens and they find themselves face to face with the enemy'[19] – but also by using sexual connotations to increase this sense of vulnerability. Facing the enemy – the soldier's task – is unthinkable for a woman soldier not only because of her lesser strength but also because of her vulnerability to sexual attack.

In this, as in other items, the construction of women soldiers as sexual objects in terms of male heterosexuality is maintained. Indeed, the debates concerning the presence of women soldiers in the newspapers frequently drew upon this construct – women would only be a distraction to the 'troops': 'When men are living in the desert they start tingling. They see a female and their heads aren't clear.'[20] Sexuality is an important signifier in the construct of the male soldier as warrior: 'Hot-blooded but cool-headed, some young close cropped US Marines are given a war briefing'.[21]

Heterosexuality is prioritized, the emphasis being on male soldiers' need for sexual release. The only references to female soldiers' sexuality is in terms of their availability for men's pleasure. In a report on the use of HMS *Cunard* as a recreational facility, male sexual needs were constructed as the most important both through the use of sexual innuendo – 'In local circles it is known as HMS Pussy or the Loveboat'[22] – or more explicitly: 'sadly for the men, only 5% of the customers are servicewomen'.[23] Implicitly here women's sexual role is being constructed as an essential element in the conduct of war within patriarchal society. Traditional notions of difference in relation to male and female sexuality, the male need for release and the female need for romance and love, are foregrounded in items such as the following:

Despite the imbalance between men and women, male soldiers boast that about half manage to score with the women on board. 'Mind you they're military women. You gotta talk to them and all that,' said one. . . .[24]

Even when women soldiers' sexuality is acknowledged as being independent of male heterosexuality, as in the limited number of representations of women's sexuality in terms of lesbianism, these representations maintain the dominant ideologies where images of lesbians are constructed as at best exceptional:

When war breaks out we can be sure to be seeing plenty of women in the frontlines . . . showing courage, even, perhaps the occasional lesbian or gay soldier serving his or her country[25]

– or as a way of avoiding military duty: 'a gay deceiver'.[26]

The challenge to traditional ideologies is accommodated by reconstructing traditional notions of femininity within the specific context of war. Women's subordinate role is maintained by constructing women soldiers as potential – and actual – victims, mothers or sexual objects, all of which might detract from the military role. Combat remains inscribed as a male arena. However, constructing representations of women soldiers in terms of patriarchal notions of femininity endorses rather than questions the parallel ideologies of militarism; even women who are not 'naturally' equipped to participate in war are willing to be involved as combatants in this just cause.

The next theme illustrates the way in which representations of Western female soldiers were used to endorse the stance of the Western Allies.

'American women in shorts'

Part of the just-war discourse used to underpin representations of Allied action includes a set of images which built up the anti-Iraqi stance. This was achieved by not only highlighting difference in lifestyle between Western and Arab society but also presenting the Arab way of life as inferior. The subordinate position of women in Arab society – their dress, the restrictions upon their lives, their lack of legal autonomy – became the signifiers of a lesser culture. The contrast with the values of Western society was signified by the image of the female soldier; this became symbolic of the progressive 'right thinking' values underpinning the US and British campaign and was used to endorse not only the just-war discourse but also an imperialist discourse: she is the one to deal with 'Islam's bovver boys':[27]

> One of this bunch met his match the other day when he stopped an American woman Army driver and ordered her out from behind the wheel (not permitted here). She pointed her M16 carbine at him and said 'Go on make my day . . .'[28]

Here we see the constant tendency of British newspapers to ignore differences among the various Arab states. This particular incident took place in Saudi Arabia and 'Islam's bovver boy' on this occasion was a member of the Alliance forces. The female soldier was used to justify this imperialist stance. Ironically, because of its power, this image of a Western female soldier was used as a propaganda weapon by the Iraqi government. Hence Hussein's jibe at the Saudi government who, he claimed, were being protected by 'American women in shorts'.

The First Female Prisoner-of-War

The dominant codes in the representations of female soldiers come together in the reports on the first female prisoner-of-war. The capture and later the release of Melissa Rathburn-Nealy was presented as primary news and it became a reference point for representations of other women soldiers, with her capture prompting a debate concerning the role of women in the military. The fear and vulnerability of this female soldier is summed up in the headline which announces her capture: 'Agony of Girl Marine'.[28]

Now the 'unthinkable' had finally happened, with the capture of an Allied female soldier by the Iraqis, 'The face of the war had suddenly changed'[30] because this soldier, unlike her male colleagues, was at risk from sexual assault. We have no doubt about this woman's desirability. Reports of her capture were accompanied by a series of glamour photographs, a desirable young woman posing or gazing seductively into the camera. Her vulnerability was increased by the sense that she was alone created by the constant references to her as 'the only woman listed as missing'[31] and as 'the only American servicewoman'.[32] The dramatic narrative relating the discovery of the capture adds to this sense of fear: 'The truck hit a wall and overturned. Marine rescue party found the truck with the passenger door opened and the wheel still spinning. No bloodstains were found'.[33]

The Allied cause is well served in this representation of a female soldier for at one and the same time she is positioned as vulnerable, in need of protection, but also a supporter of a just cause: 'She's patriotic ... she just wanted to do the best for her country'.[34] The safe release of this soldier was not used to endorse the idea that a female soldier has the capacity to face the risks of military service. Although images of women soldiers were used to support the rightness of the Western Allies, the high cost of equal rights for women was portrayed in the photographs of this woman in uniform which were used. Melissa Rathburn-Nealy, when released, was a tired, strained woman, 'BATTERED BUT NOT BOWED'.[35]

Conclusion

During the Gulf War, women were breaching the traditional constructs of masculinity and femininity; women were now aggressors. In representations of female soldiers, the contradiction had to be dealt with. The ideological determinants of the photographs of women soldiers were derived from traditional discourses of sexuality within the context of war. The news-worthiness of the events of war comes not just from the extremities of the situation but also from the need of a society to maintain boundaries of legitimacy, by creating a sense of moral justification (Hall *et al.*, 1978). During the Gulf War the 'just-war' discourse was translated into the everyday idiom of newspapers in which the cause of the war was personified in Saddam Hussein. Thus the values Hussein came to represent, a totalitarian regime, military rule and an Islamic way of life, were constructed as antithetical to the moral stance assumed by the Western Allies.

Representations of women soldiers can endorse the legitimacy of the war, with women presented as willing to sacrifice anything for a just cause. Further, the woman soldier became the icon of the democratic principles of free Western society, in contrast to the regime of Hussein. However, at the same time, the very construct of 'woman soldier' questions the values underpinning the Western Allies' campaign, that is, the values of Western patriarchal society. Newspapers were faced with a dilemma in the reporting on the participation of women soldiers. This dilemma, as I indicated earlier, was dealt with in two contrasting ways and depended upon the stance of the particular newspaper in relation to both the war and to gender politics.

In newspapers where there was a pro-war stance and a conservative position in terms of gender politics, there was a visible coverage of female soldiers (albeit a small proportion of the total coverage of the war). Thus the pro-war stance of papers such as the *Daily Record*, the *Daily Telegraph* and the *Daily Express* was endorsed by representations of women who were not 'naturally' equipped for war but who were willing to pay the ultimate cost. In these representations traditional ideologies of femininity were recon-structed within the context of war. Thus women soldiers were predominantly constructed as potential victims, mothers and most frequently sexual objects.

In the *Guardian*, which took a more critical stance towards both the discourses of sexuality underpinning traditional gender relationships and to the war, the construct of 'woman soldier' also posed a dilemma revealing a tension between competing positions: liberal, feminist and pacifist stances. Here was an opportunity to represent the changing role of women, but to do so might also endorse the values underpinning the Allied military action in the Gulf. There does not seem to be a way of reconciling these positions in relation to the idea of 'woman soldier'. The dilemma was dealt with by limiting the representation of women's participation in the war in all spheres, but particularly as soldiers. Although there were frequent incidental references to 'servicemen and women' there was little focused attention on women soldiers in the reports of the war. Instead this paper included a feminist analysis by Julie Wheelwright of the war and the impact of this on women, in terms of their participation in the military, as victims of war and more generally in terms of the position of women within contemporary patriarchal society.[36] Such articles however, were confined to the Women's Page.

At the beginning of this chapter, I suggested that the presence of considerable numbers of women prepared for combat posed questions about the traditional and polarized constructs of femininity and masculinity. However, from this analysis of newspaper reports concerning women soldiers, it appears that the apparent contradiction of the construct 'woman soldier' was either ignored or used to endorse a pro-war stance. In the newspaper where a more critical stance to both the war and to gender politics was taken, the issue of women soldiers was not dealt with in any substantial way. Where a pro-war stance was evident, the apparent contradiction of woman/soldier was used to support the Western Allies' stance and so was accommodated into the dominant discourses of patriarchy. Traditional notions of femininity were inscribed in these newspaper representations.

Women's relationship with the military seems a distant one, yet the military does have a critical influence on women's lives both materially and culturally within patriarchal society. Although the Gulf War only involved a minority of women, the fact that women could be combatants seemed to offer the opportunity to challenge traditional ideas of femininity, by demonstrating the changing role of women in contemporary society. However, what has become apparent from this study is that women's entry into the military is problematic. The notion of a 'woman soldier' remains a paradox, but one which can be used to endorse and further entrench traditional ideologies of femininity and masculinity. As a powerful institution within patriarchy, 'serving that state by means of organised coercion' (Enloe, 1981, p. 25), its composition remains predominantly male. More importantly, its values remain masculine. Thus women are placed in a less powerful and less valued role both within the military and in society more generally.

As any potential challenge posed by women soldiers is accommodated within the male hegemonic order of patriarchy, we should remember that the subordination of women is an inevitable outcome of increased militarization. Representations of women soldiers remain bounded within traditional discourses of sexuality; women soldiers were presented predominantly in terms of victim, mother or, most frequently, sexual object.

Women's role in the military, even in instances of engaging in combat, has reinforced rather than challenged the traditional constructs of masculine and feminine. The presence of a small number of female combatants has perhaps further reinforced it as a male area, underpinned by masculine values. Women soldiers in history have been presented at best as unusual, at worst as deviant and to be feared.[37] The myth of the Amazon is still in circulation today and is used in the dominant discourses not only as a derogatory term but as a policing construct. Many women currently in the military talk of the way in which their abilities as soldiers are undermined by constant reference to their sexual behaviour. These women find themselves in a no-win situation; 'easy lay' or lesbian (Enloe, 1981), with both terms being used in an insulting manner intended to police the women's behaviour.

The presence of women soldiers prepared for combat did not challenge the dominant discourses. Men remain the 'true' warriors and the business of war remains a male arena of activity. But perhaps more threatening for women is the fact that war is a central construct of manhood within contemporary society. Treitschke, the architect of Prussian militarism prior to the First World War, associated war with the natural state of man:

> War is beautiful . . . we must wait for it with the knowledge that when
> it strikes, it will be more beautiful and more wonderful to live forever
> among the heroes on a war memorial in a church than to die in an
> empty bed nameless. (quoted in Isaksson, 1988, p. 11)

War, whether it is international war or the warfare on the streets of a modern city, is a time for men to seek not only power and glory but their true manhood. We should consider how many cultural products such as films, television and popular literature are inscribed with this notion of masculinity. How many heroes in popular culture go out in this 'blaze of glory'?

Notes

This article is an extract from a larger study on newspaper representations of women during the Persian Gulf War. I would like to thank Deborah Cameron for advice and support and Linda Cunningham for her reading of the several versions of this chapter.

1 Recent Hollywood films of the Vietnamese War illustrate this. Films such as *Full Metal Jacket, Platoon* and *Hamburger Hill* focus on male participation, despite the large numbers of women who were part of the military as combatants (women were a substantial part of the North Vietnamese army) and as medical and ancillary staff in the US armed forces.
2 The newspapers included in the study were the *Daily Telegraph*, the *Daily Express*, the *Daily Record* and the *Guardian*.
3 The *Guardian* included only a small number of photographs in the reports on the Gulf War overall so there were only a limited number of photographs of women. Of these, more than half portrayed women in traditional roles as wives or mothers. There were very few of women in non-traditional roles, and these were mainly MPs and journalists. This newspaper did, however, carry the largest number of photographs of women in oppositional roles, especially women peace campaigners and female MPs who opposed the war.
4 *Daily Record*, 9 January 1991, p. 8.
5 *Daily Record*, 18 February 1991, p. 4.
6 *Daily Record*, 3 January 1991, p. 1.
7 *Daily Express*, 13 February 1991, p. 2.
8 *Daily Telegraph*, 26 January 1991, p. 3.
9 *Daily Record*, 3 January 1991, p. 1.
10 *Daily Express*, 25 February 1991, p. 13.
11 *Ibid.*
12 *Daily Telegraph*, 7 March 1991, p. 11.
13 *Daily Express*, 22 January 1991, p. 23.
14 *Daily Record*, 21 February 1991, p. 9.
15 *Ibid.*
16 *Daily Express*, 2 February 1991, p. 9.
17 *Daily Express*, 25 February 1991, p. 8.
18 *Daily Record*, 7 February 1991, p. 3.
19 *Ibid.*
20 *Daily Telegraph*, 26 January 1991, p. 3.
21 *Daily Record*, 18 February 1991, p. 4.
22 *Guardian*, 18 February 1991, p. 3.
23 *Daily Express*, 21 February 1991, p. 8.
24 *Guardian*, 18 February 1991, p. 3.
25 *Daily Telegraph*, 16 January 1991, p. 14.
26 *Guardian*, 9 January 1991, p. 19.

27 *Daily Express*, 10 January 1991, p. 8.
28 *Ibid.*
29 *Daily Record*, 1 February 1991, p. 3.
30 *Daily Telegraph*, 1 February 1991, p. 22.
31 *Daily Express*, 4 February 1991, p. 4.
32 *Daily Telegraph*, 11 February 1991, p. 3.
33 *Daily Record*, 1 February 1991, p. 3.
34 *Daily Record*, 4 February 1991, p. 3.
35 *Daily Record*, 5 March 1991, p. 11.
36 Three articles were included in the Women's Page during this period: 'Women at War', 24 January 1991, p. 24; 'The Sexual Heat of Battle', 31 January 1991, p. 36; 'War's Hidden Horror', 13 February 1991, p. 36.
37 Wheelwright (1989) charts the involvement of women soldiers participating in a number of wars, from the Napoleonic Wars to the First World War. Benefiting from the strict dress codes of the time, women were able to enter the army or the navy with some ease. These women did participate in combat, but only covertly, because by donning male clothing they took on a male persona. This was apparent even in instances where the individual was known to be a woman. Flora Sandes fought in the Serbian army during the First World War. Sandes was expected to act like a soldier, that is, like a man, especially in the presence of other women. In the area of combat within the military only masculine qualities are valued and accepted. Faderman (1985) also illustrates the way in which women found to be cross-dressing were dealt with severely, such behaviour being seen as dangerous and deviant.

References

CHAPKIS, WENDY (Ed.) (1981) *Loaded Questions: Women in the Military*, Amsterdam, Transnational Institute.

ELSHTAIN, JOAN BETHKE (1987) *Women and War*, Brighton, Harvester Press.

ENLOE, CYNTHIA (1981) 'The Military Model', in CHAPKIS, WENDY (Ed.) (1981) *Loaded Questions: Women in the Military*, Amsterdam, Transnational Institute.

FADERMAN, LILLIAN (1985) *Surpassing the Love of Men*, London, The Women's Press.

FLORENCE, M.F., MARSHALL, C. and OGDEN, C.K. (1987) *Militarism versus Feminism*, London, Virago (first published 1915).

GOLDMAN, NANCY LORING (Ed.) (1985) *Female Soldiers – Combatants or Noncombatants: Historical Perspectives*, London, Greenwood Press.

GREENBERG, SUSAN (1991) 'The New Face of Battle', *Newsweek*, 10 September, pp. 18–21.

HALL, STUART (1972) 'The Determinations of Newsphotographs'. in *Working Papers in Cultural Studies No. 3*, Birmingham, University of Birmingham.

HALL, STUART, CRITCHER, CHARLES, JEFFERSON, TONY, CLARKE, JOHN and ROBERTS,

BRIAN (Eds) (1978) *Policing the Crisis, Mugging, the State, and Law and Order*, London, Macmillan.

HUSTON, NANCY (1982) 'Tales of War and Tears of Women', *Women's Studies International Forum*, vol. 5, no. 3/4, pp. 271–82.

ISAKSSON, EVA (Ed.) (1988) *Women and the Military System*, Hemel Hempstead, Harvester Wheatsheaf.

LLOYD, GENEVIEVE (1986) 'Selfhood, War and Masculinity', in PATEMAN, C. and GROSS, E. (Eds) *Feminist Challenges*, London, Allen and Unwin, pp. 63–76.

MICHELETTI, ERIC and DEBAY, YVES (1991) *Operation Desert Shield: The First 90 Days*, London, Winrow and Greens.

MUIR, KATE (1992) *Arms and the Woman*, London, Sinclair-Stevenson.

STIEMH, JUDITH HICKS (1982) 'The Protected, The Protector, The Defender', *Women's Studies International Forum*, vol. 5, no. 3/4, pp. 367–73.

THOMPSON, JANNA (1991) 'Women and War', *Women's Studies International Forum*, vol. 14, no. 1/2, pp. 63–75.

WARNER, MARINA (1985) *Monuments and Maidens: The Allegory of the Female Form*, London, Weidenfeld and Nicolson.

WHEELWRIGHT, JULIE (1989) *Amazons and Military Maids: Women who Dress as Men in the Pursuit of Life, Liberty and Happiness*, London, Weidenfeld and Nicolson.

Section III
Practising Sexual Politics

Chapter 8

Writing Women's Friendship: An Intimate Experience?

Ruth Hamson

If we look ... we may find an untold story of friendship between women, sustaining but secret. (Heilbrun, 1989, p. 98)

In front of me, above my desk, hangs a photograph. Two young women, immaculately dressed and carrying gloves and handbags, walk along the seafront holding hands. They are laughing, happy and confident. The photo is dated 1949, the year before I was born; yet I have become another figure in this picture. I set out to record and explore the life history of this one friendship. Where should I place myself: following behind, watching? Facing them as they walk towards me? Or walking with them hand-in-hand? Looking at this photograph will no doubt elicit varied responses, depending on the viewpoint of the spectator. The nature of the relationship will be constructed according to the observer's particular frame of reference. Different words and perceptions spring to mind. I wanted the women to speak for themselves, to tell me their story as they see it. My initial aim was to hear their experience and how they conceptualized it.

Iris was my mother's sister. Aged 79 when I began this story, both she and her friend Joan, ten years younger, were part of my family background; from childhood I was aware that they belonged together and loved each other. They met during the war, were close friends for nearly half a century and for twenty-five years shared a house together. Neither ever married: for most of their lives they lived in London, travelling into the city every day to pursue careers within commercial shipping companies. When I approached them about this study, they were living quietly in a Buckinghamshire cottage

where Joan made home-made bread and jam and cared for Iris, disabled through arthritis. I found them hand-in-hand, a rug over their knees, watching snooker on the television. They agreed to tell me the story of their lives.

As They Walk Towards Me: Women's History and Women's Friendship

When I first read Heilbrun's words, quoted above, I was coming to the end of my research. In writing women's history, we are told, we 'have the task of making women visible where they have been hidden in the past' (Purvis, 1992, p. 274). The study of oral history is an area of contemporary interest not confined to Women's Studies. *The Handbook of Oral History*, published in 1984, expresses the hope that 'In re-writing history "from below", oral history can create a more accurate and authentic picture of the past. It can give back to people a sense of the historical significance of their own lives' (Humphries, 1984, p. x). Women are acknowledged amongst those whose history has been little heard, and in the past decade, women ranging from academics to community groups have attempted to redress this neglect. There are, however, questions to be asked about our use and understanding of women's historical experiences. Deirdre Beddoe warns against looking to the past only to seek 'explanations for the present' (Beddoe, 1983, p. 3), and as feminist debates become increasingly complex, remaining clear-sighted about our work is not always easy. We have to make 'the knife edge decision . . . between using feminist insights to analyse women's lives and avoiding the danger of projecting present ideals and values back in the past' (Purvis, 1992, p. 277). How can we be sure that our interpretations represent the intentions behind the words we are given? We ourselves are positioned in the research, and must recall Liz Stanley's words, 'we can now *never* understand the past as it was understood by those who lived it' (Stanley, 1992, p. 169). Further, in using reminiscence, there are questions related to memory, which, rather than being a mirror image, is surely reshaped and reconstructed over the years as we assimilate new perspectives and attitudes: 'the past that is constructed orally can never be fixed; it will change to the degree that the present changes' (Cornwell and Gearing, 1989, p. 43).

In addition to these considerations, current debates about the possibility/ desirability of 'objectivity', of keeping a distance between the researcher and the researched, become key issues in relation to studying friendship. From the outset I recognized that experiences and feelings which have shaped my life would be part of my research: as women we all have experiences of friendships with other women, both positive and negative. These informed not only the reasons behind my decision to study women's friendship, but also my methodology. At the same time, the actual process of the work I carried out, the sharing of stories and confidences, enriched and changed those experiences and understandings.

If women's history generally has remained hidden, friendship between women has been particularly well-concealed or even ignored. However, on Easter Monday 1994, an article on women's friendship appeared in the *Guardian*, bringing some significant comments on the subject into the public arena:

Despite its key roles in most women's lives ... friendship between women has been consistently overlooked by historians, philosophers and artists.... Women's friendships have always been depicted as peripheral to their roles as wife and mother. The tendency to define women in relation to men and to children, rather than to one another, has meant that their friendships have been persistently trivialised, eroticised or marginalised. (Abrams, 1992)

The definition of friend in my English dictionary reads: 'a person with whom one enjoys mutual affection and regard (usually exclusive of sexual or family bonds)' (*Concise Oxford Dictionary*), whilst Maggie Humm, in *The Dictionary of Feminist Theory*, defines friendship as 'a form of women's emotional bonding' (Humm, 1989, p. 81). Other feminists would want to label relationships between women in different ways and despite Abrams' claims in the newspaper article cited above, it is not always evident that feminism has clarified what friendship between women means and how it is experienced. Labelling and categorization are undoubtedly difficult but I believe this should not deter us from exploring women's friendship or recognizing its importance. Pat O'Connor claims that 'work on friendship between women can be said to lie at the heart of our understanding of key issues in women's lives' (O'Connor, 1992, p. 193).

Despite assertions from within Women's Studies about the importance of female friendship, I found comparatively little research into the subject. In fiction, however, friendships between women have often assumed a high profile, from the schoolgirl genre onward. Rosemary Auchmuty, citing reasons for the popularity of school stories well into the 1960s, suggests that the girls portrayed provided strong role models and a temporary escape from the male world. Friendship not only between schoolgirls but between adult women too is 'comfortable, constant, supportive and accepted' (Auchmuty, 1992, p. 133). As a child I was an avid reader of schoolgirl fiction. As a student of Women's Studies, reading women's fiction in which friendship played a significant part provided an incentive for further study, uncovering the potential of women's friendship in a multiplicity of situations. I went on to discover a certain amount of biographical writing of women friends, though these of course tend to follow the normal pattern of our culture in valuing what is public and successful; the private lives of hidden women have continued to remain largely unexplored. Other texts around women's friendship are theoretical studies of women's friendship as it is portrayed in fiction – literary criticism. This seemed to me to be looking at the image, rather than the experience. Whilst I accept the importance of images in informing my own ideology and expectations, creating role models, they cannot be substituted for real experience, what actually happens for women.

The tendency of male-based society to trivialize women's friendships is one explanation for the lack of texts in this area, but I believe there are problems of definition and understanding amongst women themselves, which problematize such research.

Following Behind: Lesbian Issues in History and Friendship

The recent work of Pat O'Connor acknowledges the problematizing of the word 'lesbian' in studying friendships between women. Indeed, many writers of texts on female friendship are lesbians who are searching for a lesbian history and identity. Lillian Faderman, for example, in *Surpassing the Love of Men*, uses a variety of historical resources, including letters, diaries and fiction, to uncover a world apparently full of close emotional and romantic relationships between women. Both she and others have argued that such friendships in the past were both common and accepted within society but have become hidden and 'suspect' since the work of the sexologists and Freud at the beginning of this century. Others have explored all-women communities within history. Janice Raymond argues that within such communities the true history of women can be found and that we need to restore what she terms the 'prime order' in women's lives, where women's affections are self directed and where women put each other first (Raymond, 1986, p. 43). She makes it very clear that she is talking here about friendship relationships, not about sexually based love relationships, and speaks out against the tendency in some lesbian groups to emphasize the sexual aspect.

Martha Vicinus, writing recently in *Feminist Studies*, openly pursues lesbian-centred research but in doing so criticizes others, such as Faderman, for being less clear-sighted in their work. 'Historians', she writes, 'are more confined to their evidence than writers of fiction and cannot create utopias, but they can and do create myths' (Vicinus, 1992, p. 490). This is echoed by Lisa Moore: 'Faderman's . . . studies obscure the wariness and even prohibition that sometimes surrounded women's friendships' (Moore, 1992, p. 501). But whilst attempting a critique of a certain brand of lesbian-based history, Vicinus and Moore are themselves still part of that type of research. Moore uses the term 'friendship' in the context of arguments about sexuality. Lesbian writers seem to be making assumptions that friendships between women are to be identified as lesbian. At one point Vicinus states: 'By the 1950s, everyone knew what a lesbian was' (p. 489). We need to understand that whilst this may be true as part of her own history, it may not be part of others' reality.

Is it possible to look at history and not to create our own myths? In exploring epistemological issues related to lesbian history, Liz Stanley addresses problems raised in studies of 'romantic friendship'. According to her, scholars have begun with theories and 'the nature of actual friendship is then deduced from the theory' (1992, p. 161). She argues that we should listen to what women actually say, rather than look for what we expect them to say. Her argument is made in the context of her own recognized desire to build a lesbian history. In her vision of female friendship, Raymond too claims to be looking for a balance, where women's friendship is seen not as a poor alternative to heterosexual relationships, nor as 'lesbian' in a prescribed sense, but as a chosen, carefully considered existence, which allows women to be free for themselves and live fulfilled lives (1986, p. 239). Both Stanley and Raymond are involved here not only in an investigation of other women's lives and history, but in labelling and identifying themselves and their own position. Stanley, in her criticism of Faderman's labels, imposes her own; for example, her definition of Faderman's creation of an age of 'innocence' was more probably seen by Faderman herself as an age of 'ignorance'. In expressing my intention of using an open approach, I needed to recognize similar factors. The women I talked to have labels and definitions both for themselves and for other women. And as I listened to them I had my own understanding and application of the word 'friendship' to negotiate, not only in interpreting their story, but in my own life.

I was concerned to avoid an essentialist approach in classifying Iris and Joan. Issues around sexuality and identity undoubtedly need to be explored, as do the contexts within which relationships between women are played out, but rigid categorization is one of the criticisms that we in Women's Studies have levelled at the male world; we view the need to compartmentalize and label as a male paradigm. 'Lesbian', 'gyn-affection' or 'friendship' are equally forms of labelling. However, I recognize that the purpose of language is to name and categorize, so that in attempting to interpret the narrative as it was told to me, I have been linguistically defining these women's lives. I sought definitions, for example, for areas such as their class and their sexuality; I attempted to explain their childhood experiences and represent their developing relationship. My work is a construct of their life stories through language and, as such, inevitably uses labels. I hope, though, that in exposing contradictions between their lives and existing texts and theories around unmarried women, I have raised questions about the ways in which women's lives are categorized. My aim has been 'the recovery of women's experiences' (Lubelska, 1991, p. 44), to discover what women themselves say about their friendship.

Hand-in-hand: Feminist Methodology

It was suggested to me by other Women's Studies students that knowing these two women was a problem, that their position as 'relatives' made them too close for objects/subjects of research. I felt, though, that this was a positive aspect, an opportunity to practise feminist principles of research. Ann Oakley, for example, argued over a decade ago that 'A feminist interviewing women is by definition both "inside" the culture and participating in that which she is observing' (Oakley, 1981, p. 57). Given the direction of my own study, it is interesting to note in her chapter outlining her objectives for feminist interviewers, a subheading, 'The transition to friendship?'. This reminded me of an essay by Elizabeth Minnich which I discovered whilst reviewing literature on women's friendship. She suggests that the relationship between author, subject and reader in biographies of women offers a model of friendship. It seems that, according to feminist epistemology, in researching the life story of a friendship between two women, I myself take on the role of friend, an 'achieved and genuine reciprocity' (Minnich, 1985, p. 287). Knowing them already should facilitate and enrich this process, I felt. At the same time, I recognized the need for sensitivity in working with older members of my family. They were not familiar with feminist ideas nor with academic terminology. As a friend, awareness of their perceptions and feelings was important; to push for more than they were willing to tell me, to interpret according only to my own understanding, might contravene all ideas of friendship between women. I needed, from a position of understanding my own Self, to meet and accept their perception of their Selves so that together we could attempt to write their story in a context both supportive and self-affirming, a context of friendship.

I had no fixed agenda of questions, I wanted them to do the narrating. I asked them to tell me things such as how they met, what they thought of each other at that time and how their friendship developed, and to describe the circumstances of their lives. Once started, I didn't need to say much. I spent two mornings interviewing them about their lives together and also talked separately with each about childhood memories. The typescript of these interviews runs to over a hundred pages. My main contributions were promptings for them to expand on things they mentioned, or to bring them back to fill in gaps in their narrative. I also looked and nodded and affirmed and we all laughed quite a lot. I spent time sharing lunch with them. From being known but rather distant aunts, coloured for me by the family view that they were different because they lived without men, they became friends, whose comments and understanding around family issues were shrewd and well-observed, especially as they began to understand from my response, that I was not, as I think they had imagined, devoted to a patriarchal way of life.

From these interviews, I wrote their story, using their words as much as possible. I looked at their childhood, the way class and family experiences had formed their attitudes and expectations. I considered their working lives, the context of their developing friendship, and their relationships with others in the public world. I explored their life together; both socially, in a largely women's world they inhabited, and privately, in living together, the images they created of themselves, their perceptions of their own identity and sexuality. Having recorded their words and understandings around each issue, I compared the theoretical assumptions given in other texts. This went beyond questions pertaining simply to friendship and women's identity to given information about the public world of work and historical events, compared with their experience as they lived it. My aim was to recover their story and compare it with existing assumptions, and to avoid using theories as the basis for deduction, in the way that Liz Stanley criticizes. Stanley has called for 'a middle way, one which does not impose a theoretical structure on the lives and experiences of historical people, but which recognizes that love between women could take many shapes and meanings' (Stanley, 1992, p. 169). She suggests a combination of history and biography, 'looking closely at particular lives' and listening to what women actually say, rather than what we expect them to say. In my own experiences of women's friendship, certain roles and attitudes have often been expected of me: in contrast, I wanted to offer openness, a willingness to listen.

Images of Friendship: Iris and Joan's Story

In listening, I became part of their story as they expressed it to me; the possibilities and strengths they had offered each other made real the potential suggested by writers such as Janice Raymond describing what she terms 'passionate friendship [which] has its own depth and intensity and is characterised by strong feeling and often physical affection' (Raymond, 1986, p. 227). Here are two women who told me they love each other deeply, who shared their lives for more than fifty years and a house for twenty-five. But they retained their own selves, their separate identities, free from any sense of possessiveness or competition. As young women they discussed living together and wanted to do it, but Iris chose to stay with her mother and care for her for another ten years. Joan felt she was unable to stay with her parents and set up her own home – an unusual move for a single woman in the 1950s. She pursued a significant career within the male world of a shipping company. Throughout this time they remained devoted to each other but without feelings of envy or regret. They shared whatever they could and celebrated that sharing but each was secure within herself and accepted both her own and the other's position. Even when they bought a house together, they maintained their own spaces – separate rooms and kitchens – for many years. They did not assume ownership of one another through joint ownership of a house.

'Respecting the other's privacy', O'Connor notes in her study, appears to be a 'universal rule' in successfully working out the tensions in relationships (O'Connor, 1992, p. 51), whilst Stephanie Dowrick describes the choice 'for two selves to live alongside each other, rather than in and through each other, but that is rarely easy to achieve' (Dowrick, 1992, p. 207). In talking about how they lived, Joan explained it as 'giving somebody room to live their own life if they want' (Hamson, 1993, p. A66). Joan and Iris knew very little about feminism and had never heard of any of these writers or books but at times the resemblance of their words to existing texts was remarkable. In discussing the fact that for many years they were not able to live together, Joan says:

> I think ... this might not have been so successful had we done it earlier, when I was younger and perhaps more impetuous and more demanding, that because we've let it take its course ... I believe it was really meant to be. (Hamson, 1992, pp. A59–60)

Compare this with Raymond's words:

> time becomes a crucial factor ... because it conveys practical wisdom about what form the friendship should take. Time provides the context for internal judgement to operate so that discernment leads to meaningful choices in the friendship and not spent emotion. (Raymond, 1986, p. 228)

Iris and Joan clearly stepped outside of the 'normal' life expected for women both by not marrying and by making their relationship with each other central to their lives. What of the way they label themselves? Joan's comment on men was 'you can do very well without them dear, I'd say' (Hamson, 1993, p. A36), whilst Iris said 'I've never been really attracted to men at all' (p. A38). Similar comments are to be found from older women in books such as Neild and Pearson's *Women Like Us*. These women, however, eventually came to identify themselves as lesbians, usually after a period of struggle or crisis about their own sexual identity. Iris and Joan appear to have had no such crisis; their perception is that sexuality is tied up with men and children, and as such is outside of their experience. They reject the word 'lesbian', claiming: 'when Iris and I were friendly, getting together, there wasn't all this – let's be blunt about it – all this homosexuality nonsense about, and being gay and being lesbian and one thing and another' (p. A47), contradicting Vera Brittain's assertion (quoted in Lewis, 1984, p. 134) that during the 1950s such matters were widely discussed. They are apparently unconcerned about labels others might put upon them: as Joan says, 'if anyone likes to think anything, they can ... think it. I think we've got past that stage now ... It doesn't worry us' (Hamson, 1993, p. A87). They have, however, chosen to comply very much with the norms of femininity in, for example, standards of dress, and in devotion to their families, which may have been an unconscious way of defending themselves against the prevailing ideology of women's place within a heterosexual domestic sphere. Perhaps this is an endorsement of Adrienne Rich's argument, that acceptance within a male-dominated society depends on pretending 'to be not merely heterosexual but a heterosexual *woman*, in terms of dressing and playing the feminine, deferential role required of "real" women' (Rich, 1984, p. 221).

Although their friendship with each other and without men might be expected to have put them outside heterosexual society, on the margins, they choose to emphasize the normality of their lives and insist they have not been unusual. From Faderman's study of women's friendship over 150 years to Neild and Pearson's snapshots of contemporary women, the consensus seems to be that after the Second World War the stigmatization of the label 'lesbian' drove women further into a heterosexual family life. Iris and Joan's narrative suggests that this was less inevitable than has been suggested. For example, their memories of their first holiday in 1946, where they stayed amongst heterosexual couples described as being on a second honeymoon, indicate that it had an almost honeymoon quality for them too. Yet they were not consciously aware of prohibition or stigmatization and claim to have had no sense of being outsiders. The implication that by the mid-twentieth century all relationships were judged in sexual terms is not borne out by their words. Stanley has criticized Faderman for romanticizing women's friendships, making them appear simple and innocent when in fact they were always regarded with suspicion. I resist romanticism in a sentimental sense: Iris and Joan's is not an instant love story, but involved years of waiting and working before they felt able to share their lives. Yet there is a simplicity and innocence about the progress of their friendship; or is it, as Stanley suggested, not innocence, but ignorance?

Towards Understanding: Interpretation and Response

Within the context of interviewing and talking, the sharing of the friendship was a two-way process between them and me. When it came to writing the story down, though, I was the one at the word processor, the one choosing which words to use and selecting interpretations. Katherine Borland in *Women's Words* poses the question 'who controls the text?' and cites the example of her grandmother, on whom she conducted some research, who on reading the finished text said 'the story is no longer MY story at all' (Borland, 1991, p. 70). Of course, Iris and Joan themselves as narrators will, in the words of June Purvis, have shown 'an inevitable bias in the selection and presentation of content' (Purvis, 1992, p. 291). There is validity in my interpretation, but it is equal only to theirs, and if they felt misrepresented it would be a breach of the trust of friendship that they had shown in allowing me to write. For this reason, when I had written the main body of the story, I sent it to Iris and Joan, asked them to read it and then visited them again to discover their reactions. I then used this interview as the basis for the concluding chapter of my dissertation.

They took this seriously. When I arrived, four days after they had received the script, they were prepared for me, with carefully written notes. Although a certain amount of this was correction of detail, I feel it indicated ownership for them; they were claiming the story as theirs. There was very little they disagreed with. Joan used the word 'shattered' in describing her reactions to the text, but this referred to surprise rather than anger or hurt. She expressed amazement

> at the number of references where you said our lives or our feelings or our thoughts fitted in with some of these works that have been done by various people over the years ... [and that] what up to now I had regarded as two quite ordinary people, living a mundane life, could provide so much food for thought. (Hamson, 1993, p. A105)

Friendship between women has been described by many who have written about it as being 'self-affirming'; one of the hopes in using oral history is the validation of women's lives. Iris and Joan's reactions to their story as I wrote it seem to indicate that this has been realized. They discovered that their story is worth telling and that it consists of more than they have hitherto recognized, and they felt reassured by the way it 'fits in'. Joan also commented that she and Iris had 'both learned a lot about each other ... It's made us think a great deal about our relationship and each other'

(p. A106). I felt that they found discussing their relationship a positive experience.

Throughout the five months I was working on the project, they maintained great interest and enthusiasm. When finally I had the work bound, I took them a copy. It was wet and windy and Iris was far from well, so they refused to let me take them out to lunch. But they had prepared a special plate of sandwiches and opened a bottle of champagne for me; they felt it was something to celebrate. Rosemary Auchmuty has written 'I would like to be able to celebrate women's love for women affirmatively and joyfully' (Auchmuty, 1992, p. 210) and we were able to do that. Our celebration went beyond the fact that I had completed a piece of research. It was a celebration of a lifelong friendship that had been confirmed as sustaining, fulfilling and supportive through speaking it out; a friendship that had been hidden behind the family-based environment around which it was lived. Beyond that, though, we were celebrating a new friendship, built between these two women and myself. Sharing something of our lives had involved acceptance and trust on both sides. I too had experienced the support of their friendship and found self affirmation in writing their life. During our final interview, they had expressed some apprehension about people reading it, but when they saw it in book form, it became a precious possession, and they asked me for cheap copies which they passed around to be read amongst family and friends. They were proud of their story.

Less than a year on, Iris died. There is another story of friendship in their last weeks together at home. As a friend, I continued to visit them; we discovered the genuine reciprocity that Elizabeth Minnich described. More than once, one or other of them said how glad they were that I had written their story. Now that Joan is on her own, she knows she can share her most poignant memories with me, because in a way I have been part of them.

If power lies in deciding which stories are to be told, then the writing of this life story is empowering, for those who read it as well as for the narrators and the writer. In sharing with Iris and Joan, I have not just written about their lives. I became a friend and received friendship: it has been, and remains, an intimate experience.

References

ABRAMS, REBECCA (1994) 'You've Got a Friend', *Guardian 2*, 4 April, p. 8.
AUCHMUTY, ROSEMARY (1992) *A World of Girls*, London, The Women's Press.
BEDDOE, DEIRDRE (1983) *Discovering Women's History*, London, Pandora.
BORLAND, KATHERINE (1991) '"That's Not What I Said": Interpretive Conflict in

Oral Narrative Research', in GLUCK, SHERNA BERGER and PATAI, DAPHNE (Eds) *Women's Words: The Practice of Oral History*, New York, Routledge, pp. 63–75.

CONCISE OXFORD DICTIONARY (1990) Oxford, Oxford University Press.

CORNWELL, J. and GEARING, B. (1989) 'Biographical Interviews With Older People', *Oral History*, 17, pp. 36–43.

DOWRICK, STEPHANIE (1992) *Intimacy and Solitude: Balancing Closeness and Independence*, London, The Women's Press.

FADERMAN, LILLIAN (1981) *Surpassing the Love of Men*, London, The Women's Press.

HAMSON, RUTH (1993) *Our Lives ... Our Feelings ... Our Thoughts: A Friendship Between Two Women in the Twentieth Century*, MA Dissertation, University of Leicester, Nene College, Northampton (unpublished).

HEILBRUN, CAROLYN (1989) *Writing a Woman's Life*, London, The Women's Press.

HUMM, MAGGIE (1989) *The Dictionary of Feminist Theory*, Hemel Hempstead, Harvester Wheatsheaf.

HUMPHRIES, STEPHEN (1984) *The Handbook of Oral History: Recording Life Stories*, London, Inter-Action.

LEWIS, JANE (1984) *Women in England 1870–1950: Sexual Divisions and Social Change*, Brighton, Harvester Wheatsheaf.

LUBELSKA, CATHY (1991) 'Teaching Methods in Women's Studies: Challenging the Mainstream', in AARON, JANE and WALBY, SYLVIA (Eds) *Out of the Margins: Women's Studies in the Nineties*, London, Falmer Press, pp. 41–8.

MINNICH, ELIZABETH KAMARCK (1985) 'Friendship Between Women: The Art of Feminist Biography', *Feminist Studies*, 11, pp. 287–305.

MOORE, LISA (1992) '"Something More Tender Still Than Friendship": Romantic Friendship in Early-Nineteenth-Century England', *Feminist Studies*, 18, pp. 499–510.

NEILD, SUZANNE and PEARSON, ROSALIND (1992) *Women Like Us*, London, The Women's Press.

OAKLEY, ANN (1981) 'Interviewing Women: A Contradiction in Terms', in ROBERTS, HELEN (Ed.) *Doing Feminist Research*, London, Routledge and Kegan Paul, pp. 31–58.

O'CONNOR, PAT (1992) *Friendships Between Women: A Critical Review*, Hemel Hempstead, Harvester Wheatsheaf.

PURVIS, JUNE (1992) 'Using Primary Sources When Researching Women's History from a Feminist Perspective', *Women's History Review*, 1 (2), pp. 273–309.

RAYMOND, JANICE (1986) *A Passion for Friends: Toward a Philosophy of Female Affection*, London, The Women's Press.

RICH, ADRIENNE (1984) 'Compulsory Heterosexuality and Lesbian Existence', in SNITOW, ANN, STANSELL, CHRISTINE and THOMPSON, SHARON (Eds) *Desire: The Politics of Sexuality*, London, Virago, pp. 212–41.

STANLEY, LIZ (1992) 'Epistemological Issues in Researching Lesbian History: The Case of "Romantic Friendship"', in HINDS, HILARY, PHOENIX, ANN and STACEY,

(Eds) *Working Out: New Directions for Women's Studies*, London, Falmer Press, pp. 161–72.

VICINUS, MARTHA (1992) '"They Wonder to Which Sex I Belong": The Historical Roots of the Modern Lesbian Identity', *Feminist Studies*, 18, pp. 467–97.

Chapter 9

Journeying with Jeanette: Transgressive Travels in Winterson's Fiction

Cath Stowers

> Why not put her back into man? Return to man his femininity and the problem of Women disappears. The perfect man. Male and Female. (Winterson, 1994a, p. 196)

There recently seems to be turmoil over Jeanette Winterson's public persona, with certain instances of media coverage creating a pathologizing of her life story in which her work often almost disappears.[1] Hence a recent letter in the *Guardian* (Briggs, 1994) berated Winterson for being 'obsessed with escaping her mother' while Philip Hensher's review of *Art and Lies*, also in the *Guardian*, launched a scathing attack on her. To my mind, the media seems obsessed with Winterson's personal past and displays an apparent inability to read her novels as texts. In an interview for *The Late Show* (1994), for example, despite Winterson bemoaning the fact that women writers are all too frequently reduced to their autobiography, and despite her assertion that she 'made' herself 'into a fictional character', Jeremy Isaacs appeared doggedly determined to focus on Winterson's personal history, her relationship with her parents and so forth. And yet in spite of this scavenging around Winterson's autobiography, her lesbianism is frequently decentred in much reception of her novels. Ever since the reassuring bildungsroman form[2] of *Oranges Are Not The Only Fruit*, it is rare for her fictions to be interpreted as lesbian texts, and it is consequently worth questioning whether such a reaction represents a displacing of lesbianism.[3] Whilst I do, of course, acknowledge recent work by, for example, Lynne Pearce and Gabriele

Griffin which does not ignore Winterson's lesbianism, my point is that very little criticism has engaged with Winterson's works *as a whole* as lesbian texts, or considered the possibility of a consistent lesbian aesthetic running through her novels.

It is not only much of Winterson's recent reception by the media that has made her portrayal of gender a contentious issue. As Lynne Pearce has pointed out, many feminist readers and critics have felt 'cheated' by Winterson's handling of gender (Pearce, 1994), while Winterson herself has further problematized the issue with her reluctance at being cast as a straight-forward 'feminist' or 'radical lesbian'. In her 1994 *Late Show* interview, the stress Winterson laid on her fiction's striving to create an 'enchanted place' made it clear that this differing world which 'doesn't exist' and 'never did', which is unconcerned with 'authenticity' or 'realism', is being increasingly equated by Winterson with art. And doesn't this suggest that these novels are becoming concerned only with positing and reaching some universal realm of 'art' which transcends such practicalities as gender? I believe, on the contrary, that gender is not being left behind, but rather is an inextricable – and ultimately transformed – part of Winterson's alternative 'world of art'. For Winterson is without doubt not only a self-promoting, visible author, but also decidedly *out*, at other times making it abundantly clear that the contours of female authorship are here defined in specifically lesbian terms.[4] By positing her works in a discourse of specifically *lesbian* desire, this essay aims to correct any tendency that would elevate the meaning of Winterson's texts to a realm supposedly separable from sexual politics.

Winterson's recent *Great Moments in Aviation* teems with images of travel. Set aboard a 1950s boat sailing from the Caribbean to England, the film script features maps and aeroplanes, hot air balloons and golden angels, while in her introduction Winterson states 'My work is always concerned with journeys' (Winterson, 1994b, p. vii). I want to show in this chapter how and why all of Winterson's novels are veined with kaleidoscopic voyages and explorations, with, as in *Sexing The Cherry*, 'journeys folded in on themselves like a concertina' (Winterson, 1990a, p. 23). We need to ask why these metaphors of travel pervade Winterson's novels. What purpose do they serve? Can her repeated emphasis on cartography be read as symptomatic of a concern to reclaim woman and femininity, to write both onto the patriarchal map? Is fluidity of travel somehow connected with an attempted dissolution of gender binaries? Should the association that is being made between sexualization, gender and travel be seen as a strategy to allow the free play of sexual difference and the subsequent release of female desire?

These questions arise because travel in Winterson is unconcerned with the conquest, mastery and exploitation of its traditional patriarchal paradigm, an Otherizing where 'woman' is deeply implicated as the mysterious *object* to the male *subject*. In undertaking my very own explorations, and to clarify the gendered nature of travel writing, I will be drawing on Sara Mills' and Mary Louise Pratt's researches into the differences between male and female travellers, to see what distinctly feminist paradigms of travel might look like. As I hope will become clear, when the characteristics of female explorers which Mills and Pratt have identified are juxtaposed with Winterson's fictions, her male explorers often display decidedly female attributes as they travel – if only in part – across gender boundaries.

Given that this chapter necessarily aims to address problems of sexual difference in Winterson's work, I will be utilizing a range of influential explorations into *l'écriture féminine* as a major source of inquiry into the question of how woman's body and sexuality has been represented and how it could be (re)written. It is, of course, vital to acknowledge the vastly differing critical and political orientations of Winterson and Cixous, Irigaray and other theorists. Nonetheless, I believe plausible cartographic connections can be made between their arguments and Winterson's rethinking of gender and sexual difference. My method, then, aims to employ aspects of French feminist critique to accentuate and draw out the ambitions of Winterson's metaphors of travel. I stress at my outset, therefore, that it is the metaphors at work in Cixous and Irigaray that are significant here. Cixous' 'Sorties', for example, alludes to an especially female form of travel, a metaphor contrasting masculine linearity with female subjectivity and modes of being, while Irigaray has claimed that woman is in fact 'a projective map' for 'guaranteeing the totality of the system'. Viewed as occupying a marginal position within the Symbolic, she becomes constituted as the borderline of that order (Cixous, 1986; Irigaray, 1985a). I aim to determine whether Winterson's travelling characters threaten the hegemony of such borders. Yet it is not my intention to use these theoretical writings to force Winterson's fictions into some sort of feminist allegory. Her texts, after all, resist such closure and continually slither away thematically and generically from critical mastery.

Winterson is without doubt highly popular. Her books often reach the best-seller list, while viewing figures for the 1989 television adaptation of *Oranges Are Not The Only Fruit* recorded audiences of 2.9, 4.4, and 3.9 million, considered a success for a mid-week screening.[5] And yet little critical work has been devoted to her. It is worth considering whether this absence of any great critical analysis of her novels is a symptom of what her fiction does. Does the prevalence of travel imagery in her work somehow figure its resistance to the Otherizing of traditional literary theory and her reluctance to be pinned down or pigeonholed in critical terms? Winterson has spoken, after all, of the evasiveness of her writing in terms of journeying: 'It's all on the move. I don't like to do the same thing again. So now that people think they know what I'm about, I'm on the move' (Winterson, 1990b). So the traditional paradigm of practical criticism which determines to find and fix a 'true meaning' in a text will find no way into Winterson's fiction. Bearing this point in mind, I shall offer readings of how Winterson's texts might 'mean' rather than any definitive arguments of what they mean. This method should stress the patterns of resistance in her texts to structures of critical authority, and open the issue of the productive role of the reader of her work, rather than engage in any hermeneutic exercise in which meaning is fixed and frozen in a single interpretative act.[6]

Although the imagery of exploration and travel is meticulously consistent and constructed in Winterson's work, her texts are simultaneously supremely fluid, flowing across differing genres and very much alive. The reader responds to them with a sense of fantastic pleasure. Questing may well be the source of this frequently engendered delight. A tension exists, however, between seduction and subversion, and although considering this aspect of pleasure, I nonetheless believe that the dissidence of Winterson's work should not be lost. Part of its pleasure lies in the way it problematizes gender and sexual difference. Although Michele Roberts has recently argued that 'the quest for the elusive and mysterious feminine' in Winterson's work is linked to a contempt for femininity, I hope to stress the ways femininity is not 'cut off' but allowed to feminize, re-sexualize, the masculine (Roberts, 1994). Instead of merely reversing gender, Winterson's travel tropes reinvent masculinity into a flux of genders. As her male explorers ultimately turn towards the maternal, tropes of travel finally come closer to Adrienne Rich's representation of lesbian orientation as 'a journey back to the mother' (Rich, 1980). But Winterson's maternal journeys are distinctly *male*, yet not at the expense of the mother or lesbian desire. To my mind, this special interest in feminizing men is a somewhat unusual lesbian preoccupation – one that certainly warrants further consideration. In this way, while recognizing poststructuralist suspicions of direct equations between the author and her text, I hope to achieve a vital counteracting of the frequent disavowal or de-centring of Winterson's lesbianism in the reception of her texts.[7]

It is perhaps in *The Passion* that travel and cartography are first established as a prominent feature of Winterson's work, and it is to this text I first turn. Set in the Napoleonic Wars, the novel consists of the dual narratives of Henri, the French peasant boy travelling as cook after his hero Napoleon, and Villanelle, the magical, bisexual water-borne woman he falls in love with as he ends up in Venice. Travel is figured in two differing paradigms. On the one hand, there are Henri's infantry expeditions and questing after Napoleon; on the other, the alternative model of Villanelle's shape-shifting, fluid Venice. Napoleon personifies the masculine linear force of history-making, rationality and war, where the feminine, woman's history, becomes charted out of sight, considered to have no place on patriarchy's official map of world events. Yet these tropes of travel are gradually reworked in *The Passion* to disclose how history is not as indisputable as patriarchy would have us believe.

Set against the uniformity of Napoleon's military whereby 'straight roads follow, buildings are rationalised, street signs … are always clearly marked' (Winterson, 1988, p. 112) is the alternative non-uniform, multi-form model of Venice, which 'Not even Bonaparte could rationalise' (p. 112). It is expedient to recall here that Winterson prefaces *The Passion* with a quotation from *Medea*: 'You have navigated with raging soul far from the paternal home … and now you inhabit a foreign land.' Immediately a rebellious voyaging to new realms is made explicit, the focus on Henri's disobedient and contravening travels away from the masculine paradigm of Napoleon towards the fantastic – and decidedly female – Venice. Although the feminine is 'other', represented as it is by the watery realm of Venice, an other medium, it does not remain denigrated, or feared, for Henri dives deep into that streaming female fluidity, his battle lines changing course to labyrinthine water-borne wanderings. This 'city of mazes' (p. 49) is suggested by the weavings of Villanelle's stories, her name itself hinting at a poetic form that interlaces repeated lines. Maps are rendered useless here, hence Villanelle explains to Henri that 'Your bloodhound nose will not serve you here. Your course in compass reading will fail you' (p. 49).

Already it should be clear that the innovative mercurial paradigm to which Henri turns has parameters which are not rigid or immovable, and that this new female model spirals back and forth across time. Throughout *The Passion*, Winterson unsettles the taken-for-granted distinctions between past, present and future, in this place freed from linear temporality. Journeys, moreover, turn to a form of travel which is no longer based on the coherent, conquering self, being transposed instead to a mercurial interior exploration into a feminine multiplicity, a 'travel along the blood vessels' to 'the cities of the interior', 'another place whose geography is uncertain' (p. 68). Yet it may not be necessarily obvious why these reworkings of travel tropes, leading to this protean apparition of a city, should be viewed as distinctly feminizing and female. Venice's rheumy realm in *The Passion* provides a seductive figuration of influential feminist theories on time, matter, space and self. Feminist theory has extensively argued that time itself is highly gendered. Annie Leclerc, for instance, speaks of 'another sense of time', cyclical, not closed or repetitive like man's linear perception of time, man who 'can only see History', whose 'sexuality is linear' (Leclerc, 1990, 1974). With the reassurance of such concepts as reality and matter erased in this novel, Henri's feminized travels could be said to be an attempt to fulfil Antoinette Fouque's plea for women to occupy imaginary spaces, inventing what the Symbolic cannot (will not) define and providing the doorway to a journeying 'beyond the reality principle', that 'reality principle' which here is history and representation (quoted in Ward Jouve, 1991, p. 72). The reconceptualization of the self in Venice is undoubtedly further congruent with feminist deconstructions of the unitary and universal subject of literary realism and history.

Winterson goes further, however, than simply writing women into history. In keeping with feminist arguments, that we need to be aware of how much that very model of history owes to the patriarchal model which excluded women in the first place, Winterson has made clear the highly differing nature of women's history, in terms which figure a tracing of a female palimpsest: 'Women's history is not an easily traceable straight line.... Following us is to watch for the hidden signs, to look in the gaps and be prepared for strange zig-zags' (Winterson, 1990c, p. xxi). Henri offers just such an alternative anti-linear paradigm, countering the notion that history is composed of exceptional individuals and the public sphere of predominantly male activities.[8] He veins the novel with his traces and memories of the home, the feminine, which has been lost: 'I was homesick from the start. I missed my mother' (p. 6). Executing a re-positioning of history, a remapping of a palimpsestic her-story, he sets the 'stories' of his notebook against that history where 'old men blurred and lied' (p. 28). Rejecting any claims to truth, stressing the subjective, story-telling nature of his accounts, Henri becomes reminiscent of what Mills and Pratt have identified as a rejection of any authoritative narrative voice by *female* travellers. Investigating history in previously unexplored sites, he begins to resemble those women travel writers who often made themselves and their houses into what Pratt has called 'privileged sites of political understanding and action' even though official histories were being made on the battlefield (Pratt, 1992, p. 164). Henri thus treks, I believe, to a new fluidity far removed from that conquesting linearity of military expedition and history-making represented by Napoleon to Catherine Clément's more female 'history arranged the way tale-telling women tell it' (Cixous and Clément, 1986, p. 6).

So in *The Passion* imperialism becomes demystified and its legacy in the creation of official culture and history is indeed confronted by a distinctly feminist paradigm. Yet there is more going on here than any simple excavation of the feminine. For the masculine is not banished from *The Passion*. Instead, it is reworked and feminized. The novel makes it clear that the two spheres of 'Soldiers and women' which is 'how the world is' (p. 45) are by no means mutually exclusive, and Henri delights in crossing over the limits between the two. His homesickness aligns him with that female sphere, as he unsettles rigid gender boundaries, hesitating over heterosexuality and explaining that he 'came to women late like [his] father' (p. 12). His abandonment of that male sphere represented by Napoleon consists not only of a rejection of linear travel in favour of a female fluidity, but also of the certainties of strict gender roles for a flux of mixed genders in 'the city of disguises' (p. 49). Here gender is opened to imitation and masquerade and, like most things in watery Venice, is not water-tight after all. Though banned from the boating profession by her gender, Villanelle still 'learned the secret ways of boatmen', and, as 'There aren't many jobs for a girl' (p. 53), she 'cross-dresses for a living' (p. 61). Throughout *The Passion* unstable sexual identities create uncontrollably multiple identifications. Here 'what you are one day will not constrain you on the next' (p. 150), suggesting the possibilities of release offered by the deconstruction of gender.

Although originally wishing to be heroic, following and worshipping Napoleon as 'my own need for a little father . . . had led me this far' (p. 81), Henri's journeys in *The Passion* are ultimately transposed into a yearning for the maternal. He turns increasingly to that feminine sphere represented by his reminiscences of his mother, his travels ultimately leading him away from the father figure and into that pre-Oedipal Venice where he can rediscover the sense of the maternal with Villanelle: 'I had never lain like this with anyone but my mother' (p. 140).

Like *The Passion*, *Sexing the Cherry*, set in the seventeenth and twentieth centuries, is also narrated by two characters – Jordan, the boy-foundling who journeys the world after both the travelling naturalist Tradescant and the elusive dancing Fortunata; and Dog Woman, his gargantuan, bawd-like mother. Clearly in this novel too the mother of the travelling male protagonist is of great significance. Why, then, is this male journeying away from and back to the maternal home becoming a prominent motif in Winterson's work?

In *Sexing the Cherry* the masculine paradigm of representation and travel is largely figured by images of mapping, with cartography's lines of official definitions suggesting colonizing, fixing and categorizing. This model is symbolized by Tradescant, whose name implies all the cant of trade and places him in a lineage committed to collecting and classifying.[9] The journeys he makes are concerned with certainty, with trophy-collecting, 'can be tracked on any map . . . he knows what he's looking for. He wants to bring back rarities and he does' (Winterson, 1990a, p. 101). But, synonymous with narrowness, inflexibility, pedestrianism, maps are negated and it is those journeys normally left unmapped, unrepresented, 'the path not taken and the forgotten angle' (p. 10), which Jordan wishes to trace.

As the narrative progresses, Jordan's longings to be more like Tradescant present him enmeshed in gender expectations which define appropriate masculine and feminine behaviour. Throughout the novel he expresses anxiety at his inability to fulfil that masculine, teleological model of travel represented by Tradescant, whereby 'voyages can be completed. They occupy time comfortably. With some leeway, they are predictable' (p. 102). Like Henri, Jordan is surely more reminiscent of women travellers, in whom, as Pratt argues, 'a curiosity (desire) marked as female is in need of control' (Pratt, 1992, p. 104). Indeed, his travels are infinite and labyrinthine: 'there is no end to even the simplest journey of the mind. I begin, and straight away a hundred alternative routes present themselves' (p. 102).

Unlike those male explorers who often proudly display a coherent and authoritative self, Jordan shatters into a plethora of selves, reminiscent of female travellers' concern with self exhibition and exposure.[10] From the very first page where Jordan 'traced the lineaments of my own face opposite me' (p. 9), the tracking of the palimpsest of his possible selves is delineated as a major theme. Yes these self-seeking journeys do not uncover any unitary male self. Rather he suggests a journeying into self knowledge which is never-ending, discovering a marvellous multiplicity where 'Our lives could be stacked together like plates on a waiter's hand' (p. 91). This, then, is a split subjectivity, similar to Woolf's transgendered Orlando where the 'selves of which we are built up' are 'one on top of another' as 'plates are piled on a waiter's hand' (Woolf, 1977, p. 235). Suggesting that representation and identity do not have to be phallogocentric, Jordan frequently digresses from any coherent account of linear travels, travelling down tangents on the nature of 'reality', time, the self and so forth, situating him closer to those female travellers who used diversions and digressions to authenticate their journeys.[11] *Sexing the Cherry* can even be read in parts as an example of that 'anti-conquest' travel narrative which includes the female gaze (Pratt, 1992, p. 82). Given that the majority of the people Jordan encounters on his travels are female – the Dancing Princesses and so forth – the returning gaze of others now demanding recognition is female, creating that subsequent female voyeurism which Pratt claims frequently 'feminizes' the male explorer (Pratt, 1992, p. 82).

Jordan is further associated with the escape from linear time, re-presenting time as a turning globe instead of that mapping which attempts to name, categorize and fix Otherness. Encountering a town where buildings are 'never in the same place from one day to the next' (p. 42), and a floating city with no floors or gravity, where 'everyone . . . learned to be acrobats' and 'used their town as a raft to travel' (pp. 96–7), his feminization finally extends into his dissolution of space and matter.[12] These fluid, air-borne towns, like the Venice of *The Passion*, figure alternative models of language and representation. Yet it is again necessary to stress why these reconceptual-izations of self, time and space should be viewed as specifically feminine. What does it mean, for instance, for a feminized male to lose the unitary self? What are the political implications of such multiplicity? What we are witnessing is the female unsettling of male-identified selfhood which many French feminist writers have theorized. Such a positive fragmentation represents an allowance, perhaps, for Jordan to 'speak (as) woman', to escape from Irigaray's 'prison within which the (masculine) subject must define himself? (Sellers, 1991, p. 137), and to embark on a distinctly female form of fluid travel. Similarly, as Jordan journeys into the flowing overlapping of lives across time as his twentieth-century reincarnation Nicholas Jordan, the male dissection and compartmentalization of linear time is transposed into a fluxing time travel, a fluidity of visions. As flashbacks explode chronological time, we seem to be witnessing Irma Garcia's 'Hors-temps', the 'times-outside-time' situated on time's fringes (1989, p. 177). Arriving in history vibrantly, across centuries, 'over and over again', Jordan can be read as an example of Cixous' 'new history' of woman, 'a process of becoming in which several histories intersect with one another', which 'is always in several places at once' (Forman and Sowton, 1989, p. 177; Cixous, in Cixous and Clément, 1986, p. 160).

Yet can such strategies really be read as a radicalization, or are we still ensnared in gender binaries? This is an issue which the endlessly journeying Fortunata articulates, as she wonders whether 'if she travelled … like a hero', she would 'find something different' from 'the great division' of 'heroes and … homemakers' or discover instead 'the old things in different disguises?' (*Sexing the Cherry*, p. 131). These musings point to the most prominent question that preoccupies Winterson's work. Can a playing with or reversal of gender rules and roles really effect a genuine deconstruction of the male/female binary? Can it enable a mixed-gendered identity? Having argued for Jordan's alternative cartography and subsequent feminization, I want to suggest that *Sexing the Cherry* develops that project begun in *The Passion*, as the feminine is excavated so as to allow free play with the masculine.

In this respect, the imagery of grafting serves as a particularly poignant representation. For not only was the seventeenth century the great era of cartographical representation, it was also the period of naturalist explorations and experiments. This is one of the tropes Winterson takes as a way of further interrogating concepts of sexing, for Jordan's gender-bending and departures from traditional paradigms of exploration are further hinted at by his alignment with the naturalist's travels. No one perhaps epitomized the concepts of natural history in this period more than Linnaeus, who attempted a classificatory system of all flora based on the letters of the alphabet and on sexuality, with all plant types categorized according to their reproductive parts. This may be the model of natural history's travels, representations and gendering suggested by Tradescant. But Jordan appears far closer to that naturalist figure who, as Pratt has pointed out, 'often has a certain androgyny' (Pratt, 1992, p. 33).[13] Natural history's projects, continues Pratt, possessed 'some decidedly non-phallic aspects', and here Winterson associates Jordan with these gender-transgressive potentialities. It has been claimed by some that the very word 'homosexual' originated from experiments in the fertilization of flowers (Bristow, 1992, p. 3), and here botany becomes a matter of crossing and mixing genders, similarly hinted at in *The Passion* by Henri and Josephine's shared botanical interest.

Whereas the model of Adam which Linnaeus' system followed was one set in the primordial garden before Eve arrived, here the feminine becomes part of Jordan's gender blending. Gender is (re)rendered as shifting and complex, and grafting is 'an art' which Jordan wishes 'I might apply to myself' (*Sexing the Cherry*, p. 78). Illustrating 'the location within oneself of the presence of both sexes', Jordan exhibits exactly that 'springing up of selves one didn't know' which Cixous attributes to 'the I/play of bisexuality' (Cixous, 1986, p. 84). This feminization of masculinity has resulted, it seems, in a bisexuality which is based on a free play of identities and heterogeneous desires associated with *femininity*, for even though Jordan's cherry tree 'had not been born from seed' it 'would still be female' (p. 79).

Even more so than in *The Passion*, such a feminizing engenders a yearning after the maternal. Thinking it might make him 'a hero after all' (*Sexing the Cherry*, p. 100), Jordan's journeying is initiated by the sight of that phallic signifier, the banana, his travels an attempt 'to return to that memory, to release whatever it had begun in me' (p. 100). But throughout the text, that phallic banana symbol is actually equated with Dog Woman, and Jordan is represented by the more female pineapple; thus Winterson unsettles signifiers of gendered identity. For although initially travelling after Tradescant, whose own 'father was a hero before him' (p. 101), Jordan's yearning travels avoid becoming implicated in the possession and exploitation of colonialism's discourse. Although he ends up eternally travelling across time with Nicholas Jordan resolving that he 'would find' Fortunata's reincarnation, the book closes with Dog Woman's fleeting image of Fortunata disappearing from Jordan's side – 'she vanished and there was nothing next to Jordan but empty space' – making clear that this questing is not aiming for capture and appropriation. Just as in *The Passion* Henri negates paradigms of heterosexual desire and the male model of control of the Other, so Jordan's explorations are more concerned with discovering a reciprocal love and desire to be wanted by both Fortunata and Dog Woman.[14] As such, he represents Pratt's interactive narratives of 'anti-conquest' which consist 'of attempts to achieve reciprocity' between self and others, or 'to endure its absence' (Pratt, 1992, p. 81). Hence Jordan explains that he is not like Tradescant, for whom 'being a hero comes naturally'. Instead he simply wants his mother 'to ask me to stay, just as now I want Fortunata to ask me to stay. Why do they not?' (*Sexing the Cherry*, p. 101).

For Irigaray, identity is a male concept used to make sense of men's necessary separation from their mothers. Claiming that women have a closer relation to their mothers then men, she argues for the possibility of a female identity that is 'unrecognized, unknown, unthought, as are reciprocity, fluidity, exchange' (Holmlund, 1991). As we have seen, becoming feminized and positing the maternal over masculinity, Henri and Jordan resemble Barthes' transgressive son who plays with the body of the mother (Suleiman, 1990). Travel, therefore, becomes an attempted entry into some kind of utopian space, a conceptual territory of the future, a terrain on which notions of sexual identity are challenged. The *progression* of Winterson's playings-with-genders is now becoming clearer, tropes of travel in her work serving as increasing attempts to escape from, to reconceptualize, gender. Yet these two earlier novels apparently did not go far enough, for in *Written on the Body* she attempts to establish what happens if the very mark of sex is lost.

Narrated by an ungendered, bisexual, Lothario-like character, *Written on the Body* tells a tale of love and loss as the beloved Louise is diagnosed with cancer. Whereas much of the text reads like the narrator's intimate journal of numerous seductions, the novel's middle sections mimic a medical text book, divided into various bodily parts. Here we reach the height of Winterson's sexualization of journeying, for her travel tropes are now figured as specifically bodily explorations by the narrator. The unearthing of the feminine is accomplished via a celebratory reclamation of the female body. The almost neurotic, fixated yearning to hold on to Louise is figured at times in terms of anatomical possession and penetration as the narrator 'didn't only want Louise's flesh' but also 'wanted her bones, her blood, her tissues, the sinews that bound her together' (pp. 50–1). A common reaction to *Written on the Body* has consequently been the claim that Winterson is simply presenting a tale of unpleasant obsessional exploration of the Other.[15] Yet I find it hard to believe that she would suddenly contradict and negate what appears to be a central intention by replicating heterosexual patterns of travel, exploration and desire. Tropes of travel in *Written on the Body* are once again unconcerned with any conquest or possession of femininity. Instead, they enact a feminizing as, rather than backtracking on her previous works, in *Written on the Body* Winterson continues along the same trajectory, initially following masculine models only to reject them in favour of more feminine paradigms.

The use of a bisexual, ungendered narrator undoubtedly suggests that this novel is her most radical attempt to escape from both sex and gender. Yet the controversy and criticism with which *Written on the Body* has been met is largely due to this very character.[16] I want to offer my own interpretations of this contentious figure, in particular suggesting that although Winterson's narrator is not simply portrayed as a lesbian, s/he still fulfils distinctly lesbian aims. As such, s/he is an example of what Zimmerman has identified as the 'deconstruction' of the lesbian as an 'essentialist ... being' and 'the reconstruction of her as a ... subject position' (1992, quoted in Palmer, 1993, p. 30). Winterson's reasons for using an ungendered, bisexual character are, I believe, similar to Monique Wittig's arguments in *The Straight Mind*. For just as Wittig aligns the sign 'lesbian' with neither masculinity nor femininity, so too it is possible to view Winterson's genderless narrator as an attempted escape from the effects of gender dichotomies. For Wittig, the 'imposition of gender' denies women 'any claim to the abstract, philosophical, political discourses that give shape to the social body' (Wittig, 1992, p. 81). Ambiguously and provocatively ungendered, the narrator of *Written on the Body* is free to pick and plunder varying masculine discourses, especially dissecting and analysing the language of medicine and exploration. Her/his narratorial position surely resembles Wittig's arguments that the 'refusal to become (or to remain) heterosexual always meant to refuse to become a man or a woman' (Wittig, 1992, p. 81). For not only does the narrator negate the traditional role of woman as passive object of exploration by following masculine paradigms, but also, in ultimately rejecting such models in favour of reciprocity, s/he becomes an almost perfect illustration of Wittig's claim that lesbianism is far more than 'a refusal of the role "woman"; it is also the refusal of the economic, ideological, and political power of a man' (Wittig, 1992, p. 81). The absence of any declaration of gender is not suggesting that gender has no power, but rather that gender dichotomies can be upset,[17] as that trajectory of mixed-gendered bisexuality I have been following from Villanelle's cross-dressing to Jordan's grafting meets its apotheosis.

So in *Written on the Body*, Winterson puts the very concept of 'woman' under erasure and displaces the phallic body and subject (of exploration, of medicine, and of language) with a lesbian body and subject founded on reciprocity. This displacement is achieved by the use of tropes of bodily journeys and explorations. The narrator's excursions into Louise's body are not reiterations of masculine penetrative pioneering into passive, idealized femaleness. Instead they are an instance of Catharine Stimpson's claim that lesbianism 'represents a commitment of skin, blood, breast and bone' (1982, p. 244, quoted in Duncker, 1986, p. 169). For the 'cocked and ready to fire' female body explored here is as highly-charged as Emily Dickinson's 'Loaded Gun',[18] the 'thin white smoke' of orgasm set in opposition to that clinical body posited by medical discourse with 'what doctors like to call the olfactory nerves' (*Written on the Body*, p. 136). Ultimately Winterson's narrator analyses and parodies paradigms of anatomical investigation only to reject them. S/he tries to 'embalm' Louise 'in [her/his] memory', to 'hook out' her 'brain through ... accommodating orifices'. But although stating 'Now that I have lost you I cannot allow you to develop, you must be a photograph not a poem' (p. 119), s/he finally rejects the masculine, clinical, dissecting language of male science. 'Within the clinical language, through the dispassionate view of the sucking, sweating, greedy, defecating self', s/he finds 'a love-poem to Louise' (p. 111). Following the trajectories of medical exploration to find that 'The logical paths the proper steps led nowhere' (p. 92), the linearity of attempted penetration and possession becomes refigured in imagery reminiscent of Winterson's labyrinthine towns and interior cities rich with pluralities of interpretation: 'My mind took me up tortuous staircases that opened into doors that opened into nothing' (p. 92).

If, then, travel tropes of anatomy are rejected, what does Winterson offer in their place? The answer lies in patterns of journeying which, as in the two earlier novels, remap the old mythic, heterosexual structure of desire where woman as sexual Other is the goal of the quest. Negating the heterosexism of medical discourse which has no space for lesbian desire – 'No, it doesn't come under the heading Reproduction. I have no desire to reproduce but I still seek out love' (p. 108) – exploration only leads to a reciprocal lesbian desire, a female sexuality theorized by Irigaray where individuality and singularity are meaningless. Instead of the linear goal-orientated plot of traditional treasure hunts, the narrator has no investment in any simple taking or conquest of the Other, giving her/his self as a source of pleasure: 'you will redraw me according to your will. We shall cross one another's boundaries and make ourselves one nation. Scoop me in your hands for I am good soil' (p. 20). The alliance between Self and Other becomes so strong that disease too becomes dual; hence the initial discovery of Louise's cancer leads to the narrator's own bodily disintegration as 'my body slithers away' (p. 101). Ultimately s/he can only plead, in the lyrical language of love poetry, to be rescued from the battlefield of anatomy's discourse: 'Do you see me in my blood-soaked world? Green-eyed girl, eyes wide apart like almonds, come in tongues of flame and restore my sight' (p. 139).

Judith Mayne has argued that one of lesbianism's 'strategically important' functions lies in the problem it poses for representation, questioning its
'alignment of masculinity with activity and femininity with passivity'
(Mayne, 1991, p. 127). These are precisely those gendered binaries which
Winterson's travel tropes disrupt. Deconstructing the category of the lesbian
Other, Winterson suggests that lesbian narrative has no investment in
conventional travel writing's avoidance of similarity between authoring Self
and unauthorized Other.[19] The efforts to penetrate and write Louise's body
entail making the narrator's own body into the text: 'Your hand prints are all
over my body.... You deciphered me and now I am plain to read' (p. 106).
In contrast to traditional male writing of the female body as something
penetrable, knowable and possessable, this is no simple translation of body
into text, of sexuality into textuality. The 'body' of the title which is 'written
on' is that of the narrator, 'translated' by Louise's 'reading hands' into 'her
own book' (p. 89). But any revelation is only of a reciprocity which is written
on the body, and which even then consists of a 'palimpsest', 'a secret code'
like 'braille' beneath the surface. This, then, is a release from the stultifying
binary of heterosexual authoring and narrative, resulting in a similar effect
to Cixous' 'other bisexuality': 'starting with this "permission" one gives
oneself, the multiplication of the effects of desire's inscription on every part
of the body and the other body' (Cixous, 1986, p. 85).

Detonating medical discourse, the lesbian body produces its own
innovative narrative, an excess best symbolized in the final scene of *Written
on the Body*. Although set in a microcosm – 'The world is bundled up in this
room' (p. 190) – it is a microcosm which erupts, as if lesbian desire cannot
be confined: 'The walls are exploding' (p. 190). Since the novel 'closes' (if
it can be said to do so) in circularity, *Written on the Body* becomes an
especially literal illustration of that spiralling return to the beginning so
favoured by female travellers: 'This is where the story starts, in this
threadbare room' (p. 190). In an ambiguous, infinite, open-endedness, we are
left with the image of the two female lovers embarking on another never-
ending journey as the lesbian subjects exchange the castrated space of
erasure for a never-ending horizon of desire. Travel finally figures not that
male sexuality which 'only inscribes itself within frontiers', figured as 'Loss'
which 'comes back to him as profit', but rather that female sexuality
characterized by Cixous, where woman is 'not the being-of-the-end (the
goal)', but 'is able not to return to herself, never settling down, pouring out,
going everywhere to the other' (Cixous, in Cixous and Clément, 1986, p. 87).
This may not be the traditionally assured 'happy ending' for, as Lynne Pearce
has claimed, the reason for the prominence of journeying in lesbian works

may be the fact that romantic love between women is without the possibility of institutional legislation, the 'bid for unity' thus 'permanently set against a sense of invisibility, transience and exile' (Pearce, 1990). One thing, however, is certain – that Winterson's reworkings of travel tropes have ensured that this will be a decidedly female journeying, a wandering into an expansion rich with possibilities of swaggering dual travel:

> Beyond the door, where the river is, where the roads are, we shall be. We can take the world with us when we go and sling the sun under your arm. Hurry now, it's getting late. I don't know if this is a happy ending but here we are let loose in open fields. (*Written on the Body*, p. 190)

Winterson's fiction thus provides innovative and seductive decodings and recodings of mixed gendered and fluid identities, achieved, as I hope I have illustrated, by recurrent journeys – often back to the maternal – which effect a feminization of male travelling characters. I would suggest that future explorations of Winterson's writings need to engage with the tropes of travel which uphold her (re)formulations of gendered identities and sexual difference. In this way, her fiction could provide insights into what a distinctly lesbian aesthetic may look like, suggesting potential figurations of an enduring lesbian battle with gender binaries. It would, for example, be useful to question whether she is experimenting with a lesbian use of bisexuality as a subject position and narrative tactic to escape from heterosexual gendering. Future research could thus question the interaction of bisexual and lesbian subject positions, considering the ways that dissident sexualities engender new configurations of narrative practice and textuality.

The centrality of travel in Winterson's work further suggests that we are witnessing the emergence of a definite tradition of journeying in lesbian texts. Given that belief systems such as that of 'the natural' map social orders on to domains of human experience such as sexuality, demarcating acceptable and unacceptable behaviour, it is not surprising to find that travelling to a new land plays a prominent role in lesbian aesthetics.[20] I believe that Winterson's use of travel represents an interrogation of that map of meaning which places heterosexuality at the centre. Her reworkings of travel paradigms ultimately lead us to that distinctly lesbian desire which does not circumscribe the realms of exploration, but rather opens up space and breaks down boundaries, as in *Written on the Body*: 'You set before me a space uncluttered by association. It might be a void or it might be a release. Certainly I want to take the risk' (p. 81). Although the prominence of such a trope in lesbian writing may have negative connotations of exile and exclusion, it also surely suggests a more positive freedom. In this way, it becomes possible to consider the forms a lesbian emancipation from patriarchy, heterosexuality and gender binaries may take. A reading of Winterson's metaphorics of travel could expand into a wider consideration of movement as metaphor, countering the tendency of literary criticism as yet to avoid any real analysis of metaphor which, as Irigaray has argued, is by definition elusive. To interpret a metaphor may be to close off the play of meaning it sets into motion, but by proffering many possible meanings, an interactive practice of feminist literary criticism could genuinely engage with the pleasure of Winterson's work.

Notes

1 The controversy surrounding Winterson is too vast to examine in depth here. Numerous arguments have raged in the media recently concerning Winterson's self-promotion and apparent arrogance. I do not have the space – or the intention – to establish just how much of this public persona is based on an ironic, camp mocking of the literary establishment. I believe there is little doubt, however, that Winterson's reception is inextricably bound up with issues of gender, sexualities and authorship, and remind the reader here of Nicci Gerrard's point that although Martin Amis has expressed a desire 'to be remembered in the same breath as Shakespeare . . . no one says that he is mad' (Gerrard, 1994).

2 I take this term to refer to what critics have variously named the 'novel of development', 'novel of formation' or 'apprentice novel'.

3 See also Pearce, 1994; Wisker, 1994.

4 See, for example, Claire Messud's interview with Winterson in the *Guardian*, 26 August 1992.

5 For further discussion of the reception of the televised *Oranges Are Not The Only Fruit*, see Hinds, 1992, and Wisker, 1994.

6 These points are also made by Judy Giles, who has argued that 'Winterson's texts, of course, invite the reader to explore how rather than what they mean and make it difficult to impose a single meaning'. (Giles, 1991).

7 For further discussion of such de-centring see Hinds, 1992.

8 Similarly, in 'Women's Time', Julia Kristeva has spoken of the need both for woman's '*insertion* into history and the radical *refusal* of the subjective limitations imposed by this history's time' (Kristeva, 1989, p. 198).

9 His father, also John Tradescant, established the Musaeum Tradescantium in Lambeth, London, and father and son were memorialized by Linnaeus, who named the flowering plant genus Tradescantia after them.

10 Such concerns about displaying the self are well illustrated, for example, by Sarah Lee, the author of *Stories of Strange Lands and Fragments from the Notes of a Traveller* (1835) who complains in her introduction: 'The number of I's that I have scratched out, the sentences that have been turned and twisted, to avoid this provoking monosyllable, almost surpass belief' (Pratt, 1992, p. 107).

11 Frequently women travellers also remarked on the way the narrator must seem to the native peoples of countries they visited. When Jordan is surrounded by women while disguised as a woman, it is he who is made to feel as alienated and de-territorialized as women normally are under what Dale Spender has termed 'man-made language': 'In my petticoats I was a traveller in a foreign country. I did not speak the language. I was regarded with suspicion' (Winterson, 1990a, p. 31).

12 Pratt has argued that in *women's* travel accounts towns and rooms become allegories of the female explorer's 'subjective and relational states' (Pratt, 1992, p. 159). In Winterson's texts, on the one hand there is the imagery of buildings, houses and towns, but on the other – and subverting the fixity and sense of place of the architectural imagery – is the imagery of travel. Whereas the imagery of habitations is often related to metaphors for single, unified methods which build an organized knowledge and representation, here travel imagery represents fluidity and a concern with the production of such ordering systems.

13 Both John Tradescants were, after all, memorialized by none other than Linnaeus (see note 9 above).

14 Indeed, refiguring patriarchal history – which, as characterized by Cixous, depends on 'the distinction between the Selfsame' and the 'Other' (Cixous, 1986, p. 70) – *The Passion* effects an innovative experimenting with patterns of desire. The linearity informing masculine paradigms of conquest where the male Self quests after the female Other emerges here through the analogy of the military campaign, with all its repercussions of heterosexuality's penetrations and withdrawals. In Venice, however, desire becomes figured as a mysterious, fluid travel with no final possession. Villanelle's masquerades enable her to confound gender dichotomies and follow her lesbian desire which, after all, Kristeva has described as 'the operation of a cross-gendered masquerade' (Roof, 1991, p. 49). In rejecting Napoleon in favour of Villanelle, Henri too negates paradigms of heterosexual desire and posits female paradigms over that male model of control of the Other, finally realizing that 'I am in love with her; not a fantasy or a myth or a creature of my own making. Her. A person who is not me. I invented Bonaparte as much as he invented himself' (Winterson, 1988, pp. 157–8). Hence, ironically exiled on an island like Napoleon, Henri ends up with no interest in that naming and appropriation linking the traditional dynamics of travel, history and representation and explains of the bird that becomes his pet in prison, 'I won't give it a name. I'm not Adam' (p. 156). By the end of the novel, he prefers the female world of love, compassion and support to that of the male military: 'If we had the courage to love we would not so value these acts of war' (p. 154).

15 See, for example, Smith, 1992; Hughes-Hallett, 1992; Miner, 1993.

16 Hence, for example, Valerie Miner has claimed that although initially 'the concealment of [the narrator's] sex forecasts interesting theoretical questions about essentialism', Winterson fails to 'carry these identity questions beyond the gimmick' (Miner, 1993).

17 I remind the reader here of Judith Roof's arguments that it is possible to perform a masculine persona without necessarily accepting it (Roof, 1991).
18 I refer here to Emily Dickinson's poem, 'My Life Has Stood A Loaded Gun'.
19 Consequently, the narrator further negates conventional travel writing's model of representation which, as Jon Stratton has pointed out, 'requires a separation, requires two entities to be distinct' (Stratton, 1990, p. 10).
20 See, for example, Wittig, 1989; Cruikshank, 1980; the film *Desert Hearts*; and Miner, 1982.

References

BRIGGS, BARRIE (1994) Letter to the *Guardian*, *Guardian Weekend*, 25 June.
BRISTOW, JOSEPH (Ed.) (1992) *Sexualism Sameness: Textual Differences in Lesbian and Gay Writing*, London, Routledge.
CIXOUS, HÉLÈNE (1986) 'Sorties', *The Newly Born Woman*, Manchester, Manchester University Press.
CRUIKSHANK, MARGARET (Ed.) (1980) *The Lesbian Path*, Monterey, Angel Press.
DUNCKER, PATRICIA (1986) *Sisters and Strangers: An Introduction to Contemporary Feminist Fiction*, Oxford, Blackwell.
FORMAN, FRIEDA JOHLES with SOWTON, CAORAN (Eds) (1989) *Taking Our Time: Feminist Perspectives on Temporality*, Oxford, Pergamon.
GARCIA, IRMA (1989) 'Femalear Explorations: Temporality in Women's Writing', in FORMAN, FRIEDA JOHLES with SOWTON, CAORAN (Eds) *Taking Our Time*, Oxford, Pergamon.
GERRARD, NICCI (1994) 'The Ultimate Self-Produced Woman', *The Independent on Sunday*, 5 June.
GILES, JUDY (1991) 'Storytelling and Identity in Jeanette Winterson's *Oranges Are Not The Only Fruit* and *The Passion*', University of Ripon and York St. John, unpublished essay.
GRIFFIN, GABRIELE (1993) *Heavenly Love?: Lesbian Images in Twentieth-century Women's Writing*, Manchester and New York, Manchester University Press.
HENSHER, PHILIP (1994) 'Sappho's Mate', *Guardian*, 5 July.
HINDS, HILARY (1992) '*Oranges Are Not The Only Fruit*: Reaching Audiences Other Lesbian Texts Cannot Reach', in MUNT, SALLY (Ed.) *New Lesbian Criticism: Literary and Cultural Readings*, Hemel Hempstead, Harvester Wheatsheaf.
HOLMLUND, CHRISTINE (1991) 'The Lesbian, the Mother, the Heterosexual Lover: Irigaray's Recodings of Difference', *Feminist Studies*, 17 (2), Summer.
IRIGARAY, LUCE (1985a) *Speculum of the Other Woman*, trans. Gillian C. Gill, Ithaca, Cornell University Press.
IRIGARAY, LUCE (1985b) *This Sex Which Is Not One*, trans. Catherine Porter with Carolyn Burke, Ithaca, Cornell University Press.
JACKSON, ROSEMARY (1981) *Fantasy*, London, Methuen.

KRISTEVA, JULIA (1989) 'Women's Time', in BELSEY, CATHERINE and MOORE, JANE (Eds) *The Feminist Reader*, Basingstoke, Macmillan.

The Late Show (1994) 'Face to Face', BBC2, 24 June.

LECLERC, ANNIE (1990; original publication 1974) 'Woman's Word', in CAMERON, DEBORAH (Ed.) *The Feminist Critique of Language*, London, Routledge.

MAYNE, JUDITH (1991) 'Lesbian Looks: Dorothy Arzner and the Female Authorship', in BAD OBJECT-CHOICES (Eds) *How Do I Look: Queer Film and Video*, Seattle, Bay Press.

MILLS, SARA (1991) *Discourses of Difference*, London, Routledge.

MINER, VALERIE (1982) *Movement*, The Crossing Press (reprinted London, Methuen).

MINER, VALERIE (1993) 'At Her Wit's End', *The Women's Review of Books*, April.

PALMER, PAULINA (1993) *Contemporary Lesbian Fiction: Dreams, Desire, Difference*, Milton Keynes, Open University Press.

PEARCE, LYNNE (1990) 'Jane Eyre Eat Your Heart Out: Jeanette Winterson's Re-reading of Romantic Love in *Oranges Are Not The Only Fruit*' (unpublished essay).

PEARCE, LYNNE (1994) *Reading Dialogics*, London, Edward Arnold.

PRATT, MARY LOUISE (1992) *Imperial Eyes: Travel Writing and Transculturation*, London, Routledge.

RICH, ADRIENNE (1980) 'Compulsory Heterosexuality and Lesbian Existence', *Signs*, Vol. 5, No. 4.

ROBERTS, MICHELE (1994) 'Words Are Not The Only Art', *The Independent on Sunday*, 19 June.

ROOF, JUDITH (1991) *A Lure of Knowledge: Lesbian Sexuality and Theory*, New York, Columbia University Press.

SELLERS, SUSAN (1991) *Language and Sexual Difference*, Basingstoke, Macmillan.

SMITH, JOAN (1992) 'Grazed Anatomy', *The Independent on Sunday*, 12 July.

STIMPSON, CATHARINE R. (1982) 'Zero Degree Deviancy: The Lesbian Novel in English', in ABEL, ELIZABETH (Ed.) *Writing and Sexual Difference*, Brighton, Harvester.

STRATTON, JON (1990) *Writing Sites*, Hemel Hempstead, Harvester Wheatsheaf.

SULEIMAN, SUSAN RUBIN (1990) 'Mothers and the Avant-Garde: A Case of Mistaken Identity?' in ROSSUM-GUYON, FRANCOISE VAN (Ed.) *Avant Garde (Femmes, Frauen, Women)* Vol. 4.

WARD JOUVE, NICOLE (1991) *White Woman Speaks With Forked Tongue*, London, Routledge.

WINTERSON, JEANETTE (1988) *The Passion*, London, Penguin.

WINTERSON, JEANETTE (1990a) *Sexing the Cherry*, London, Vintage.

WINTERSON, JEANETTE (1990b) 'Unnatural Passions', *Spare Rib*, No. 209 (February), p. 26–9.

WINTERSON, JEANETTE (1990c) 'Foreword' in REYNOLDS, MARGARET (Ed.) *Erotica*, London, Pandora.

WINTERSON, JEANETTE (1992) *Written on the Body*, London, Jonathan Cape.

WINTERSON, JEANETTE (1994a) *Art and Lies*, London, Jonathan Cape.

WINTERSON, JEANETTE (1994b) *Great Moments in Aviation*, London, Vintage.

WISKER, GINA (Ed.) (1994) *It's My Party: Reading Twentieth Century Women's Writing*, London, Pluto.

WITTIG, MONIQUE (1989) *Across the Acheron*, London, The Women's Press.

WITTIG, MONIQUE (1992) *The Straight Mind and Other Essays*, Hemel Hempstead, Harvester Wheatsheaf.

WOOLF, VIRGINIA (1977) *Orlando*, London, Grafton.

ZIMMERMAN, BONNIE (1992) 'Lesbians Like This and That: Some Notes on Lesbian Criticism for the Nineties', in MUNT, SALLY (Ed.) *New Lesbian Criticism*, Hemel Hempstead, Harvester Wheatsheaf.

Chapter 10

Lesbian Studies: An Opportunity Not To Be Missed

Patsy Staddon

As Lesbian Studies makes its appearance, whether as an independent study area or as a module in first and higher degree courses in Women's Studies or Cultural Studies, an almost unique opportunity presents itself. Surely academic arrogance will not continue to assume that the basis and structure of such a subject area, let alone criteria for its assessment, may be devised solely by the academic body politic? Surely news of such feminist approaches as student-centred learning, and participatory and collective study, has by now permeated Senate Committees? Is this not the (long-delayed) moment when it becomes accepted that no one of us can be an expert as to another woman's life, nor fit to judge her account of it, nor able to instruct her as to her own experiences, much less to grade her accounts of them? Lesbians, after all, are known for being argumentative, even uncooperative. Surely we will not allow Lesbian Studies to become another plastic construction, inappropriately devised and assessed, of what women's experience of life is really like? Or will we all watch, in helpless fascination, as the study area most likely to incorporate politics and lifestyle, using the most innovative and grounded of methods, fizzles away into Gender Studies, Sexuality Studies, and Lesbian and Gay Studies, as structured and predictable and orderly as any establishment might wish?

A Background to the Development of Lesbian Studies

As long ago as 1982, Maggie Humm pointed out that feminists 'must attack the *processes* of knowledge transmission, attack academic production and reproduction itself and its fallacious concepts of "courses" and assessment'. She asserted then that for feminist systems to develop within institutions, it was necessary for feminist academics to 'start with each student's intentions rather than offering their own, tightly organised programmes of study'. Students might design their own course, while staff acted as resources. Consideration of the content of courses was of no use unless structures were also altered to fit a feminist agenda. In 1987, she wrote of her own use, at the North East London Polytechnic, of such learning and accreditation techniques as the writing by students of autobiographies, as part of their course planning, in a contract system of learning.

Further attention was given to these issues in 1990, when Ellen Rooney drew attention to the problems involved in the application of feminist theory to the actual production of knowledge. If this production were interrogated, the progress of Cultural Studies would be hindered; yet, if the construction of theory were resisted, and politics compromised, Cultural and Women's Studies were likely to be assimilated into the disciplinary structure of the University (Rooney, 1990).

That these problems remained unresolved, and politically smouldering, was acknowledged by Dawn Currie recently. She felt that, despite the postmodernist celebration of multiplicity, a failure to theorize race, class, and gender has led to unaddressed questions as to power within the academic system (Currie, 1993). Such questions may well have been debated within that system, but there is little sign of action having been taken in many Women's Studies courses to deal with issues of authority, assessment, and basic structure; nor have I yet seen an awareness of them in the development of Lesbian and Gay Studies. For example, at one university, as a higher degree course is proposed in Women's Studies, frequent repetitions of the term 'feminist' in the description of the course modules does not prevent the methods of teaching from being described as 'methods of instruction' and there is no mention whatever of such feminist approaches to learning as those referred to by Humm. Another university, planning a Lesbian and Gay Sexuality module dealing with the sociological and political perspectives of sexuality, expects its teaching methods to consist of lectures and seminars, while assessment techniques will consist of coursework and an examination. The political perspectives referred to appear not to have been applied to the construction of the course!

Lesbian Studies does not merely offer us a second opportunity to explode such traditional academic approaches as those in which an expert in her subject instructs a group of students who are less expert. It presents us with the necessity of so doing. The essence of being lesbian is the experience of being other than the expected norm, and the woman who sets herself up as an expert in such a field is rash indeed. Equally, the employment of skill-sharing needs to be prioritized, as does that of mutual assessment, with no lesbian accepting an academic situation which implies her superior knowledge in the area of, say, lesbian lifestyle. This would, admittedly, be something of an extension of Liz Stanley's suggestion that students, at least in part, might be seen as co-producers (Stanley, 1990, p. 6). She has also addressed the academic dichotomy, for the feminist, whereby 'the known are also the knowers ... divisions between students and teachers ... are ... neither simple nor absolute' (*ibid.*, p. 11). With due credit given to these and to other thinkers, it does seem to me that facilitation would appear to be the skill of the future, in this as in many other departments, with a far more fluid approach brought to the issues of course construction, experience and accreditation.

Changing the Structures

For the purposes of this chapter, the definition of feminism which I should like to apply is that of Adrienne Rich: 'feminism is the place where in the most natural, organic way subjectivity and politics have to come together' (Gelpi and Gelpi, 1975, p. 114). Traditional ways of constructing, producing, packaging and distributing knowledge have long made it more difficult for women to own information about themselves and their history. Cathy Lubelska has already drawn attention to the incongruity of developing new 'knowledge' in Women's Studies, without paying attention to the methodology. Consequently, 'the methods which we employ in our teaching remain, by and large, traditional, mainstream and oddly incongruous with our goals' (Lubelska, 1991, p. 41).

For those of us constructing an area called 'Lesbian Studies', there is not only the opportunity, but the absolute requirement, to define not only what we will study, but how we will study it. The development and interpretation of lesbian awareness is unlikely to be served or suited by the implementation of traditional – i.e. male-oriented – teaching and grading methods, so long bedevilling Women's Studies courses. This is a difficult problem for women who are making their careers in the academic, and male-defined, world. It is hard enough to challenge the content of degrees and research, without declaring the very structures of the system, within which one is gainfully employed, to be inimical to the intellectual development of women. Consequently, it is understandable that anxious voices have been raised, within my hearing at least, by lesbians in different departments of different universities, to affirm the importance of conforming to existing practices, lest

Lesbian Studies not be taken seriously as a discipline. The fear seems to be that if we are not careful, 'too many' lesbians will 'qualify'; 'academic standards' may not be upheld; dare one suggest, careers may not after all be pursued to such advantage? There seems to be some desire to pull up the drawbridge.

Escaping the Dilemma?

Some women have suggested that what should happen is the development of less academic, yet empowering courses, open to all lesbians, to run separately from universities' more academic first and higher degree modules. Something of the sort has already been done, for example, in London, where it has been possible to attend courses in Lesbian History and in Lesbian Culture, at community centres and at Birkbeck College, for interest only, or to follow a course leading to the Certificate in Applied Women's Studies, which includes courses on lesbian issues.

During the spring term of 1994, in Bristol, I set up two short contrasting courses in Lesbian Studies, since research among fellow lesbians had appeared to suggest that some women greatly disliked the idea of academic learning, but still wanted to learn, in an informal setting, more about being lesbian. Others still were keen to see the magical words 'Lesbian Studies' appear as soon and as frequently as possible in academic literature, and were eager to see formal courses set up. One of the courses was formally structured, and took place at the University of Bristol; this was entitled 'An Introduction to Lesbian Studies'. The other course, called 'Alternative Lesbian Studies', took place in a local community centre, and was to be constructed and planned by the women present, possibly with speakers being invited, as was the case on the university course.

There is, on the surface of it, no harm in such schemes, although it is true that funding is increasingly difficult to find for courses which do not lead to some form of accreditation; of this, more later. But I came to realize, as the term progressed, that such a division is not the ideal answer, as far as Lesbian Studies are concerned. Anything which could be seen as a two-tier system of lesbian education will not only anger and alienate the majority of the community, but will also create a completely inaccurate picture of what lesbian culture and politics are about. In other words, *it will not be academically valid.*

We are not considering the development of a subject with no political implications – if indeed such a subject exists. In my view, Lesbian Studies may appropriately be used, as Women's Studies might have been, in the liberation of a less empowered group in society, and it is not likely that structures which were put in place to facilitate the holding together of that society will be appropriate for study in this instance. Lesbian Studies is most certainly a challenge to a patriarchal system, and it is a denial of its power and identity to attempt to limit its thought and achievements by the imposition of academic structures evolved for the benefit of such a system, and already discredited by feminism. This remains the case even when such structures, incredibly, seem to remain largely unchallenged in Women's Studies courses. Lesbian, and also heterosexual, academics have to deal with this now, or face the contempt of later generations of women. We can no longer afford to design and offer courses whose content is fixed, and whose culmination is to be an examination, since this method of assessment involves the assumption by some women of greater knowledge and awareness of the subjective experience of other women.

New Alternatives

What, then, are the alternatives on offer? Are there alternatives which can be produced confidently and with pride whether within an academic context or outside it? How can being a lesbian be studied and assessed, in such a way that we do not end up in the situation of some organizers of Women's Studies courses: with disillusioned feminist students leaving the course half way through, while course administrators and tutors continue to practise outdated, discredited, and ineffective methods?

Facilitation has appeared to be the most useful skill to date. The meaning and experience of being lesbian will be different for every woman on every course, and a rich and varied forum for learning can be very quickly created by doing little more than rearranging seating to form a circle. New ways of learning and presenting soon emerge, satisfactory to students and 'teachers' alike.

By what appears to be a happy coincidence, the emergence of Lesbian Studies has been accompanied, in Britain, by a government economy which could make very much easier the adoption of such new philosophies and practices. University Departments of Continuing Education, frequently the testing grounds for new subject areas, have been warned that funding is to be cut back for courses which do not lead to some recognized qualification. This has caused some concern, since another traditional role of Continuing Education Departments has been to provide 'interest only' courses, for many different age groups, and it is feared that such courses may now become prohibitively expensive.

However, a positive result of this economy has been the making of plans, within the Departments of Continuing Education at least, for the development of forms of course structure and of academic ratification which enable students with different agendas to study successfully in a mixed group. Such learning mechanisms have been used for many years in the country's primary schools, and have long been included in feminist methodologies, yet, when we come to look at the teaching even of feminist subjects within universities, the old ways of teaching and assessing have prevailed. Now, assisted by the power of economics, the idea of very much more diverse and student-centred techniques are finally infiltrating such august bodies as University Senates, and are likely to be employed in a wide variety of subject areas.

For the benefit of those not yet acquainted with this new system of learning and accreditation, in order to make the most of modularization, it has been decided to award Open Studies Certificates and Diplomas. These would benefit part-time students, and would maximize H.E.F.C. funding. They would be based on an accumulation of credits, and could be used as part of a first degree course at a university. This would be particularly advantageous in the case of Lesbian Studies, since students who did not want, on all occasions, to announce their degree as being in Lesbian Studies, could instead refer to the other subject areas studied in other modules.

The credits, assessed on a pass/fail basis only, would be awarded for a number of pre-arranged criteria, designed to allow for multiple means of self expression, and for many different ways of displaying knowledge within the area concerned. At a recent study day, to consider possible methods of assessment, suggestions included: changing the word 'assessment' to 'response'; a reflective diary/journal, to be read by the tutor; questionnaires to test self-awareness and knowledge, which could be self-assessed; student presentations; peer review, decided by the other students; collective determination of desirable criteria in written work; case studies, pieces of local research, letters to journals etc.; production of tapes and video-tapes; and discussion of the methods and criteria of assessment as a part of the learning process.[1]

These forms of course response, otherwise known as assessments, would need to have been discussed and agreed beforehand, in order to agree the number of credits to be allocated in each case. However, there is the potential for a huge increase in flexibility and in depth of response. Some methods would require more work by the Facilitator, or Course Tutor, than do conventional procedures; others would require less.

Recent Action and Development

When I launched the pilot course, 'An Introduction to Lesbian Studies', in January 1994, I had not yet had the benefit of this study day, and hence my ideas were in a more rudimentary form. However, it was preceded by much discussion among lesbians, 'academic' and 'non-academic', as to what kind of course would be best, and as to whether it should run at all. I also leafleted pubs, clubs and discos, the Women's Centre, Lesbian Line, and the local radical women's bookshop. I hoped that women who might not have thought of learning more about being lesbian at a university might perhaps change their minds if the presentation and approach was right. Originally, as I mentioned earlier, there were to be two courses, both open to any women interested, one run on conventional lines, with a pre-arranged tutor and speakers, at the university, and the other to be held more informally, at a local community centre. There was to be an interchange of ideas between the two courses. However, the informal course did not last more than four weeks, while the university one ran for its full ten-week length, plus one extra session for evaluation. This may have been because women on the formal course had had to pay in advance, whereas attendance at the informal course was free, but I think another factor was the excitement of being able to debate lesbian issues in a university setting.

All who took part in the university course saw it as being experimental, both in design and in management. (At this time there was no difficulty in running a course for interest only.) I had advertised it as approaching Lesbian Studies from a feminist perspective, and had brought a number of feminist principles to bear on its initial construction. These included: a very high degree of group participation; ample opportunities for criticism and discussion; a class diary; examination and evaluation of the processes of knowledge exchange undertaken; and the subsequent formation of a group of ex-students, to act in an advisory capacity on the construction of Lesbian Studies degree modules. Throughout the course, and whatever the central theme of the session, the issues of 'what is Lesbian Studies?', 'who is it for?', 'who should teach it?', 'how should it take place?', and 'is it an area of study that can or should be accredited?' were continually being raised.

Each session was introduced by a lesbian speaker, with particular knowledge and experience in the area under consideration. The speakers included both academics and non-academics. Discussion followed, and sometimes group work. Speakers with particular knowledge in each field introduced sessions on lesbian history, queer politics and lesbian feminism, lesbians' use of alcohol, lesbian fiction, lesbians and psychology, lesbian racism, lesbian sexuality, lesbians and social class, and on what it means to be lesbian. Reading lists had been recommended at the start of the course, and vigorous discussions invariably followed the presentations. There was no possibility of a speaker not having to deal with very down-to-earth and searching questions; the atmosphere was a combination of the research seminar and the political meeting. It seems likely that lesbians, who have already challenged society's conventions merely to exist, are likely to be extremely critical of anyone who sees herself in any way as an expert, no matter how much work she may have done in her area of interest. This in itself calls for innovative communication and report procedures.

Evaluative discussion among women involved in the course, in whatever capacity, indicated success for the movement away from a situation where those present are divided into those who know and those who don't, and a real enthusiasm for the sharing of information. There was disagreement over the issue of whether men might be allowed on Lesbian Studies courses, and, if not, how we might exclude them, and over the degree of intellectual content a course of this sort should contain. It was suggested that future courses might give more time to working in groups, to facilitate more specialist discussion.

In general, women judged the format of the course to have been a success, but there was a real awareness of the difficulties (some thought, the impossibilities) involved in producing packages of learning, for certification, given the organic and diffuse nature of lesbian knowledge. (Even so, a sizeable minority of women on the course had, in fact, hoped for more formality, with aims clearly defined in advance by the course leader, thus showing that whatever may be hoped for politically, in the long run, there may still be a place, in the short term, for a traditional framework for Lesbian Studies.) However, at the conclusion of the course, most of the participants agreed that the structure of the course needed to reflect the subject, and that conventional methods were quite inapplicable to the creation of academically valid Lesbian theory.

My own feeling was that, whatever it is that we are striving for, as we try to interpret and define our world, we have to be careful to avoid labelling as 'excellence' the very aspects of knowing which are pre-defined, circumscribed, and circumscribing. At the same time, we need to find ways to include ways of knowing which are intuitive and inspirational, hard to pin down and to reproduce, and which escape only too easily from the structures of learning which universities have employed heretofore. Is it possible that if we actually employ the tools designed by feminist methodology, and adopt the idea of consensus education, we can abandon the discredited ways of knowing which are fixed, trammelled by an outdated and unjust system, and which do not accurately reproduce the experience of women, and perhaps in particular of lesbian women? Is it also possible that we can additionally let fall the outmoded and convoluted language still being employed in much feminist writing, despite earlier assertions that it was inappropriate for us to use it? After all, even Einstein noted that the most fundamental ideas are essentially simple, and may be expressed in a language comprehensible to everyone (Born, 1971). The employment of clear, simple language on all our courses makes it very much easier for such courses to be accessible to all women, so that a continuum of studying, rather than a gulf, may exist between women who would like their study to lead to qualifications and those who study for interest.

Current Work for Change

As a result of this preliminary course, and of a public meeting in Bristol during Pride Week 1994, a consultative group has been formed. Avon Lesbian Studies Advisory Group comprises lesbians from inside and outside the academic world, who have a commitment to the development of a Lesbian Studies which is of high quality, is student-centred, employs the methods of accreditation to first degree level previously described, and is securely grounded in authentic lesbian experience. This Advisory Group will attempt to maintain effective links between the university and the community, as accredited Lesbian Studies courses develop. In addition to this local Advisory Group, some lesbians outside Bristol, with particularly relevant experience, have agreed to act in an informal consultative capacity. These include Jane Hoy, who has organized many Lesbian Studies courses at London's Birkbeck College, Carol Ann Uszkurat and Celia Kitzinger. All are committed to the ideal of constructing and presenting Lesbian Studies in such a way as to be consistent with active feminist politics.

My own immediate plans include the development of a number of Level One first degree modules in Lesbian Studies, at the University of Bristol's Continuing Education Department. These might be taken independently, as units of Open Studies, or, hopefully, be considered ultimately as comprising part of a Certificate or Diploma in Lesbian Identity and Politics. As well as meeting frequently with the Advisory Group, I expect to be liaising closely with various lesbian interest groups, to ensure that modules are produced which involve them wherever possible, and which accurately reflect their experience. It is my intention that a considerable amount of the subject-matter for these modules will come from non-academic lesbians, who have expressed an interest in taking part in facilitating sessions in their particular areas. For example, women with knowledge and experience of the representation of lesbians in film and video hope to be providing material within one module, and women with knowledge and experience of lesbian racism hope to provide material in another. Obviously, adopting such practices is dependent upon the cooperation of women within the lesbian community, as well as a broadly based approach from the university. However, this in itself should serve to safeguard the groundedness of the Lesbian Studies, the necessity of which I outlined earlier.

The first draft of the modules aim 'to explore from a variety of perspectives the meaning and experience of being a lesbian in the modern period (*c.* 1890–1990s); to involve students in archive exploration; and to produce both a video and a volume of original material, to aid future studies, and to be suitable for publication'. Any one or more of the modules could be taken independently of the others. Areas currently under consideration, several suggested and supported by women from the Introductory Course, or from the Advisory Group, include: patriarchy, racism and class; lesbian history; politics of lesbian feminism and internal conflicts; strength marches and Clause 28; lesbophobia, outing, the law and lesbian sexuality; custody and pretend families; sexuality: meaning and importance, non-monogamy and celibacy; sexual identities, butch/femme, lipstick lesbians; pornography and erotica, sado-masochism and transgression; the 'scene': discos, bars, cruising, magazines, newspapers; artistic interactions: films, videos, television series; representations: stereotypes, icons, body image, fashion; ageism and ablism; self help: helplines, discussion groups, courses, drama groups, shared living, holidays, retirement schemes; lesbian fiction and writing our own; lesbian thinking today, to include the placing of issues studied in a more general social context.

As I indicated above, course assessment will rely on adequate attendance and work produced, with the latter to include evidence of background reading, reports on interviews and archive research, and individual and group class presentations.

Conclusion

It is my hope that these Lesbian Studies courses, and those being created elsewhere in the country and internationally, will authentically represent aspects of what it means to be lesbian. To do so, they must ensure that our *ways* of learning from each other express our desire to be free to be ourselves, as much as *what it is* that we learn. This will imply a reluctance to acknowledge expertise, unless it may be in the role of facilitator; an insistence on learning techniques which acknowledge and bring out the knowledge and experience of all present; an uneasiness around set syllabuses; and a demand for adequate access to such resources as the Feminist Archives, the Lesbian Archive, the Fawcett Library, and university libraries.

It is my conviction that a Lesbian Studies course should not proceed, cannot be perceived as valid, without a dynamic theory as to its political and analytical approach and content. One way that I can see of achieving this is by reversing the more usual academic pattern, whereby new subject areas are tested out as modules in Masters courses, before spreading downward to the rest of the populace, as finance and public opinion allows. This tends to impose the set form, the tried and tested pattern, to the great disadvantage of new and original material coming from the students themselves. This cannot be in the interests of heightening the quality of the knowledge obtained. Instead, the student-centred, high quality patterns of learning which are being devised in the name of Open Studies, so particularly well suited to a genuinely feminist approach, may be able to infiltrate 'upwards', from the Continuing Education Department's Introductory Courses and first degree courses, into other university departments. If this happens, it will be a belated, but nevertheless intensely important achievement for feminists, whether lesbian or not, and certainly one upon which it is worth hazarding one's academic reputation.

Note

1   For the compilation of these suggestions, I should like to thank Dr Elizabeth Bird, of Bristol's Continuing Education Department.

References

BORN, MAX (1971) *The Born-Einstein Letters: Correspondence 1916–1955*, London, Macmillan.

CURRIE, DAWN (1993) 'Unhiding the Hidden: Race, Class and Gender, in the Construction of Knowledge', *Humanity and Society*, 17, 1 (February), pp. 3–27.

GELPI, BARBARA CHARLESWORTH and GELPI, ALBERT (1975) *Adrienne Rich's Poetry*, New York, W.W. Norton.

HUMM, MAGGIE (1982) 'Women's Studies and Institutional', unpublished paper.

HUMM, MAGGIE (1983) 'Women in Higher Education', *Women's Studies International Forum*, Vol. 6, No. 1, pp. 97–105.

HUMM, MAGGIE (1987) 'Autobiography and "Bell-Pins"', in GRIFFITHS, VIVIENNE *et al. Writing Feminist Biography 2: Using Life Histories*, Manchester, Manchester University Press.

Patsy Staddon

LUBELSKA, CATHY (1991) 'Teaching Methods in Women's Studies: Challenging the Mainstream', in AARON, JANE and WALBY, SYLVIA (Eds) *Out of the Margins: Women's Studies in the Nineties*, London, Falmer Press.

ROONEY, ELLEN (1990) 'Discipline and Vanish: Feminism, the Resistance to Theory, and the Politics of Cultural Studies', *Difference*, 2, 3 (Fall), pp. 14–28.

STANLEY, LIZ (Ed.) (1990) *Feminist Praxis*, London and New York, Routledge.

UNIVERSITY OF BRISTOL COMMITTEE ON CONTINUING EDUCATION (1994) Annex A, SN/94/23, Open Studies Certificates and Diplomas, February.

Chapter 11

The Micropolitics of Women's Studies: Feminism and Organizational Change in the Academy

Louise Morley

The provision of Women's Studies in higher education has a micropolitical significance, raising questions about institutional reflexivity, organizational culture, policy discourses and effectiveness of feminist agency and inter-vention for change. It could also be claimed that as feminist scholarship has entered into conventional reward systems and power networks in dominant organizations, it has its own micropolitics. In spite of New Right policies and the transition from welfare to market values in education, Women's Studies continues to flourish. The subject is long established in Britain, the USA, Canada, Australia, and in many countries in Western Europe. It is also developing rapidly in Southern and Eastern Europe, as well as in the Indian sub-continent, South East Asia and several African countries including Nigeria and Zimbabwe. The growth of Women's Studies raises questions about the presence of liberatory or oppositional discourses, about feminist strategies to influence change, and about the micropolitical consequences of creating feminist knowledge within the structures of dominant organizations of knowledge production.

Keller and Moglen (1987, p. 494) believed that as women have been historically located as outsiders in the academy, marginality was part of the strategy women devised in response to oppression. In science, Keller argues elsewhere (1984) that this location was advantageous for women, as the impulse to fathom the secrets of nature, or scientific creativity, was enhanced by being outside the rigidities of patriarchal paradigms. Early thinking about Women's Studies problematized the margins/mainstream or revisionist/

revolutionary duality, with concerns that knowledge about women was inserted on an additive basis in unreconstructed courses. More recently, the focus has been on the need to reconceptualize knowledge production in terms of gender/power relations. The audit of gender invariably exposes other aspects of power and domination in organizations. Gender has also been problematized in relation to 'race', social class, sexuality and disability. The challenge continues to exist for Women's Studies to generate theories that can articulate commonalties and differences in women's experiences and socio-economic locations. De Groot and Maynard (1993, p. 4) argue that 'Recuperation, reconstruction and reflexivity all remain important constituent elements of women's studies practice'. It could be argued that whereas reconstruction and reflexivity are important elements of all disciplinary knowledge, it is recuperation, facilitated by the principles and practices of feminist pedagogy, that distinguishes Women's Studies.

Calas and Smircich (1992, p. 230) maintain that feminist scholars have been re-examining and revising the production of knowledge in their disciplines from 'exclusionary institutional arrangements' and have shifted attention 'from equity issues to examination of the consequences of women's absence as knowledge producers'. Women's Studies has been described as 'a source of creative innovation in the concepts, theories and methods applied to social and cultural inquiry' (de Groot and Maynard, 1993, p. 3). The importance of Women's Studies as a system of recovery and relocation of power in the academy is widely celebrated by students and feminist academics (Morley, 1993). Women's Studies provides an important theoretical and political service in facilitating those deemed as 'other' to analyse their own histories and voices. The subject has developed a power-sensitive discourse that supports a subordinated and excluded group to make sense of the gendered social world.

A Feminist Micropolitics

The radical feminist mantra, 'the personal is political', recognized that intrapersonal and interpersonal relationships form an arena in which macro processes of patriarchal power are enacted and challenged. The notion of the personal as political, while a useful campaigning slogan, can be criticized for its reductive totality. By suggesting that there is no distinction between the personal and the political, it could be implied that raised individual consciousness and lifestyle politics can have an impact on larger global issues such as racism, poverty, rape, hunger and homelessness. However, it can be a useful summary of the extent to which macro discourses of power invade our psychic and social landscapes. The interconnections between feminism and postmodernism have been theorized in relation to concepts of power. Both have challenged grand theories, have privileged an analysis of how power operates on a localized level and have elaborated on the politics of everyday life (Kenway, 1990, p. 176). Micropolitics constructs the organization as a political arena too. The concept of micropolitics entered organization studies in the 1980s, suggesting that there is a subtext of organizational life in which conflicts, tensions, resentments, competing interests and power imbalances influence everyday transactions in institutions. Hoyle (1982, p. 87) described micropolitics as 'an organisational underworld which we all recognise and in which we all participate'. Micropolitics is about influence, networks, coalitions, political and personal strategies to effect or resist change. It involves rumour, gossip, sarcasm, humour, denial, 'throwaway remarks', alliance-building.

Blase (1991, p. 1) defines micropolitics as being

> about power and how people use it to influence others and to protect themselves. It is about conflict and how people compete with each other to get what they want. It is about cooperation and how people build support among themselves to achieve their ends.

Rational strategies, policy development and decision-making processes can be disrupted by the 'organisational pathology' (Hoyle, 1982, p. 87). Micropolitics renders the competition of interests visible, exposing processes of stalling, sabotage, manipulation and power bargaining. Early theorists ignored gender, 'race', social class and sexuality as important aspects of continuity and change within power relations and competing discourses in organizations. When micropolitics did include gender, women's experiences were treated as if uniform, conflating differences of class, 'race' and sexuality. Decoding of meaning invariably excluded consideration of how institutional racism, sexism and heterosexism are embedded in individual, group and organizational practices.

When micropolitics becomes gendered in the academy, there is the added dimension that feminist academics can be repeatedly disempowered by the necessity to engage with the exercising of patriarchal power (Morley, 1994). Feminism, through theory and practice, can make subterranean meanings of the academy visible, and expose them as gendered processes of power. Micropolitics and feminist theory can be complementary paradigms for analysis of organizational life. Like many aspects of racial and gender oppression, bullying and sexual harassment at work, micropolitics can also be subtle, elusive, volatile, difficult to capture, leaving individuals unsure of the validity of their readings of a situation. What appears trivial in a single instance acquires new significance when located within a wider analysis of power relations. Both label unnamed feelings, experiences, practices and transactions, as the language in which oppressed groups express these is often politically and socially subjugated. Feminism and micropolitics privilege processes, rather than structures. Paechter and Head (1994) indicated that gender/power relations operating at the micro level within a professional group do not necessarily follow the structural apportionment of power. By this analysis, men without structural power can exert more influence than women in senior positions, as a consequence of the cultural association of masculinity with authority.

A Genealogy of Women's Studies

In terms of a Foucauldian approach to the archaeology of knowledge, it is interesting to consider how the conception and development of Women's Studies interact with the organization's micropolitics. Equally, there is a necessity for feminist academics to evolve micropolitical strategies to promote and defend women's interests in the academy. The micropolitical perspective recognizes control and conflict as essential and contradictory bases of organizational life. Aspects of feminist theory would apply the same analysis to gender relations. The struggle to establish and maintain Women's Studies in particular, and feminist education in general, can represent a powerful conjunction of patriarchal power relations enacted micropolitically.

The discussion about what constitutes and necessitates Women's Studies has been rehearsed for the last decade. Debates continue as to whether feminist influence is best sustained within disciplinary boundaries, or separated out and constellated in the form of Women's Studies. The margins/ mainstream location of Women's Studies has been extensively theorized over the years (hooks, 1984; Aaron and Walby, 1991). There are parallels with the micropolitical location of other counter-hegemonic discourses in the academy, such as Black Studies and Lesbian and Gay Studies, with fears of increased visibility leading to enhanced vulnerability and political incorporation. Speaking in relation to homosexuality, Jonathan Dollimore (1991, pp. 225–6) indicates that 'the concept of reverse discourse suggests another dialectic sense that the outsider may be said to be always already inside: a return from demonized other to challenging presence via containment'. A question therefore exists as to whether one micropolitical purpose of Women's Studies is to contain and constrain challenges to regimes of truth in the academy.

A Reverse Discourse?

By constantly challenging dominant discourses in the academy by exposing the partiality of knowledge, and gender bias in concepts such as logic, reason, objectivity and embodiment, Women's Studies could be said to represent a 'reverse' or 'counter' discourse (Ramazanoglu, 1993). Feminists have indicated a need for academic disciplines to broaden their parameters of inquiry. It has become an orthodoxy of feminist analysis to draw attention to the micropolitical functions of academic disciplines, believing that separation mirrors and reinforces the fragmentation of most spheres of social life, and it is through this separation that gender differences and inequalities are maintained (Campbell, 1992, p. 11). Furthermore, development of feminist knowledge is obstructed by male-defined conceptual boundaries. Women's Studies has consistently challenged the growth and spread of disciplinary mechanisms of knowledge. The promotion of qualitative research methods, interdisciplinary or transdisciplinary approaches to learning and feminist pedagogy for empowerment suggests that those involved in Women's Studies refuse to think and act in accordance with the 'rules' of knowledge and academic life. As such they risk the discursive construction of demonized Other in the academy, with material consequences. Micropolitically, this is reinforced in resourcing, academic legitimacy and professional recognition of feminist academics. If Women's Studies represents a model of feminist education, it is worth remembering Virginia Woolf's micropolitical observations of gendered resource allocations in *A Room of One's Own* (1929) when she draws attention to the symbolic status of women in the academy as represented in the dessert of prunes and custard, as opposed to the gourmet fare enjoyed by the men.

Women's Studies has been described as the intellectual arm of the Women's Liberation Movement (de Groot and Maynard, 1993), yet activists and change agents in the wider community question whether the struggle against sexist oppression can be effectively mounted in academic provision, where elitist, class-bound traditions of white male abstract logic threaten to dilute or co-opt radicalism. In such an analysis, Women's Studies is firmly located as a reformist measure. But concern with feminist praxis also suggests that Women's Studies might play a role in change agency (Stanley, 1990). Whereas feminist theory has become increasingly sophisticated since the early days of second-wave feminism, complaints abound about a particular configuration of feminist theory that comes across as incomprehensible and disempowering to women readers. Equally, levels of abstraction and academic rigour have not necessarily been matched with women's social and political advancement (Faludi, 1992; hooks, 1993). Fears exist that the cleavage between academia and political activism is widening. Nor has the position of women academics in the UK significantly improved since the introduction of the first MA at the University of Kent in 1981 (Evans, 1993; Morley, 1994). In her research with women professors in the USA, Brown Packer (1994) discovered that there was a distinct relationship between involvement with Women's Studies and lack of opportunities for career advancement. Campbell (1992, p. 17) believes that 'for many women, electing to pay attention academically to their identity as women para- doxically requires either considerable sophistication or a not-minding that . . . seems to verge on mindlessness (or . . . opportunism)'. If career development is a micropolitical function of Women's Studies, scarcity of opportunities will create its own competition, cutting across feminist principles of cooperation and collaboration. Calas and Smircich (1992, p. 247) draw attention to the paradoxical position of feminist academics who, through their academic work, help to sustain the circumstances they are supposedly rethinking. Keller and Moglen (1987, p. 508) highlight the complexity of feminists negotiating power in the academy. They ask:

> But what does it mean to be a good feminist in a real world, where
> real power, real issues of professional survival and real opportunities
> are at stake ... where power, excellence and the capacity or ability
> to influence are not ever distributed equally?

Foucault described how power grips us at the point where our desires and our very sense of possibilities for self definition are constituted. Women's Studies can serve as a vehicle for realization of ambition and provide opportunities for self definition for feminist academics, thus running the risk of replicating and perpetuating hierarchical power relations. If Women's Studies is a counter discourse, which produces new knowledge and speaks new truths, it would follow that it also constitutes new power (Ramazanoglu, 1993). Sawicki (1991, p. 102) locates this phenomenon within a post- modernist analysis and draws attention to how Foucault was sensitive to the fact that oppositional discourses often unwittingly extend the relations of domination that they are resisting. In the macro context of global recession, uneven distribution of wealth, mass unemployment and the consequential disempowerment of the labour force, the gulf between rhetoric and action is growing. It is increasingly questionable whether the role of feminism is to change the world, or to respond sensitively to wider global changes. It is important to consider to what extent Women's Studies describes a universal, or is a product of a specific time, place and group. Black feminists have drawn attention to the need for Women's Studies to develop an overarching analysis of oppression which incorporates understanding of 'race', sexuality and social class as important intersections with gender (Lorde, 1984; Collins, 1990; hooks, 1984).

The role of the intellectual in the change process has been problematized in postmodernist thought. Foucault suggests a facilitative role for the intellectual – 'not so much a creative place in the discursive vanguard as the job of clearing the road blocks' (Cain, 1993, p. 88). Another interpretation for Women's Studies teachers is to compare their role to that of midwives in relation to an emergent discourse (*ibid.*, p. 89). One branch of Italian feminist theory describes the micropolitical function of feminist teachers as 'madre simbolica'. At the heart of this role lies the practice of 'affidamento' (entrustment): a relationship in which one woman entrusts herself, symbolically, to another woman. Without this symbolic placement, they argue 'the female mind is afraid, exposed to unpredictable events'. (Milan Women's Bookstore Collective, 1990, p. 31). One criticism of this perspective is that it reinforces the micropolitical function of feminist academics as mothers, defining them out of academia, and into an undifferentiated group of nurturing women. It also disempowers feminist academics by essentializing a highly evolved process and interpersonal skills.

Women's Studies and Equality Discourses

A micropolitical analysis of an organization can reveal gaps, inconsistencies and discrepancies between the process of policy formation, text and implementation. Ball cautions that changes in policy should not be confused with changes in practice because micropolitical strategies can be deployed to promote or defend the latter (1987, p. 40). The question is whether equity policies enable or impede the development of Women's Studies in the academy. Do equity policies assert and conceal power relations simultaneously, or is Women's Studies an example of equity in practice? The term 'Women's Studies' can be the linguistic antithesis to standard patriarchal provision in higher education. Gender continues to be an unmarked category for men, with women constructed as the repository of difference, and knowledge associated with them viewed as 'special' or a 'minority' interest. The existence of Women's Studies can signify a performance indicator of an organization's commitment to change. But processes of change remain largely untheorized in relation to feminist intervention in the academy. Compared with other public sector institutions, local authorities, schools and colleges of further education for example, the equity discourse has scarcely permeated the academy. Only two out of five universities offer equal opportunities training for staff responsible for recruitment, and in half these cases training is not compulsory. When policies and statements do exist, it is questionable how much impact they have had on employment practices, organizational culture, dominant academic discourses, and pedagogy in the academy. So, does the equality discourse fail feminist interests because it is conceptually flawed, or because the implementation is too susceptible to micropolitical interference, as it demands the resocialization of stakeholders?

Critics claim that the equity discourse is inappropriate for the complexities of difference, diversity and pluralism as it is embedded in rationalist trajectory analysis (McNeil, 1993, p. 159). Kulke (1993, p. 132) argues that equality discourses of modern times have not fundamentally altered the gender hierarchy, because concepts of equality and gender differences have been formulated and constrained by the form of patriarchal rationality within which they are embedded. Postmodernist analysis draws attention to the connection between ideas of equal rights and opportunities for all human beings, and the Enlightenment concept of freedom.

Troyna (1994, p. 73) analyses micropolitical functions of the equality discourse in education in terms of Edelman's concept of 'symbolic political language' and 'condensation symbols' (Edelman, 1977). Troyna explains how 'condensation symbols' are designed to create symbolic stereotypes and metaphors which reassure supporters that their interests have been considered. But they are framed in ways such that the proposed solutions may also be contradictory or ambiguously related to the way supporters originally viewed the issue. To use this model, it is debatable whether 'equality' or 'Women's Studies' represents the condensation symbol for feminism in the academy. In terms of the well-established triad of definitions of feminist theory (radical, socialist and liberal), the equality discourse is firmly located within liberal, reformist ideology. McAuley (1987, p. 162) argues that equal opportunities policies are damaging to women, because the statement of intent comes to be accepted by men as a representation of the truth. However, equality discourses can operate to make oppression more visible.

A common criticism of the equality discourse is that it has a relativity problem. Franzway *et al.* (1989, p. 96) ask 'equal with what, or whom?' They believe that 'equality' fails to challenge the model by which the male is taken as the universal case. Normative connotations of policies for equality can separate the individual from the wider social context and perpetuate hegemonic value systems. Burton (1991, p. xii) outlines two views on the effectiveness of equal opportunity programmes in addressing women's subordinate status in organizations. The first, postulated by Game (1984) questions whether these programmes are anything more than a liberal update providing new and more subtle forms of patriarchal domination. The second view, held by Eisenstein (1985), suggests that equal opportunity programmes might be a critical leverage point for more fundamental social change. Eisenstein described affirmative action programmes for women's equality as 'feminist judo' – 'throwing with the weight of the state'.

Paradoxically, equality policies seeking to further the interests of oppressed groups frequently remain in the hands of the dominant group, members of which will inevitably deploy micropolitical activities to safeguard their interests. When the powerful group draws attention to 'race' and gender, albeit in policy discourses, there is a danger that power relations are confirmed, rather than challenged. Micropolitically, this can serve to pathologize and disempower members of oppressed groups, who are discursively located as victims or 'losers'. Their inclusion in either employment or service delivery in the academy is not ascribed to skills, quality or experience, but is attributed to organizational policies and the progressive views and generosity of the dominant group. This feature is particularly apparent in nomenclature adopted by universities to describe mature students as 'non-traditional', thereby insidiously reinforcing normative constructions of students (Morley, 1993).

In Britain the laws covering gender equality relate to sex discrimination and equal pay. As in cases of racial discrimination, the process of individuation is institutionalized as the onus is on individuals to prove discrimination, with obvious micropolitical consequences. Lovenduski and Randall (1993, p. 190) point out that

Taking an equal opportunities case to the tribunals or courts is extremely hard on the complainant, who may find herself isolated at work, unsupported by her union, and at the end, in receipt of inadequate compensation and victimised at work.

Micropolitical harassment and disempowerment of oppressed groups is notoriously difficult to prove, whilst the organization's micropolitics can also make the prospect of grievance procedures and industrial tribunals unthinkable. Attitudinal changes are notoriously difficult to measure, and play only a limited role in the wider matrix of social change. The Equal Opportunities Commission has no mandate to conduct organizational equality audits. Wider policy initiatives and programmes for action are the political choice of local authorities or individual organizations. As a result they are fragile, temporary and easily overridden by state policies and internal micropolitical interference. In the 1990s, with the emphasis on quality rather than equality, the New Right has been intent on policing higher education through initiatives such as quality audits, appraisal and research selectivity exercises. In this climate, it remains a welcome surprise that Women's Studies has survived the onslaught. Kate Campbell shares this fear:

> As ... the prevailing straitened economic climate seems hostile to all but narrowly economic considerations, it seems especially important to maintain momentum and prevent feminism becoming stalled at this point. (Campbell, 1992, p. 20)

Feminist Change Agency and Organizational Culture

Negotiating male organizational culture is a key micropolitical function in the establishment and maintenance of Women's Studies in the academy. In organization terms, innovation is still viewed as installation of a product. In relation to Women's Studies, the arrival of the feminist product highlights the gendered micropolitics of the institution. Lacey (1977) claimed that change or possibility of change brings to the surface those subterranean conflicts and differences which are otherwise glossed over in the daily routines. As change agents, feminist academics have to destabilize current culture and practices in order to establish a new order (Morley and Walsh, 1995). Challenges to patriarchal provision can be dismissed as the work of radical feminist academics representing minority interests. Gender has traditionally been an unmarked term in organization studies, with organizational culture defined as a system of shared values and beliefs that interact with an institution's people, control systems and structures to produce behavioural norms. Burton (1991) argues that the concept of organizational culture can be used coercively to restrain the equal opportunities officer 'who displays enthusiasm for altering customary ways of doing things'. Organizational culture is presented as if it were 'not constituted by power relations, but rather something which expresses the general interests and orientation of the organisation' (Burton, 1991, p. 31). It is also argued that it is the masculine culture of organizations that impedes women's progress within them (Mills, 1988). It is questionable whether masculine culture is static or whether it is dynamic, reproducing itself in a multiplicity of micropolitical actions and interactions.

The academy, like any other organization, is full of contradictions – structures are both fixed and volatile, enabling and constraining. It is important to consider whether Women's Studies requires a broader cultural shift in the academy. Asymmetrical gender power relations shape organizational culture, and organizational culture reinforces gender, class and racial oppression. This is highly significant in terms of feminists' role as change agents in academia, and raises questions about how women mediate effects of policy and make a difference in organizations. Association with Women's Studies in a gendered organizational culture can serve to underpin women's micropolitical identity as 'other' in the academy.

A postmodernist analysis of organizations highlights how there are multiple meanings for the everyday terms used in organizational power networks (Hassard, 1993, p. 136). Whereas there may be a dominant culture in the academy, it is unlikely to be a unitary one, as culture is fragmented and unstable. A postmodern view of power is that it is not monolithic, but capillary, with the potential to constantly reproduce itself. In this analysis, power and difference remain ungendered and unracialized. Alcoff (1990) criticizes Foucault for appealing to micropolitics without providing any analysis of the overall structures of domination. Developing this analysis, it could be said that organizational culture reinforces wider cultural norms as it is sanctioned by wider power relations. Hence, women are discriminated against, sexualized and disempowered in the academy because that is the cultural construction and condition of femaleness.

As a subject area, Women's Studies provides access for individuals, communities, life experiences and knowledges which have been traditionally excluded from the academy. Conversely, educational institutions control the access of individuals to various kinds of discourses. The motivating forces behind an organization's decision to introduce Women's Studies can be economic, rather than political – identifying a gap in the market and recognizing the academic hunger many mature women students have as a result of limited educational opportunities in their youth (Edwards, 1993). Another influence could be ideological and related to needs interpretation, or institutional reflexivity, reminiscent of Giroux's description of the political project of modernism, that is 'rooted in the capacity of individuals to be moved by human suffering so as to remove its causes' (Giroux, 1991, p. 11). More often than not, change comes about as a result of massive feminist agency, intersecting with the personal biographies and political beliefs of people in power and with organizational receptivity.

Foucault's concept of discourses maintains that they are constituted by exclusions as well as inclusions, by what cannot, as well as what can, be said. Discourses make statements possible, and discursive formations are made up of groups of statements (Cain, 1993, p. 76). Whereas language is central to the processes of power, change and agency, discourses are not just linguistic formations, but are fused with power and institutionalized in practices. Discourse-oriented theory assists in decoding the micropolitics of an organization. Feminist academics can be knowledge agents, micropolitically making interventions, not only in course provision and organizational practices, but also about the discourses and regimes of truth that inform them.

Opportunity 2000 was launched in Britain with an express purpose of increasing the number of women in management. But this was in the context of the New Right discourse of 'opportunity' without the qualifier of 'equality'. In the current economically driven enterprise culture of the academy, it is questionable whether management can facilitate counter-hegemonic discourses. As Ball indicates, the discourse of management plays an essential role in achieving the 'radical right' shift in education by gaining closer and more precise control over educational processes. Ball argues that management encapsulates what Foucault describes as a 'moral technology', or a technology of power, and constitutes an 'all-embracing conception of organizational control' (Ball, 1990, p. 156). He concludes that 'management is a "micro-physics of power".... The primary instrument is a hierarchy of continuous and functional surveillance' (Ball, 1990, p. 165). A cynical view could suggest that Women's Studies 'manages' women and is part of the conspiracy discourse to make women into 'docile bodies', diverted away from revolution and social action, with its membership more focused on the production of the written word than on social revolution.

Conclusion

Feminisms and micropolitics have contributed to decoding organizational practices of domination and disempowerment. As a vehicle for recovery of subjugated knowledges and a challenge to established epistemologies, Women's Studies may have a micropolitical function, symbolizing resistance to patriarchal dominance of the academy. The presence or absence of the subject could act as a gender audit and provide valuable information about organizational culture, the critical mass of feminist academics employed, their power and influence and strategic effectiveness. The establishment of Women's Studies highlights how discursive and material power are exercised and contested in dominant organizations. Feminist education problematizes power and privileges empowerment. Micropolitics and conceptually flawed organizational policies can account for the spaces between intention and outcome.

Note

I would like to thank John Head of King's College, London, for helpful critical comments.

References

AARON, J. and WALBY, S. (Eds) (1991) *Out of the Margins: Women's Studies in the Nineties*, London, Falmer Press.

ALCOFF, L. (1990) 'Feminism and Foucault: The Limits to a Collaboration', in DALLERY, A. and SCOTT, C. (Eds) *Crises in Continental Philosophy*, New York, State University of New York Press.

BALL, S. (1987) *The Micropolitics of the School*, London, Routledge.

BALL, S. (1990) 'Management as Moral Technology: A Luddite Analysis', in BALL, S. (Ed.) *Foucault and Education*, London, Routledge.

BLASE, J. (Ed.) (1991) *The Politics of Life in Schools*, Newbury Park, Sage.

BOWLES, G. and KLEIN, R. (Eds) (1987) *Theories of Women's Studies*, London, Routledge and Kegan Paul.

BROWN PACKER, B. (1994) 'Gender Equity for Women Professors at Research Universities', paper presented at 7th International Conference on Women in Higher Education, Orlando, Florida, USA, January.

BURTON, C. (1991) *The Promise and the Price*, St. Leonards, NSW, Allen and Unwin.

CAIN, M. (1993) 'Foucault, Feminism and Feeling: What Foucault Can and Cannot Contribute to Feminist Epistemology', in RAMAZANOGLU, C. (Ed.) *Up Against Foucault*, London, Routledge.

CALAS, M. and SMIRCICH, L. (1992) 'Rewriting Gender into Organisational Theorising: Directions from Feminist Perspectives', in REED, M. and HUGHES, M. (Eds) *Rethinking Organisation: New Directions in Organisational Research And Analysis*, London, Sage.

CAMPBELL, K. (Ed.) (1992) *Critical Feminism*, Buckingham and Philadelphia, Open University Press.

COLLINS, P. HILL (1990) *Black Feminist Thought*, Boston and London, Unwin Hyman.

DE GROOT, J. and MAYNARD, M. (Eds) (1993) *Women's Studies in the 1990s: Doing Things Differently*, Basingstoke, Macmillan.

DOLLIMORE, J. (1991) *Sexual Dissidence: Augustine to Wilde, Freud to Foucault*, Oxford, Clarendon Press.

EDELMAN, M. (1977) *Political Language: Words that Succeed and Policies that Fail*, New York, Academic Press.

EDWARDS, R. (1993) *Mature Women Students*, London, Falmer Press.

EISENSTEIN, H. (1985) 'The Gender of Bureaucracy: Reflections on Feminism and the State', in GOODNOW, J. and PATEMAN, C. (Eds) *Women, Social Science and*

Public Policy, Sydney, Allen and Unwin.

EVANS, M. (1993) 'A Faculty for Prejudice', *The Times Higher Educational Supplement*, 12 November.

FALUDI, S. (1992) *Backlash: The Undeclared War Against Women*, London, Chatto and Windus.

FRANZWAY, S., COURT, D. and CONNELL, R.W. (1989) *Staking a Claim*, Cambridge, Polity.

GAME, A. (1984) 'Affirmative Action: Liberal Rationality or Challenge to Patriarchy?', *Legal Service Bulletin*, 9, 6, pp. 253–7.

GIROUX, H. (1991) *Postmodernism, Feminism and Cultural Politics*, Albany, Albany State University Press.

HASSARD, J. (1993) *Sociology and Organization Theory*, Cambridge, Cambridge University Press.

HINDS, H., PHOENIX, A. and STACEY, J. (Eds) (1992) *Working Out: New Directions for Women's Studies*, London, Falmer Press.

HOOKS, B. (1984) *Feminist Theory: From Margin to Center*, Boston, Mass., South End Press.

HOOKS, B. (1993) *Sisters of the Yam*, London, Turnaround.

HOYLE, E. (1982) 'Micro-politics of Educational Organisations', *Educational Management and Administration*, 10, pp. 87–98.

KELLER, E.F. (1984) *Reflections on Gender and Science*, New Haven, Yale University Press.

KELLER, E.F. and MOGLEN, H. (1987) 'Competition and Feminism: Conflicts for Academic Women', *Signs*, 12 (Spring), pp. 493–511.

KENNEDY, M., LUBELSKA, C. and WALSH, V. (Eds) (1993) *Making Connections: Women's Studies, Women's Movements, Women's Lives*, London, Falmer Press.

KENWAY, J. (1990) 'Education and the Right's Discursive Politics: Private versus State Schooling', in BALL, S. (Ed.) *Foucault and Education*, London, Routledge, pp. 167–206.

KULKE, C. (1993) 'Equality Politics and Difference: Approaches to Feminist Theory and Politics', in DE GROOT, J. and MAYNARD, M. (Eds) *Women's Studies in the 1990s: Doing Things Differently*, London, Macmillan.

LACEY, C. (1977) *Socialization of Teachers*, London, Methuen.

LORDE, A. (1984) *Sister Outsider*, Trumansburg, N.Y., The Crossing Press.

LOVENDUSKI, J. and RANDALL, V. (1993) *Contemporary Feminist Politics*, Milton Keynes, Open University Press.

MCAULEY, J. (1987) 'Women Academics: A Case Study in Inequality', in SPENCER, A. and PODMORE, D. (Eds) *In a Man's World: Essays on Women in Male-dominated Professions*, London, Tavistock.

MCNEIL, M. (1993) 'Dancing with Foucault', in RAMAZANOGLU, C. (Ed.) *Up Against Foucault*, London, Routledge.

MILAN WOMEN'S BOOKSTORE COLLECTIVE (1990) *Sexual Difference: A Theory of Social-Symbolic Practice*, Bloomington, Indiana University Press.

MILLS, A.J. (1988) 'Organization, Gender and Culture', *Organization Studies*, 9 (3), pp. 351–69.

MORLEY, L. (1993) 'Women's Studies as Empowerment of "Non-Traditional" Learners in Community and Youth Work Training: A Case Study', in KENNEDY, M., LUBELSKA, C. and WALSH, V. (Eds) *Making Connections*, London, Falmer Press, pp. 118–29.

MORLEY, L. (1994) 'Glass Ceiling or Iron Cage: Women in UK Academia', *Journal of Gender, Work and Organisation*, Vol. 1, Issue 4, pp. 194–204.

MORLEY, L. and WALSH, V. (Eds) (1995) *Feminist Academics: Creative Agents for Change*, London, Taylor and Francis.

PAECHTER, C. and HEAD, J. (1994) 'Power and Gender in the Staffroom', paper presented at the Women's Studies Network UK Association Conference, University of Portsmouth, July.

Personnel Management (1994) Vol. 5, No. 6 (June).

RAMAZANOGLU, C. (Ed.) (1993) *Up Against Foucault: Explorations of Some Tensions Between Foucault and Feminism*, London, Routledge.

SAWICKI, J. (1991) *Disciplining Foucault: Feminism, Power and the Body*, London, Routledge.

STANLEY, L. (Ed.) (1990) *Feminist Praxis*, London, Routledge.

TROYNA, B. (1994) 'Critical Social Research and Education Policy', *British Journal of Educational Studies*, Vol. 42, No. 1, pp. 70–84.

WOOLF, V. (1929) *A Room of One's Own*; republished 1945 etc., Harmondsworth, Penguin.

Chapter 12

Self Preservation: Feminist Activism and Feminist Jurisprudence

Jill Radford and Liz Kelly

This chapter provides an account of a venture in feminist law making, marking an explicitly activist intervention into feminist jurisprudence or feminist legal theory, a newly emerging area of feminist study or scholarship. We introduce and examine a radical (and) feminist proposal for a change in law, informed by and constructed around the experiences, material realities and circumstances of women's lives. We emphasize an interconnectedness of theory, activism and methodology, politics, policy and research in feminist practice, and we illustrate the need to work across the divisions between feminists working round the law whether as academic lawyers, legal theorists, professional practitioners, advisors, researchers, or activists and support workers.

The chapter begins with an introduction to the context for the proposal. We then discuss the general context in which a new defence to murder is needed, and introduce the proposed defence: 'self preservation'. We then proceed to illustrate how and why the currently available defences fail women, and the ways in which self preservation would not. We conclude by locating the proposal within current attempts to develop feminist jurisprudence.

From the bases we ourselves work from, the Child and Women Abuse Studies Unit (CAWSU) and Rights of Women (ROW), we are members of a network of feminists, which includes Southall Black Sisters and Justice for Women groups in London, Manchester, Norwich, Leeds and York. This network is developing and promoting the proposal; our primary aim is to make change that matters to women. Engaging with feminist jurisprudence at its most basic, our aim is the creation of feminist law; it is part of a political struggle but neither its totality nor an end in itself.

'Tasks of the Moment'

We have concerns about narrow, excluding definitions of feminist jurisprudence which define it solely in terms of contributions to feminist scholarship
or legal discourse. Carol Smart (1989), for example, has expressed concern
that there are strands in feminist jurisprudence which are in danger of playing
into the word games, formal abstractions and empty universalisms that have
lost touch with specificity and with women's material realities. In contrast,
this venture is more in tune with Martha Fineman's (1991) 'tasks in hand
approach' grounded in some very particular specificities of women's lived
experiences and located within a feminist understanding of the gendered
power relations within patriarchal law. Fineman argues that a possible and
necessary task for feminism, including feminist jurisprudence, is to set itself
in opposition to law as 'a discourse and a process of power' (1991, p. xiv).
Further, she holds that 'tasks of the moment' require questioning the values,
concepts and assumptions embedded in legal thought.

It was through working to support individual women convicted of
murder and consequently sentenced to life imprisonment for killing a violent
partner (or former partner) that we came to recognize the limitations of
existing law. It was in preparing defence arguments and grounds for appeal
that we began to question the values, concepts and assumptions embedded
in existing homicide law. It proved impossible to reach any conclusion other
than that none of the existing defences, even with reform in mind, provided
an adequate space for including women's experiences. Only a new law could
do justice to (and indeed provide justice in the context of) women's
experiences and material circumstances. Consequently, our 'task of the
moment' became the construction of a new defence based on women's
experience of domestic violence.

In drawing this work to the attention of the feminist academy, we are also
questioning current contentions within academic Women's Studies that
respecting differences between women's relation to male power makes
feminist politics non-viable. Campaigning for women who, while sharing a
common predicament, come from different backgrounds in terms of race,
class and culture ensured that this work was grounded both in the
commonalities of women's oppression and in an awareness of how these
power structures impact differently in the lived experiences of women. A
concern to avoid constructing exclusionary legal proposals which reproduced
the racism and classism which currently characterizes law in the UK has been
a key aim within the network.

We also question contentions within both academic Women's Studies
and media feminism which hold that acknowledging women's experiences

of victimization is inherently essentialist. It is currently fashionable to define feminism which works against women's oppression as 'victimhood feminism' (Paglia, 1993; Wolf, 1993). Liz Kelly, Sheila Burton and Linda Regan (1994) have argued elsewhere that this rests on a confusion of feminist politics with those of social work and therapy professionals who, albeit belatedly and within their own professional discourses, have responded in a partial way to issues of sexual violence raised by feminists. Feminist activism around men's violence has indeed stemmed from a recognition of that violence as a key element in the oppression of women and children. It has insisted that the enormity of the problem of victimization be recognized. But feminist writing and support work, in contrast to that of many professionals, took care not to construct women as 'passive victims'.[1] A key element in feminist research and campaign work has been not only to document the range and extent of victimization of women and girls, but also to expose the systematic failure of all social institutions to take sexual violence seriously. Since the early 1970s, feminist support work and concerted campaigns have emerged in many countries for women who have fought back. We have heard recently that women in India, Puerto Rico, Mexico, Turkey, Finland and Slovenia are interested in the self preservation proposal, since the injustice of how women who kill abusive men are treated by the legal system is not confined to Britain. The recent campaigns in Britain to support women who have killed their abusers are both part of a much longer tradition, and an example of how the realities of women's lives can be the basis for international connections.

Why a New Defence is Necessary

Feminist jurisprudence, like feminist attempts to create change in other spheres, begins from the basic precept that 'adding women and stirring' is a problematic approach. There are inherent difficulties in reform strategies which simply attempt to map women's experiences, situations and circumstances onto man-made law – laws developed through statute or the common law system, which have been constructed by powerful men in response to situations in which men have commonly found themselves. Rather than promoting amendments which will still leave women on the margins or struggling through loopholes, a more coherent strategy for promoting legal change lies in a shift from the 'margins to the centre' through the construction of new laws which are grounded in the experiences, material situations and cultural contexts of women's and children's lives.

Homicide law is designed, rightly, to place limits on the circumstances in which killing another person can be defended. Two kinds of defences exist: total and partial defences. The total defence is self defence and where this can be proved the accused will be found not guilty. Partial defences reduce the charge to one of manslaughter; whereas the sentence for murder is mandatory life imprisonment, that for manslaughter is at the judge's discretion. Provocation and diminished responsibility are the current partial defences available in British law. We demonstrate later how these defences cannot, even if amended, take account of the reality for women who kill their abuser.

Self Preservation: The Proposal

The proposal we are introducing here is for a new defence to the charge of murder using what we intend will become a new legal concept, 'self preservation'. The proposed defence has been constructed around the experiences and circumstances of women who have been subjected to continuing violence from men with whom they are, or have been, in a familial or intimate relationship. While the proposed new defence is based on circumstances in which women find themselves more commonly than adult men, the proposal is not gender specific, and while we foresee that it would be very unusual for adult men charged with murder to use this defence, they are not excluded by definition. The concept of self preservation is understood here as a rational act, in the same way as self defence is, but located in the context of the prevalence and long-term consequences of domestic violence in women's lives and the concerted failure of social institutions and agencies to intervene to protect women and sanction men. The aim of the proposed defence of self preservation is thus to add to the available legal options and thereby increase the situations where a shift from murder to manslaughter charge is possible.

SELF PRESERVATION

Draft prepared by an ad-hoc group formed at the national meeting of Justice for Women in London and amended following discussions at the national Justice for Women meeting in Manchester, 1993 and discussed at the Rights of Women, Women and the Law conference, in London in March 1994 and finalized following further discussions at a national Justice for Women meeting in Leeds, August 1994

1(i) A person who but for this section would be liable, whether as principal or as accessory, to be convicted of murder shall be liable instead to be convicted of manslaughter if:

a) the deceased person had subjected the defendant or another person, with whom the defendant was at the time of the deceased person's death in a familial relationship, to continuing sexual or physical violence and

b) the deceased person was at the time of their death or had at any time been in a familial or intimate relationship with the defendant or with the other person as described in (a) above and

c) the defendant honestly believed that but for that action, the deceased person would repeat the violence, as stated above, so that her/his life or the other person described in (a) above was in danger and

d) the defendant honestly believed that s/he had no alternative but to kill the deceased or to cause him grievous bodily harm;

(ii) On a charge of murder, it shall be for the defence to prove that the person charged is by virtue of this section not liable to be convicted of murder;

(iii) In Section 1(i) above:

a) 'familial' means related or co-habiting

b) 'intimate' means any sexual relationship not included in the definition of familial

c) 'continuing' means an act of violence as defined below on more than one occasion

d) 'violence' means any act that would constitute an offence under the Offences Against the Person Act 1861 or the Sexual Offences Act 1975

If and when this proposal is accepted, the law would begin to incorporate women's experiences into the construction of the individual, or – more accurately – of the rational citizen. Interestingly, this was picked up by the Home Affairs Select Committee in their response (in 1993) to this proposal. After noting that it was submitted by several women's organizations, they comment:

However, now that the courts recognise that a history of abuse can result in diminished responsibility, the new defence would imply that the killing was a rational choice. We do not believe that this is acceptable. Furthermore, the defence of self-preservation is one unknown to English law. (para 96, xxxii)

It would indeed be 'unknown' for English law to be founded on the experiences of women; this is precisely part of the challenge of the proposal to create such a precedent. And women's actions can indeed be regarded as rational, rather than vengeful or the consequence of a pathological syndrome, or temporary insanity, if viewed from the woman's standpoint, that is, one which is constructed out of the irrationality of the abuser's behaviour and the failure of others, both individuals and organizations, to either protect her or challenge him.

Such an approach has many parallels with what Liz Kingdom (forthcoming) has referred to, in the context of feminist legal theory, as the 'transformative model of feminist jurisprudence' which proposes 'the transformation of male legal categories and concepts to address women's experiences'.

The transformative model of feminist jurisprudence differs from the liberal feminist 'equality' or 'parity' model which, like liberal feminism more broadly, is rooted in classical liberalism. Liberalism holds in principle that all are equal under the law. The law here is constructed as a fair, neutral and rational institution, protected by due process, which defends individual liberty and provides for the protection of the individual and personal property. Liberal feminism recognizes a disjuncture between liberal ideals and legal practice, in that women, and, in anti-racist versions, black people, are excluded by the (white) male monopoly of law, and hence treated unequally. Problematically the liberal equality model assumes that these exclusions and biases in law are somehow blips in an otherwise fair and just legal system which can be remedied by writing excluded groups into law or through equality legislation. The resulting law would thereby live up to its legitimizing claims of being an impartial institution.

Diana Majury recognizes the contradictions of attempting to treat dominant and subordinate groups equally, and the problems of treating women and men in the same way when their realities are not the same. She views the goal of liberal equality as an oxymoron:

if women and men were treated 'equally' then equality would have no meaning, there would be nothing or no-one with whom to be 'equal'. However, in the absence of an 'equal' world, the dominant groups set the standards for 'equality'. (1991, p. 323)

In the following sections we demonstrate how men have set the standard for what will count as provocation, diminished responsibility and self defence, and how impossible or how potentially damaging it is for women to use these defences 'equally'.

Provocation: An Inherently Male Defence

In public forums, feminist activists, including ourselves, have made careful strategic statements welcoming the parliamentary attention accorded to women who kill and the acknowledgment by some politicians of the failure of existing law to provide an accessible defence to women in this situation. However, we have serious misgivings about recent attempts to write women's experiences into law through marginal amendments to provocation, a defence which we believe has been an intrinsically male one.

The self preservation approach contrasts with other proposals to reform the homicide laws. One such proposal is the Private Member's Bill introduced in 1994 by Labour MP Harry Cohen. This Private Member's Bill, which received widespread support amongst women's organizations like the Townswomen's Guild, the Women's Institute and the National Organization of Women's Organizations, attempts to write in women's experiences of domestic violence by legally defining it as constituting 'cumulative provocation'.

Provocation has throughout a long period of history been used successfully by men who kill women with whom they are, or have been, in familial or intimate relationships. All that this defence requires is for a man to argue that he was provoked, as any man might reasonably be, by something that the woman said or did, or did not do, which resulted in him losing his temper and killing her, in the heat of the moment. As we have argued elsewhere (Kelly and Radford, 1991; Radford, 1992a), the concept of provocation assumes a skill and experience in the use of spontaneous physical violence, more customary among men than women in patriarchal societies.

Provocation relies heavily on the legal concept of 'reasonableness', defined by the standard of the 'reasonable man' on the Clapham omnibus. Such an obviously male-defined, discriminatory concept should have no place in law. In our self preservation proposal, rather than attempting to devise an objective standard, we have drawn deliberately on the subjective criterion of 'honest belief' – as in the Morgan ruling on rape (see Edwards, 1981). As well as eliminating the obvious discriminatory element, using a notion of 'honest belief' would enable a woman or child to contextualize her action in the entire history of abuse and violence to which a man had subjected her. This would be the basis on which the reasonableness of her action would be assessed by the court. A subjective criterion would also enable the reasonableness of the action to be evaluated against the particular situation of the woman and thus allow her culture, her race, her class location, her age and her circumstances in relation to disability to be considered relevant to her 'honest belief' and hence whether her action is deemed reasonable or not.

In the existing provocation defence what counts as 'reasonable' has drawn on woman-blaming ideology, restrictive notions of acceptable femininity and presumptions of stereotypical masculinity, whereby a reasonable man might reasonably be provoked by such behaviour as a woman's 'nagging', having a drink problem, moving mustard pots or speaking to other men. These definitions of reasonableness have all been accepted in recent judgments (see Justice for Women, 1993) and have been the subject of feminist criticism since the early 1980s (see Radford, 1982b).

A second example of a move to enscript equivalence into the defence of provocation which still fails to question its underlying concepts and categories is one of the defence arguments in the Appeal Court judgment in Kiranjit Ahluwalia's case.[2] The argument was in fact accepted and has created a new precedent, although it was not the argument which won her freedom (see Radford, 1993).

It was argued that removing 'sudden' from the current definition of provocation as 'sudden and temporary loss of control' would redress a 'gender inequality' by recognizing that whereas men, when provoked, lose control and hit out immediately, women brood and their rage boils more slowly creating a time gap before they act. Previously the law held, as at Sara Thornton's[3] appeal, that any passage of time between the provoking act and the response was a 'cooling off' period and a provocation defence was disallowed in these circumstances. Delayed reaction constituted retaliation or revenge murder in this interpretation.

This change of definition may be of assistance to women in certain situations. It could have made a difference to Sara Thornton. But the problem of seeking equivalences between women and men outside of any recognition of the power relationships between them highlights a major limitation of liberal individualism. The nature of the provocation is not examined. What presumed equivalence exists between moving mustard pots and being subjected to extensive domestic violence for a ten-year period? Indeed, some feminist organizations have argued that rather than extend provocation we should be campaigning for its restriction, especially that neither 'words alone' (as in 'nagging') nor the fact of adultery should on their own constitute provocation (McNeill, 1991).

Provocation also presumes an equivalence in the physicality of violence. The standard is based on the expectations and experiences of adult men who are accorded a capacity to kill while 'out of control'. It takes no account of the differences in women's childhood and adult socialization and circumstances in cultures which educate women into subordination and men into dominance, no account of the positioning of sexual violence within this. It overlooks the reality that women's methods of countering violence often involve the use of weapons and can rarely be spontaneous, because of fear of being overwhelmed by a physically stronger man with competencies in violence. 'Loss of control' is harder, and in some cases impossible, to establish in court, for example, where there is evidence of advance planning on the part of the woman. 'Loss of control' in this context is an inherently male standard and will, therefore, continue to close off this defence for some women. In contrast, one of the key strengths of self preservation is that, based in genuine belief, it can accommodate rationality, including an element of planning.

An examination of the concepts and assumptions of provocation reveals that it is an intrinsically and inherently male defence, with key concepts and standards constructed through male experience. Attempting to write women into law in terms of equivalences to men reproduces the male norm, and will continue to work in men's interests and at women's expense, bearing in mind that men who kill women considerably outnumber women who kill men in intimate and familial contexts.

Diminished Responsibility: Medicalizing Oppression and Resistance

Similar and additional conceptual problems exist in relation to diminished responsibility, the other partial defence to a murder charge. One judicial response to the campaigns around women who kill has been to allow the importing, from the USA, of syndrome defences, particularly 'battered women's syndrome' and possibly 'post traumatic stress disorder'.

We are not disputing that domestic violence is harmful and damaging to women, nor that of necessity women and their lawyers have to make the best use of the limited legal options available under present law. Notably it was a syndrome defence which won Kiranjit Ahluwalia her freedom after the Appeal Court ordered a retrial. We have supported individual women who have used these defences, but remain both critical and suspect of their underlying concepts and categories.

Diminished responsibility, including the fashionable use of recently created syndromes, pathologizes women's behaviour and denies context and meaning to women's determination to resist and survive male violence. Through the processes of medicalizing women's experiences and behaviour, diagnostic concepts such as 'learned helplessness' are constructed. These define and categorize certain responses and reactions to domestic violence (and sexual abuse in the case of post traumatic stress disorder) as classic symptoms. Others are excluded. Some women are able to represent events in ways which can be accommodated by a syndrome. Others cannot. Symptoms and standards constructed by professional experts will be informed by their standpoint, and in societies characterized by classism, racism and heterosexism, these values will be reflected in diagnostic processes, in quite complicated ways. Cynthia Gillespie (1989) has shown that experience with the battered women's syndrome defence in the USA has resulted in as many women being excluded from its use as are included, and points to the telling fact that the majority of those who have been excluded are African American women.

Self Defence: Against Strangers and Hostages Only?

Self Defence, the only full defence to the charge of murder, is characterized by many of the difficulties we have already noted since it too is constructed around male experiences and circumstances. As such, it is rarely accessible to women.

In British law the right to take an aggressor's life to save one's own is one of the oldest common law rights. It is, however, tightly defined since it is not in anyone's interests, and certainly not women's, to sanction unnecessary killings. Through common law decisions, over the centuries, rules delineating self defence have been developed to balance this private right against the public order. As common law, however, these rules of precedent have not been passed by parliament, but made by judges, almost exclusively male. The cases have predominantly involved male defendants acting to defend themselves against an unknown assailant in a public place. Consequently law has developed which permits men to exercise their right to defend themselves in situations where men have customarily felt the need to do so; most often from strangers in public places.

Yet, as a full defence to the charge of murder, self defence is a crucial option for women facing murder charges for resisting male violence, often from men who share their homes. Outside of hostage situations, which, as John McCarthy has suggested, has parallels to living with violent men, this is very rarely a situation that men experience as adults. There is, in fact, no equivalence in the contexts in which men and women are most likely to encounter potentially lethal assaults.

Another obstacle is the exclusionary male standard 'reasonableness' paralleling its operation in provocation. Difficulties also arise with the legal concepts of 'imminence' and 'proportionality' and the requirement that there was no other possible way out of the situation such as escape or summoning assistance.

Imminence requires that the fatal act must be a defensive response to an imminent threat in an assault situation. This may not be possible for all women. If, in fear of her life, a woman, knowing that her strength and fighting skills are less than those of her attacker, tries to catch him off guard, she cannot plead self defence. It is rarely possible for a woman or child to respond immediately and effectively against a man in an assault situation. It is far more likely that this course of action would result in the death of the woman than that of the man. The law holds that, in such situations, a woman has a duty to protect herself by escaping or seeking assistance. It requires that the person under threat does not act precipitously, but allows the attacker, presumed to be an unknown entity, the possibility of changing his mind. As we know from many date rape trials, men are easily 'confused by signals', so this was a necessary protection for men in stranger assaults. However, when a woman is faced with attack from a partner or previous partner, she is facing someone whose violent potential she knows only too well, whose signals she has learned to read closely.

The presumption of possible escape is yet another exclusionary standard. When the home is the site of violence, escape or leaving is not the same as running away from a violent street incident. It is far more significant and has more far-reaching consequences. A woman may feel all manner of guilt and reluctance about leaving her home and relationships she has spent years constructing. If she has children, her options are even more limited. Both getting out and finding somewhere to go to are complex, especially since for many women the public sphere, particularly at night, is not experienced as safe.

The requirement of proportionality of force defines the first to use a weapon as the assailant. The presumption of equality in fighting skills and strength excludes a lot of women from this defence. Kathleen Lehay (1987) speaks of 'equality with a vengeance' referring to how relentlessly applying gender-neutral terms to gendered contexts can further disadvantage women.

Canadian law, in contrast to that in Britain, has defined using a weapon as 'equalizing violence' in this context, and has allowed women who have defended themselves with a weapon to enter a plea of self defence. This change parallels a transformative shift from an equality and equivalence paradigm to 'inequality-based strategies' (Majury, 1991). Whilst not removing male standards altogether it does shift focus from presumed equality to recognition of currently existing inequalities. This shift may be a route into more radical change.

Creating Feminist Law

Rooted in individualism, liberal discourse (including liberal feminism) refuses to recognize gender, race, and class relations as structural power relations. Consequently it fails to acknowledge that these power relations are encoded into the concepts and categories of law, making reform strategies which simply attempt to map women's experiences, situations and circumstances on to man-made law problematic. Whether rooted in sameness and equalities or in differences and equivalences, liberal legal discourse is constructed through a male subject and a commitment to the individual; it also is informed by and interacts with racism and homophobia. Simply including women inevitably reproduces these forces and thereby reinforces rather than challenges these oppressions. Liz Kingdom (forthcoming) argues that liberal jurisprudence can make no impact on the law's treatment of women so long as 'legal categories ... embody male norms and accordingly fail to address women's experiences'.

The Canadian redefinition of self defence recognizes that a woman may need to use a weapon to defend herself from an unarmed man, since currently this would constitute 'equalizing violence'. Diana Majury (1991) argues that legal strategies which recognize inequalities can focus on the disadvantages, risks and deprivations experienced by women and oppressed groups, and therefore on how these might be redressed. In this way the focus shifts from a comparative perspective to one of power and powerlessness, which would facilitate a focus on 'specific and concrete manifestations of women's oppression' (Majury, 1991, p. 325). This is beyond the scope of most liberal equality-based approaches to law reform.

Whilst most feminists who take the transformative approach to legal change recognize that gender differences are socially constructed, they nonetheless refuse to ignore the fact that these differences have material consequences in women's and men's lives. Legal change is one route to creating social change, within which inequality is both recognized by, and challenged through, law. Were women's oppression to be ended the law would also have to be transformed (if it had not been so already) anew to reflect this different reality.

We have argued that it is specifically because these power relations are enscripted into the assumptions, concepts and categories of law itself that a more profound level of change than amending existing law is required if the legal discourse and practice is to recognize the material realities of oppressed and traditionally excluded groups. We see the self preservation proposal as a specific illustration of this transformative approach in action.

To be fore-warned is to be fore-armed. We are under no illusion that one of the arguments some feminist theorists will make concerning this proposal is that, in beginning from the specificities of women's materiality and circumstances and naming patriarchal power, we are being essentialist. But our concern is with making a difference, a difference that matters; taking steps towards justice for women involves beginning from women's right to live without violence as an inalienable human right.

Catharine MacKinnon has argued:

> To the extent feminist law embodies women's point of view, it will be said that its law is not neutral. But existing law is not neutral. It will be said that it undermines the legitimacy of the legal system. But the legitimacy of existing law is based on force at women's expense.... It will be said that feminist law is special pleading for a particular group and one cannot start that or where will it end.... The question is not where it will stop, but whether it will start for any group but the dominant one. It will be said that feminist law cannot win and will not work. But this is premature. Its possibilities cannot be assessed in the abstract but must engage the world. (MacKinnon, 1989, p. 249)

Notes

1   It was, after all, feminist organizations which began to use the term 'survivor', in order to give recognition to the strength and creativity which many girls and women display in coping with victimization both at the time and later.

2   Kiranjit was found guilty of murder of her abusive husband in 1989. She had suffered ten years of abuse and degradation, had called the police on a number of occasions, but had never been informed about refuges. A campaign for her release was headed by Southall Black Sisters, and one element within this was searching for grounds on which to appeal her sentence.

3   Sara Thornton's case has been another of the most publicized recent cases. Sara killed her abusive husband after a violent argument while he lay sleeping on the sofa. The fact that she went to the kitchen to get a knife was seen as excluding a provocation plea.

References

EDWARDS, SUSAN (1981) *Female Sexuality and the Law*, Oxford, Martin Robinson.

FINEMAN, MARTHA (1991) 'Introduction', in FINEMAN, MARTHA A. and THOMADSEN, NANCY S. (Eds) *At the Boundaries of the Law*, New York and London, Routledge.

GILLESPIE, CYNTHIA (1989) *Justifiable Homicide: Battered women, Self Defence and the Law*, Columbus, Ohio, Columbus University Press.

HOME AFFAIRS SELECT COMMITTEE ON DOMESTIC VIOLENCE (1993) Third Report on Domestic Violence, February 1.

JUSTICE FOR WOMEN (1993) Information pack, available from Justice for Women, 55 Rathcoole Gardens, London N8 9NE.

KELLY, LIZ and RADFORD, JILL (1991) 'Change the Law (2)', *Trouble and Strife*, 22 (Winter).

KELLY, LIZ, BURTON, SHEILA and REGAN, LINDA (1996, forthcoming) 'Beyond Victim or Survivor: Sexual Violence. Identity and Feminist Theory and Practice', in ADKINS, LISA and MARCHANT, VICKI (Eds) *Sexualizing the Social: Power and the Organization of Society*, London, Macmillan.

KINGDOM, LIZ (forthcoming) 'Feminist Jurisprudence', entry in forthcoming *Routledge Encyclopedia of Philosophy*, Chief Editor: Edward Craig.

LEHAY, KATHLEEN (1987) 'Feminist Theories of (IN) Equality', *Wisconsin Women's Law Journal*.

MACKINNON, CATHARINE (1982) 'Feminism, Marxism, Method and the State: An Agenda for Theory', *Signs*, 7, pp. 227–56.

MACKINNON, CATHARINE (1989) *Toward a Feminist Theory of the State*, Cambridge, Mass., Harvard University Press.

MCNEILL, SANDRA (1991) 'Change the Law (1)', *Trouble and Strife*, 22 (Winter).

MAJURY, DIANA (1991) 'Strategizing In Equality', in FINEMAN, MARTHA A. and THOMADSEN, NANCY S. (Eds) *At the Boundaries of the Law*, New York and London, Routledge.

PAGLIA, CAMILLE (1993) *Sex, Art, and American Culture*, London, Viking.

RADFORD, JILL (1982b) 'Retrospective on a Trial', in RADFORD, JILL and RUSSELL, DIANA E.H. (Eds) *Femicide: The Politics of Woman Killing*, Buckingham, Open University Press.

RADFORD, JILL (1992a) 'Self Preservation', *Rights of Women Bulletin*, Summer; available from Rights of Women, 52–54 Featherstone St., London EC1Y 8RT.

RADFORD, JILL (1993) 'We'll be Freeing all the Women', *ROW Bulletin*, Spring.

SMART, CAROL (1989) *Feminism and the Power of Law*, London and New York, Routledge.

WOLF, NAOMI (1993) *Fire with Fire*, London, Chatto and Windus.

Notes on Contributors

Julia O'Connell Davidson is Lecturer in Sociology at the University of Leicester. She is currently involved in research on prostitution in Britain and sex tourism to economically underdeveloped countries.

Debbie Epstein is lecturer in Women's Studies and Education at the Centre for Research and Education on Gender, Institute of Education, University of London. Among her recent publications are *Changing Classroom Cultures: anti-racism, politics and schools* and *Challenging Lesbian and Gay Inequalities in Education*. Forthcoming (with Richard Johnson): *Schooling Sexualities: Lesbian and Gay Oppression, Identities and Education*.

Christine Forde is a Senior Lecturer in Education in the Department of Professional Studies at St Andrew's College, Glasgow. She is currently completing a PhD thesis on feminism and utopianism. Her other research interests include equal rights in education, personal and management development for women and women's spirituality.

Ruth Hamson completed her BA in History at Sheffield University in 1971 and then spent 20 years experiencing life as a woman. She had recently gained an MA in Women's Studies at Nene College, Northampton, where she is now a Research Associate at the Centre for Research in Women's Studies. She is currently researching female friendship and issues raised by the use of oral life history.

Stevi Jackson is co-ordinator of the MLitt in Women's Studies at the University of Strathclyde. She is a co-editor of *Women's Studies: A Reader*

(Harvester Wheatsheaf 1993), has a book on Christine Delphy forthcoming in the Sage 'Women of Ideas' series and has co-edited, with Shaun Moores, *The Politics of Domestic Consumption: Critical Readings*, to be published by Prentice Hall/Harvester Wheatsheaf. She has also published a number of articles on romance and sexuality.

Liz Kelly is Head of the Child Abuse Studies Unit, University of North London. Apart from conducting research CASU offers advice and consultancy, and organizes networking, training and conferences on the abuse of children and adult women from a feminist perspective. Liz has written many articles on child abuse as well as *Surviving Sexual Violence* (1988, Polity Press).

Mary Maynard is a Senior Lecturer in Sociology and Director of the Centre for Women's Studies at the University of York. Her publications include: *Sexism, Racism and Oppression* (with Arthur Brittan) (1984, Blackwell); *Women, Violence and Social Control* (co-edited with Jalna Hanmer) (1987, Macmillan); *Sociological Theory* (1989, Longman); *Women's Studies in the 1990s* (co-edited with Joanna de Groot) (1993, Macmillan): *Researching Women's Lives from a Feminist Perspective* (co-edited with June Purvis) (1994, Taylor and Francis); and *The Dynamics of 'Race' and Gender* (co-edited with Haleh Afshar) (1994, Taylor and Francis). She is currently working on a book on feminists and social research practice.

Louise Morley is a Lecturer in the Department of Community Studies, University of Reading, where her work includes teaching and the development of Women's Studies courses and directorship of the MA in Equity and Change in the Public Services. She has published on feminist pedagogy, equity and empowerment and her recent works include Morley, L and Walsh, V (Eds) (1995) *Feminist Academics: Creative Agents for Change*. London, Taylor and Francis.

Joanna Phoenix is an ESRC funded PhD student in Keele University's Criminology department. She has a BSc in sociology and an MSc in Gender and Social Policy from Bristol University. Her current research is on prostitution but other research interests include sexuality and feminist theory. She currently lives in Bristol with her partner, plants and two cats.

June Purvis is Professor of Sociology at the University of Portsmouth and Founding and Managing Editor of *Women's History Review*. Publications include *Hard Lessons, The Lives of Working-Class Women in nineteenth-*

century England (1989, Polity Press), *A History of Women's Education* (1991, Open University Press) and as co-editor with Mary Maynard *Researching Women's Lives from a Feminist Perspective* (1994, Taylor and Francis). Other recent articles include 'A lost dimension? The political education of women in the suffragette movement in Edwardian Britain', *Gender and Education* (1994) 3; 'Deeds, not words: the daily lives of militant suffragettes in Edwardian Britain', *Women's Studies International Forum* (1995) Vol. 18, No. 1, and 'Women's history in Britain: an overview' in *European Journal of Women's Studies* (1995) **2**, 1.

Jill Radford is a feminist activist, campaigner and researcher currently working at Rights of Women, a feminist legal project. She also teaches Women's Studies and Criminology for the Open University and at the University of Westminster. She has published widely in the area of sexual violence, and was co-editor, with Diana Russell, of *Femicide: The Politics of Woman-Killing* (1992). She was founding member of the British Sociological Association women's caucus Violence Against Women Study Group, and has remained an active member.

Caroline Ramazanoglu is a reader in sociology at Goldsmiths' College, London and a contributor to the Women, Risk and AIDS Project/Men, Risk and AIDS Project. Publications include *Feminism and the Contradictions of Oppression* (1989) Routledge; (as editor) *Up Against Foucault: Explorations of Some Tensions between Foucault and Feminism* (1993) Routledge.

Patsy Staddon is a researcher and facilitator in the field of Lesbian Studies. Her particular interests include the challenge to the academic framework presented by this area of work; the exploration of lesbian feminist methodologies; women's sexuality and the use of alcohol; and the social perceptions and interpretations of 'mental health'. Her qualifications include a first degree in English at the University of Birmingham (1965) and a masters degree in Sociology at the University of Bristol (1993). She is registered as disabled by temporal lobe epilepsy.

Deborah Lynn Steinberg teaches feminist theory and politics at Warwick University, Department of Sociology. In addition to her current work on the politics of sexuality and media representations, she has also written widely on the subjects of women's reproductive 'rights and reproductive technologies, including the co-edited (with Patricia Spallone) collection *Made to Order: The Myth of Reproductive and Genetic Progress*.

Cath Stowers is doing a PhD on emancipatory strategies in contemporary women's writing at the Centre for Women's Studies, University of York. She has recently instigated an International Academic Network on Contemporary Women's Writing and the York Women Writers Collective. She is active in local feminist politics and teaches women's studies, literature and women's creative writing in adult education programmes.

Index